*The Basket Weavers*
*of Arizona*

# The Basket Weavers of Arizona

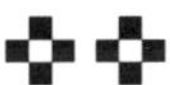

Bert Robinson

*Photographs by Robert H. Peebles*
*Foreword by H. Thomas Cain*

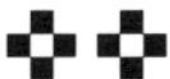

UNIVERSITY OF NEW MEXICO PRESS : ALBUQUERQUE

Library of Congress Cataloging-in-Publication Data

Robinson, Bert, b. 1889.
The basket weavers of Arizona / Bert Robinson ; photographs by Robert H. Peebles ; introduction by H. Thomas Cain.
p. cm.
Reprint. Originally published: Albuquerque : University of New Mexico Press, 1954.
Includes index.
ISBN 0–8263–1263–2
1. Indians of North America—Arizona—Basket making. I. Title.
E78.A7R65 1991
746.41'2'089970791—dc20 91–22832
CIP

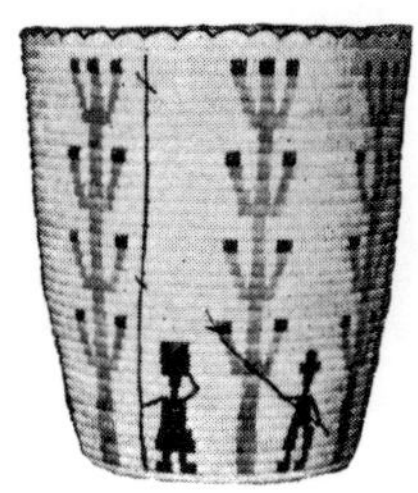

*To my wife*
*Estella*

# *Contents*

# *Foreword to the 1991 Edition*

EVERY SURVEY OF A CRAFT unavoidably must look in two directions, back over what has been covered and forward to present and future scholarship, which one hopes will complement the early findings.

*The Basket Weavers of Arizona*, by Bert Robinson, was first published in 1954 by the University of New Mexico Press. The book has been out of print for a number of years. Its usefulness has never been questioned, and its reissue is a welcome addition to the library of any serious student or collector of Southwest Indian basketry. Bert Robinson's close association with dozens of the finest Indian craftswomen from the eight basket-producing tribes of Arizona was unique. The black-and-white prints, color photographs, and maps in this book are exceptionally useful. Bert and his wife traveled extensively throughout the reservations collecting the finest examples of the weaving of each tribe as well as detailed information about the materials and weaving techniques used by the weavers. His detailed ethnographic notes are invaluable and are coordinated with the text in a thoroughly comprehensive assemblage. It is a *readable* book. Bert Robinson was no academically trained ethnologist, but his knowledge of his specialty was encyclopedic.

It was during Bert's tenure as superintendent of the Pima Indian Agency, Bureau of Indian Affairs, that he developed close personal relationships with many of the older Pima weavers. From 1935 to 1951 he collected (and commissioned) his outstanding array of Pima and Papago baskets. These were incorporated into his overall collection of Arizona Indian baskets that was rightly considered to be one of the finest in the country. It is most unfortunate that this stellar assemblage was sold piecemeal after Bert's death. The same fate befell the invaluable Birdy Brown collection of Chemehuevi baskets, which was posthumously auctioned in 1969.

It was my good fortune to know Bert Robinson in the early 1950s, when I was involved in field research on Pima Indian baskets. His ready help and encouragement with information and reservation contacts was greatly appreciated. The result was the publication in 1962 of my *Pima Indian Basketry* by the Heard Museum of Anthropology. Several of the older weavers remembered happy associations with Mr. Robinson. At this writing in 1990 I have just learned of the death of Bessie Mike of the Fort McDowell Reservation, last of the old Yavapai weavers, at the age of ninety. She was another friend of Bert Robinson's. Bessie Mike, R.I.P.

Certainly it is of interest today to evaluate the importance of *The Basket Weavers of Arizona* in relation to more recent studies of Indian basketry. A great revival of general interest in American Indian arts and crafts has occurred since the book was first published in 1954, and fine basketry has not been neglected by scholars in this field. Although nothing of the scope of Otis Tufton Mason's *Aboriginal Indian Basketry* (Smithsonian Institution, 1902; beautifully reprinted by the Rio Grande Press, Glorieta, N. Mex. in 1970) has to date been attempted, a number of regional studies have been published. Perhaps the one book that comes closest to Mason's monumental work is *Indian Baskets*, by Sarah Peabody Turnbaugh and William A. Turnbaugh (West Chester, Penn.: Schiffer Publishing, 1986). Handsome color photographs illustrate examples from all primary basketry areas. The incomparable collection of the Peabody Museum, Harvard University, is the source for most of the photographs.

Studies of specific regions are numerous. The Turnbaugh volume contains a good working bibliography of the basketry of the Southwest, the Northeast, the Plains, the Arctic and the Subarctic, the Pacific Northwest, the Cascades-Plateau region, North, Central, and Southern California, and the Great Basin.

On Southwestern basketry, the first and foremost study is certainly *Indian Baskets of the Southwest*, by Clara Lee Tanner (Tucson: University of Arizona Press, 1983). It is comprehensive, clearly illustrated, and shows the consummate clarity and attention to detail that characterize Clara Lee Tanner's many studies of Southwestern Indian arts and crafts.

A more recent scholarly catalog is *Southwest Indian Baskets: Their History and Makers*, by Andrew H. Whiteford (Santa Fe: School of American Research, 1989). Whiteford's field research included visits to all southwestern reservations to interview surviving basket makers of older generations, as well as their few younger successors.

*The Papago Indians and Their Basketry*, by Terry DeWald (1979) is the result of a very sympathetic four-year study of the Papago. It presents a poignant account of the Aw-aw-tam and life among the "Desert People." The author himself learned to make baskets from the Papago. Today the Papago produce and market more baskets than all the rest of the Arizona basketry-producing tribes combined.

What is the status of Indian baskets today? Most of those who speculate about the future of Amerindian basket production predict the imminent demise of the craft. I no longer subscribe to this approach. Who can accurately predict when or where a revival of an ancient and respected craft may occur? The basic materials are still available, and museum collections abound with examples of the finest craftsmanship. Detailed analyses have been made of all weaving techniques. Certainly there is little monetary incentive to make baskets. No one would ever pay a fair price for a basket if the time and tedious labor of collecting, preparing materials, and weaving a fine basket were taken into account. Not long ago I showed a Pima basket weaver a recent catalog for an auction at Sotheby's in New York in which an item labeled "Classic Yokuts Polychrome Coiled Gambling Tray" (diam. 66.1 cm) was given an estimated value of $20,000–$30,000. She did not quite faint! What would the prospective buyer pay for a fine old Pima basket featuring "squash blossom" designs such as the one pictured in Plate VII of this book (p. 24)?

Pride of craftsmanship may keep the tradition alive. But today you will not have much luck finding Arizona Indian baskets of the quality of those collected by Bert Robinson before 1935. Occasionally a fine old basket will surface at an Indian craft auction, and bidding will be brisk. Such baskets, fortunately, are still housed and exhibited in the Museum of Northern Arizona, Flagstaff; the Heard Museum, Phoenix; the Arizona State Museum, Tucson; and the Amerind Foundation, Dragoon, Arizona.

H. Thomas Cain
*Anthropological Consultant*
*Heard Museum of Anthropology*
*Phoenix, Arizona*

# *Foreword to the 1954 Edition*

THE BASKET WEAVERS OF ARIZONA is much more than just another book—in a sense it is the life of a man—the author, A. E. "Bert" Robinson, former superintendent of the Pima Indian Agency in Arizona. For over thirty years he lived among and served the Indian people about whom he is writing. He does not tell the reader that the lives and welfare of the Indians and particularly the Pimas, are a matter of deep emotional concern to him, but this will be self-evident from the book. He does not tell the reader that he, personally, over and above the government's program to assist Indians, has worked diligently to stimulate the sale of Indian arts and crafts through every means known to him, but he has. He has played a part in the drama of the Indians and their craft that he so ably describes. His knowledge of his subject, gained from his life's experience and backed by years of research, is only exceeded by his intense appreciation of this craft of the Arizona Indians.

Bert Robinson, as he is called by all who know him, was born on a farm in southern Illinois in 1889. He came from an old pioneer family that had homesteaded in the area early in the 1800's. His great-great-grandfather, John Robinson, with his plodding ox team had broken the prairie sod for the first time and had carved for himself a broad and fertile farm here on the frontier.

Like most farm boys of a half century ago, Bert began his education in a little one-room schoolhouse. About 1895, his family moved to St. Louis, Missouri, where he attended school and, later, Washington University.

Bert's boyhood desire to see the wide open spaces of the west was fulfilled when he stepped from a train, in 1914, at the little railway station that still stands at Central and Jackson streets, in Phoenix, Arizona.

In 1916, he married an Arizona girl. The same year, he took a job with the United States Reclamation Service, that was then operating the Salt River Valley Irrigation Project. This was the beginning of his career in irrigation and land development that extended over a period of thirty-five years.

In 1921, he entered the United States Indian Service at Sacaton, Arizona, where he supervised the clearing, leveling, and seeding to crop some 25,000 acres of Indian lands that received water from the Coolidge Dam project. In 1935, he was appointed superintendent of the Pima Agency, which post he held until his retirement sixteen years later.

In 1940, while on an official trip to Denver, Colorado, he was stricken with staphylococcic infection, which resulted in his loss of vision. Soon afterward, a friend expressed regret that Bert had not recorded the information he had acquired about Arizona Indian tribes, and especially their basket-weaving craft, on which subject he was an authority. This gave him the idea for THE BASKET WEAVERS OF ARIZONA. He began to dictate the manuscript to his wife and there followed several years of research with long trips to the remote corners of Arizona's Indian reservations. Here he collected specimens of their baskets, talked to the weavers and obtained photographs of them at work on their craft in their homes.

Bert purchased his first Indian basket in 1915 on the sidewalks of Phoenix. Since then his collection has grown to be the finest in the Southwest. His collection of Pima baskets is unequaled anywhere.

When he retired from Government Service, in 1951, he was awarded a Citation for Meritorious Service, by Oscar L. Chapman, Secretary of the Interior, which is reproduced on page 162.

WAYNE PRATT

# *Preface*

THE OBJECTIVE here is to answer some of the many questions asked about Indian crafts and the people who create them. These crafts are purely an American art, individual to the aboriginal people, the American Indians. Likewise the craftsmanship, the materials used, and the decorative patterns executed in or upon these Indian crafts are, in most instances, individual to the tribe to which the craftsmen belong. Only basket crafts will be discussed here but space is given also to the background, history, economy, and social order of the tribes who make baskets in Arizona. It would follow that, when so many subjects are pursued, their treatment will be of a discursive nature only. It is not possible, for instance, to go into the social order of the Hopi Indian in detail nor is it possible to describe the intricate weaving in the four-petal squash blossom design in a Pima basket. In one instance a few statements of fact, and in the other a picture will suffice. Often, when an Indian basket is shown, such questions as, "What tribe of Indians made it?" "Where do they live?" or "How do they live?" are asked. When these questions are answered, additional interest is created. This may be enlarged further by information regarding the material used in the basket, the manner in which that material is prepared, and some description of the decorative design which is individual to the tribe whose members make such baskets. The information herein was compiled in order that as many of these questions as possible may be answered. Historical or anthropological data were obtained from research in recognized libraries of such works. Other information was gathered through my thirty years of residence with the Indians and with their own contributions, which were given personally by them. The photographs were taken in the Indians' homes, their fields, or in whatever location the narrative describes. They are all actual and authentic. If my efforts create a better understanding of, and a more sympathetic interest in, the Indian than existed in the mind of the reader before, then my objective will have been accomplished.

## *Acknowledgments*

IN ASSEMBLING the information and data contained in this book it was necessary to have the co-operation and assistance of many people. I would be remiss in my sense of gratitude should I fail to acknowledge them here. I wish to extend my appreciation first to the entire staff at Sacaton, Arizona, headquarters for the Pima Indian Agency. "My gang," as I liked to call them, gave me every assistance possible. To Mr. C. E. Faris, United States Indian Service, retired, of Albuquerque, New Mexico, who made available to me his collection of rare old books on Indians and Indian affairs. To Mr. Mulford Winsor, whom we might call the patriarch of the Arizona state capitol. He has served there in various capacities since the dedication of the building in February, 1901. In his present position as Director of the State Library and Archives, both he and his assistant, Mrs. Alice B. Good, have been most helpful in my research into the history and background of the Arizona Indian tribes. To Mr. Donald Powell, who supplied me with many books from the research department of the library of the University of Arizona, at Tucson. To Mr. Raymond Carlson for his kindly interest and for his expert advice in the selection of the illustrations. To my editor and his good wife, Mr. and Mrs. Fred E. Harvey, for their earnest efforts in behalf of my book.

Last to be mentioned, but perhaps first in importance, are the Indian women of the various tribes discussed herein; they are truly the "Basket Weavers of Arizona." When I visited them in their homes they were most generous with their time and patience in supplying me with the information I required. To them I extend my sincere appreciation and friendship.

THE AUTHOR

# *Introduction*

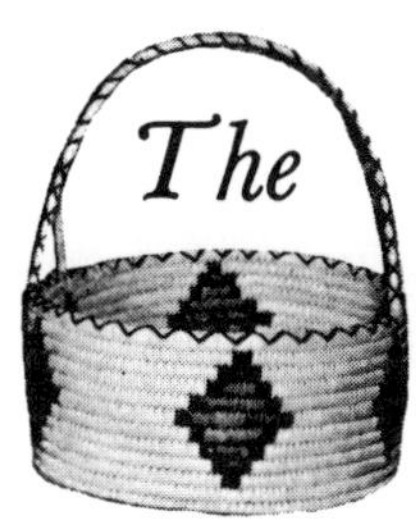


WEAVING OF BASKETS is probably the oldest of the textile arts known to mankind. No race or continent, however, can lay claim to the origin of this art, for it has been world-wide in its distribution. It seems to have been one of the first steps among primitive people in their advancement toward civilization. In gathering wild fruits, berries, nuts, and seeds, they found need for a container in which to collect these foods and transport them to their homes, so they fashioned together leaves or twigs or reeds, from the fields and marshes, into what we call baskets. Among some people this became a domestic art, and the baskets they made were used in the field or for storage or other household uses.

In America, the weaving of baskets has been given a place among the fine arts. The American Indian has given to the world an art that is unique, that is individual to his race; an art that is purely American and one in which the beauty and richness of design is such that all Americans have just cause to be proud. The Indian baskets that we see today are not of recent origin, but rather are a development of an art that has been handed down through hundreds of years.

Anthropologists have divided the primitive Americans into three groups or periods—Basket Maker I, Basket Maker II, and Basket Maker III.

Basket Maker I was a roving hunter with no fixed place of abode. The term "Basket Maker" as applied to these people is questionable, since no specimens of their handicraft have ever been found. This is not conclusive, for the type of life they lived would not furnish sufficient protection to preserve a specimen through the many hundreds of years down to the time of our own civilization. The justification for the claim that they did make baskets is based upon the fact that the technique and design of Basket Maker II, several centuries later, were so advanced that it is thought there must have been an earlier period during which some advancement in the art was accomplished.

Basket Maker II lived in caves and it is in these dry recesses that many beautiful pieces of the craft have been found. These baskets vary in size, shape, and design and show remarkable skill.

Basket Maker III had made much further advancement in that they had learned to build permanent shelters and also had learned how to make pottery. Both of these were important discoveries which vitally affected the lives of these early people. Their homes were crude affairs made of poles leaning against the framework and covered with brush and plastered with mud. They could be located near other homes, and thus we have the beginning of villages that, in time, produced the great prehistoric cultures that are being studied today.

The discovery of pottery provided the primitive home with cooking utensils that were impervious to fire, but, prior to this time, cooking might have been done in baskets in a manner similar to that practiced by more recent tribes. This was done by grinding corn or acorns into a meal or coarse flour and mixing it with water in a tightly woven basket; then heated stones were dropped into the basket until the gruel was cooked.

Basketry, like other Indian art, has been handed down through countless generations. There have been no schools, no books, no sketches or drawings, for, with an Indian, his art is spontaneous; it is part of his soul—he is a true artist. In weaving, the mother works at her basket while her daughter looks on, for she too must master the craft. She goes with her mother to the desert or into the forest or down along the river to gather the materials she will use. When they are prepared she starts to weave her basket. At first she uses only the simpler designs and the coarser weaves, but as her technique and ability improve she takes up the more intricate designs and finer weaves. She must learn all the designs that are characteristic and distinctive of her people and her tribe. These she must store away in her memory, for that will be her only reference when she wants to put them into future use.

Not only do the designs and types of baskets vary with the different tribes, but, in most instances, the materials as well. For example, the Indians on Point Barrow, in northern Alaska, make their baskets of whalebone from the mouth of the black whale of the Bering Sea, while the Attus, in the Aleutians, use soft grasses. Farther south, on the Alaskan mainland, the Thlingits use spruce roots, and across the Canadian border, in the state of Washington, the Makaws make beautiful baskets of tule leaves and dyed cedar bark. The Pomos, of northern California, weave the small feathers of birds into their baskets, and the Piutes, of Nevada, cover their baskets with attractive beadwork. The Chippewas, of Minnesota, use sweet grass and birchbark. In northern Arizona, the Hopis use rabbit brush colored with soft native dyes. Farther south the Pimas use willow and devil's claw, and the Papagos use yucca leaves and bear grass. In all, eight Arizona tribes weave baskets. Over in the Smoky Mountains of North Carolina the Cherokees use split cane, as do the Chitematchas, of Louisiana, and, in Florida, the Seminoles use palmetto leaves and wire grass. We might continue on and on, for, of the more than two hundred Indian tribes in the United States, a large number weave baskets. In Arizona, in recent years, the weaving of Indian baskets has been on a rapid decline. Certain factors contributing to this condition will require the understanding and co-operation of both Indians and whites if they are to be overcome.

In the first place, many of our Indian people are confused and distraught by the rapid-moving, ever-changing civilization that has been brought upon them. An Indian is deliberate. He seldom plunges headlong into something he does not understand. He has tried to cling to some of the old traditions of his people while he adjusted himself to the new conditions that surrounded him.

For the most part, Indians are poor. When an Indian woman weaves a basket she must sell it to buy necessities for herself and family. Often, after having spent weeks or even months in creating a basket, she is offered no more for it than a sum equal to a few days wages at common labor. As a result, she gets a job and her daughter does likewise.

In the meantime, the Great Spirit is calling more and more of the old weavers, and Indian baskets become fewer and fewer. Thirty years ago the shelves in the trading posts were filled with beautiful baskets, but today there is seldom one on display. This condition will not change until both the Indian and his white brother change their sense of values. This great heritage that has been handed down from the time of the cave people should not now be lost to the Indian. Nor should the white man consider the Indian basket merely as a souvenir to be purchased cheaply, but rather as something to be treasured as an integral part of the legend, romance, and tradition of the old West.

Although it is the newest member of our national family, in some ways Arizona is very old. As early as A.D. 600 a race of farmers had developed an extensive culture along the Gila River in the southern part of the state. They had built what was, probably, our country's first irrigation system, and were diverting water from the river onto their fields. Evidence of an ancient canal system is still to be seen in this area.

Nowhere in our country has nature, in so limited an area, created contrasts so great as we find in Arizona. In the south are found vast areas of desert wasteland with torrid heat and forests of giant cactus, while the cool mountain ranges of the north hold the greatest virgin forests of ponderosa pine in the world. In the south, where irrigation has been brought onto the desert, orange groves, date orchards, and fields of alfalfa, cotton, grain, and winter vegetables abound. Cities have sprung up where we may find nationals of a score of countries mingling with Indians whose forefathers, centuries before America was known to the white man, had tilled the very soil on which the streets are laid.

Among these aboriginal tribes are to be found cultural differences equally as great. The Pima and Papago Indians of the south are a peaceful agricultural people, but as we travel northward from their irrigated fields we are soon in the mountain country which is the home of the Yavapai and the Apache tribes.

These mountain people depended almost exclusively on wild foods. They gathered wild fruits, nuts, and seeds, and hunted wild game, which was plentiful throughout their country. They were roving marauders who raided their agricultural neighbors, pillaging and stealing the crops they had grown. While the Pimas and Papagos were noted for the peaceful acceptance of the white man into their country, the Apaches were equally notorious for the fierceness with which they opposed white immigration. The Apaches, however, were not the first to occupy this wild and rugged country, for they found the whole area dotted with the ruins left by prehistoric people who had preceded them. The comparatively narrow river valleys are strewn with the ruins of villages and homesites, some of which extend far back into the higher mountains.

In the manner that time is considered by archaeologists, in the development of civilizations and cultures, the Apache is a newcomer in this area. Three or more races or cultural groups preceded him. In the north there are evidences of a late Basket Maker occupation with an overlapping of Mogollon, who are thought to have come up from the south. Added to these at a later period were the Salados, who were the builders of the Casa Grande ruins, in the Pima country. The evolution of the Apache and Yavapai tribes, who now occupy this country, from the roving warriors that they once were to the quiet and peaceful people they are today is one of the most fascinating chapters in the history of the American Indian. Notwithstanding the wild nomadic life which they led, the women of these tribes may be counted among the finest basket weavers in the Southwest.

In Arizona, as it is today, it is difficult for us to visualize the struggle that confronted the primitive people who lived here centuries ago. This was a place of trackless forests, steep, rugged mountains, and vast areas of hot desert wasteland. Scientific research has indicated that it was plagued with great droughts that dried up the fields and caused the wild game to move away to better ranges.

Another menace, possibly greater than any other, came from the presence of bands of fierce, nomadic raiders that ranged over the Southwest and pillaged the villages of the weaker or less warlike tribes. Some of the stronger tribes were able to repel these marauding bands, while other tribes had to resort to other means of protection. This, probably, is what caused the Hopi Indians of northern Arizona to seek the security of their lofty mesas where they have lived for the past eight hundred years. These three precipice-like promontories of land extend from the plateau out onto the desert floor, from which they rise some six hundred feet. Their villages, on top of these wind-swept mesas, were beyond the range of bowmen on the plains below, and the approaches to the mesas, sometimes only a few feet in width, could be defended against a much superior attacking force.

About two hundred miles to the northwest, their friends, the Havasupais, sought refuge on the floor of Cataract Canyon, which lies

3,300 feet below the rim of the surrounding plateau. Their village could be reached only by a tortuous trail that wound along the ledges of the canyon wall. Thus their defensive position was the reverse of that of the Hopis, for an enemy had to enter single file along the exposed trail, and warriors strategically placed could hold back a much stronger invading force. The survival of the Havasupais would have been questionable if their well-filled granaries of corn, beans, and dried squash had been exposed to the fierce tribes that ranged over this area.

Their kinsmen, the Walapais, whose territory joined theirs on the west, did not have the advantage of any natural defense. Their only protection rested in the utter poverty and desolation of their country. They depended almost exclusively on the meager food supply they could wrest from the dry plateau on which they lived. Aside from a war of attrition, there was little to invite attack from an enemy.

The Chemehuevis, to the south, were more or less under the protection of their more powerful neighbors, the Mohaves. Less is known of this little Shoshonian group than any of our Arizona tribes. Whatever their alliance with the Mohaves might have been, they have lived peacefully together. In primitive times, the Mohave territory extended the full length of the Chemehuevi Valley, along the east bank of the Colorado River. Their geographic location, with respect to the larger tribe, probably afforded the protection necessary for the survival of this small agricultural group.

The four small tribes mentioned here, namely: Walapai, Havasupai, Chemehuevi, and Hopi, constitute the northern group of basket makers of Arizona. Even in the present period of decline, the greatness of their art will be recognized from the many photographs of their baskets which appear in this volume. These four tribes, together with the Apaches and Yavapais to the east and the Pimas and Papagos in the south, make up the basket-weaving tribes of Arizona. In volume of work produced, in type and beauty of decorative design, and in craftsmanship, the baskets of this Arizona group are not surpassed anywhere in the Indian country.

# *Weavers of The Desert Country*

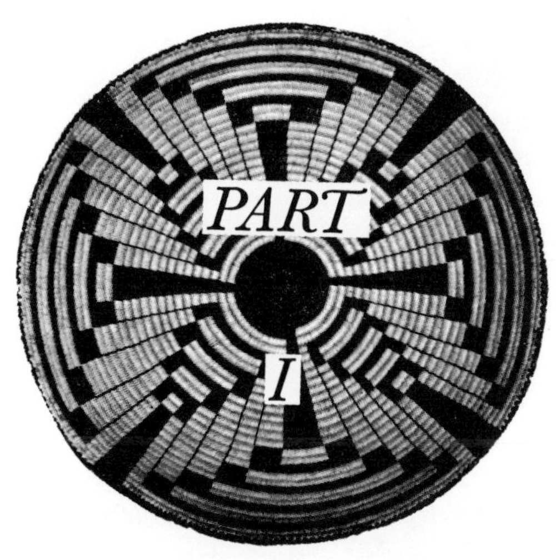

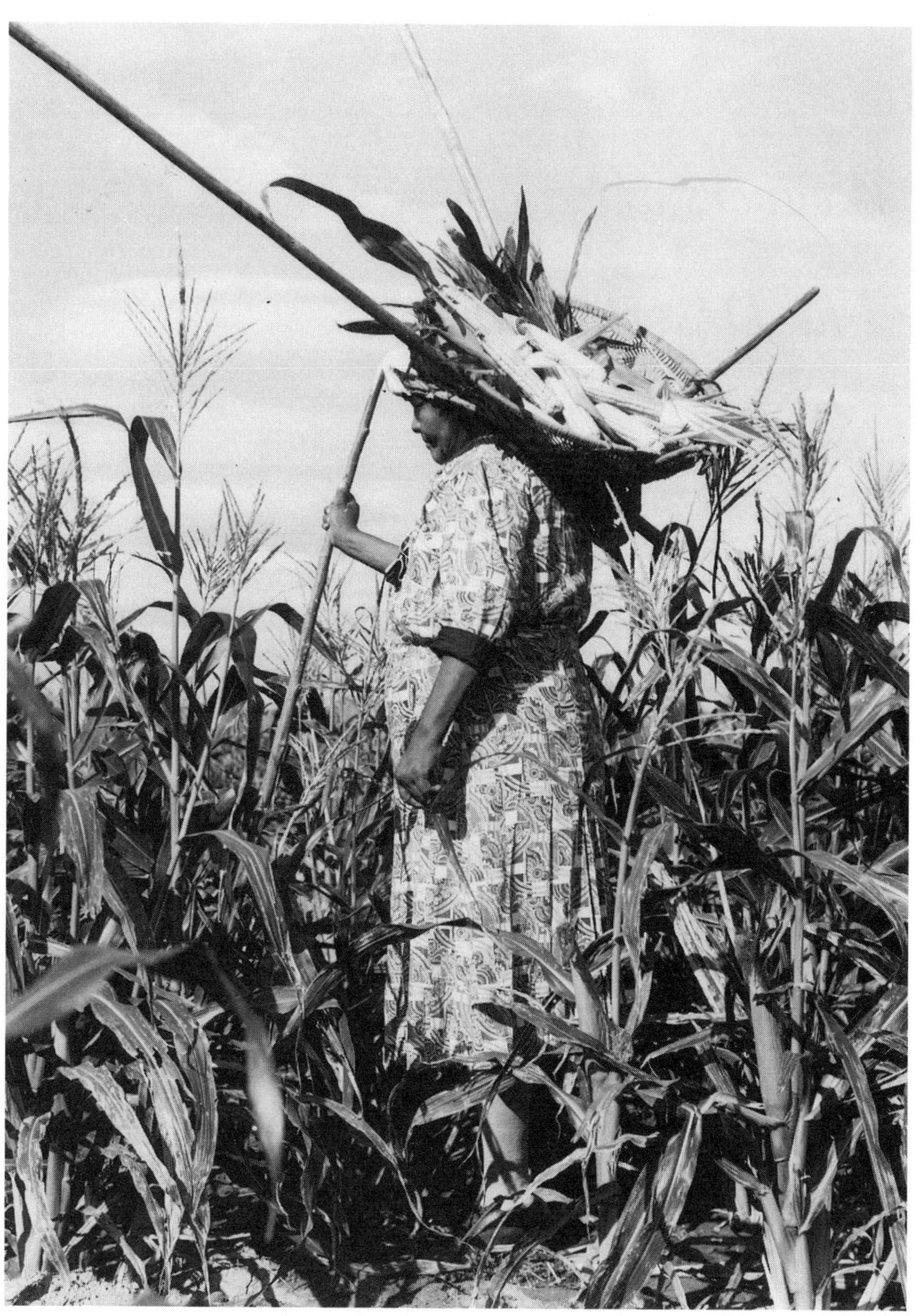

*Giho or burden basket—This probably is the oldest of Pima baskets, since it is mentioned in their old myths. It is the only Pima basket to be made by the men, and no more are now being made. These baskets are scarce*

*PLATE I*

# *Pimería and Its People*

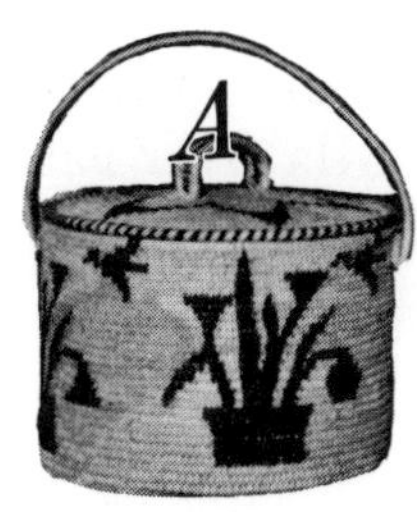

A GREAT ARID PLAIN stretches across southern Arizona from the valleys of the Salt and Gila rivers southward to the International Border and on to the Altar River, in Old Mexico. This desert plain is comparatively flat but broken frequently by short mountain ranges which rise abruptly from the surrounding desert. The highest mountain in this area is Baboquivari Peak, which reaches an altitude above 7,700 feet. Most of the other ranges attain scarcely half that height, and are rocky and barren except for the desert growth of the surrounding country. The early Spanish explorers called this region Pimería. Roughly its boundaries were as follows: The Altar River, in Mexico, on the south, the Magdalena and the San Pedro rivers on the east, the Salt and Gila rivers on the north, and the western boundary a line leading southward from approximately the junction of the Salt and Gila rivers, leaving the city of Ajo to the west and extending on down into Mexico.

The people of Pimería called themselves "Aw-aw-tam," which means "The People." However, they were not the first people to occupy this area, for they followed another race which they called "Ho-ho-kam," meaning the "People Who Went Away." Whence the Aw-aw-tam came, and when, are questions upon which archaeologists do not agree. The Indians themselves have not been able to help. The legends handed down to the present generation simply say their ancestors came from the east. Archaeologists have various other theories. Some contend these people amalgamated with the Ho-ho-kam, and others say they are descendants of this ancient race. Whatever the contact or relationship of the Ho-ho-kam to them might have been, the legend or folklore of the Aw-aw-tam makes no mention of it. The Aw-aw-tam themselves were not a close-knit tribe, but consisted of seven or more groups of the same linguistic stock scattered about over the width and breadth of Pimería.

Two groups, forming one general division of these people, have come down to the present day. The northern group, living on or near the Gila River, was called "Ak-a-merl Aw-aw-tam," meaning "River People." The other group, to the south, was called "To-ho-no Aw-aw-tam," meaning "Desert People."

Presumably the environment and economy of the different sections brought about this division in designation and name. The early Spaniards called the people along the Gila River "Pimos," from the name Pimería, and today they are called the Pima Indians of southern Arizona. They occupy reservations in both the Salt and Gila river valleys. In his report on the Pimas, Russell[1] has said, "The Pimas live in two river valleys that are strewn with the ruins of prehistoric buildings and other evidences of the presence of a considerable population that had attained probably the highest degree of civilization or culture to be found north of Mexico." The stone axes, pottery, and other artifacts of this area are exceptionally well made, and the arrowheads are almost gem-like in their perfection, indicating a much richer culture along these lines than anything ever attained by the Pimas.

Toward the end of the Ho-ho-kam period they were joined by a Pueblo people known as the "Salados," who are credited with the building of Casa Grande, the ruins of which are located a short distance east of the Pima Reservation. It is one of the most interesting spots in southern Arizona and is visited yearly by many thousands of tourists.

The first white man to visit Casa Grande ruins probably was Fr. Eusebio Francisco Kino, who said mass within its walls in 1694. Many people believe that Coronado, on his expedition in 1540, also saw Casa Grande. They believe the Chichitticalli mentioned in his report is, in reality, Casa Grande ruins, but there is no confirmation of this.

1. Frank Russell, *The Pima Indians*, 26th Ann. Report, Bur. Amer. Ethnol.

The first visit of Fr. Kino to the Casa Grande ruins and the nearby Pima villages was followed by many more such visits before his death, in 1711. He baptized many of the Indians, but did not establish any definite missions in the Pima country. He is credited with having introduced horses to the Pimas. Other missionary priests who followed him brought cattle, and wheat and other field seeds. Father Kino described the Pimas as "peaceful farmers who subsist themselves by means of irrigated agriculture." They diverted water from the Gila River to irrigate their lands, and their descendants today have rights to the water of the Gila, for irrigation, that were established by those farmers whom Fr. Kino found along the river. Their crops consisted of corn, beans, squash, and cotton. The cotton was woven into cloth for breechcloths or skirts, and lightweight blankets. Those ancient farmers little realized that a cotton bearing their name, and developed at the United States experimental station at Sacaton would be known and used throughout the world.

When we consider the many miles of irrigation canals the Pimas excavated with stone or wooden tools, carrying the earth up the bank in baskets, we realize the thrift and industry of these people. The men did the planting of the crops, and the women the harvesting and storing away for future use.[2] The seeds were planted with the aid of a sharpened stick, covered with soil, and tamped down with the foot. Boys guarded the fields from birds and animals, but substantial losses were suffered from the Apaches.

Although the Pimas relied on their farm crops for certain foods, many other foods were provided by the surrounding desert. Russell[3] mentions twenty-two desert plants of which the seed, fruit, or foliage was eaten, the two most prominent being the beans from the mesquite tree and the fruit of the saguaro cactus. Prickly pears and many other cactus fruits were cooked or eaten raw, and beans from the palo verde and catclaw and other seeds were parched, ground into meal, and eaten.

Some writers have credited the Pimas with a calendar with which the year was divided into twelve periods like our own. In the thirty-one years I have lived with them I never have heard one of their old people mention this calendar. They did have a calendar stick which

2. See Edward F. Castetter and Willis H. Bell, *Pima and Papago Indian Agriculture,* University of New Mexico Press, Albuquerque, 1942, for further information.

3. Russell, *op. cit.*

they notched to record certain important events, but only the sequence of these events was indicated and not, in any way, the date. No specific division of the year was set; nor did the moon changes figure in their measure of time.

Most Indians are not effusive conversationalists when approached by a stranger, and when a loquacious person formulates his own ideas into a question the Indian simply says "Yes," and then smiles in amusement when his interrogator is gone. When the interview appears in print, the story, along with other "facts" collected, is given as authentic. The Indian is intelligent and can express himself clearly if he cares to do so.

The Pimas did, however, indicate the time of day by the position of the sun, and the old people do so even now. It is understandable how such stories as those about the bird that has twelve feathers in its tail may, with the passing of time, become the basis of the story by which the twelve sections of the year were designated.

## *White Immigration*

IT WAS NOT until early in the nineteenth century that the trend toward western migration brought in the first white trappers and settlers. The first military invasion of the territory was under General Kearney, made during the war with Mexico in 1846. This territory was then under the control of Mexico. Kearney was followed by Lieutenant Emory, in whose report we find the following comment regarding the Pimas: "To us it was a rare sight to be thrown in the midst of a large nation of what is termed wild Indians, surpassing many of the Christian nations in agriculture, little behind them in the useful arts, and immeasurably before them in honesty and virtue."[4] Lieutenant Colonel Cooke led the Mormon Battalion through the Pima country and on to California in 1848. In his report[5] he mentions the Pimas as being friendly and honest in their contacts with his troops.

In 1849, gold was discovered in California, and the route established by Cooke became the one most favored by the thousands of gold seekers who migrated to the West Coast. Then, in 1853, the Pima

4. Ross Calvin (Ed.), *Lieutenant Emory Reports,* University of New Mexico Press, Albuquerque, 1951, p. 134.

5. Philip St. Geo. Cooke, *Conquest of New Mexico and California,* G. P. Putnam and Son, New York, 1878.

country was included in the Gadsden Purchase and became a part of the United States.

The rich soil, the favorable climatic conditions, and the abundant crops of the Pimas did not go unnoticed by the immigrants who were coming west in ever increasing numbers after the close of the Civil War. Soon settlers were coming into the Gila Valley and taking up land above the Pima country. These new farmers followed the methods of the Indians in their agriculture, and in time the diversion of water from the river to their own land almost proved disastrous to the Pimas.

The Pimas' agriculture by now had long since passed the planting stick period, which was followed by a comparatively short period during which a wooden plow, drawn by oxen, was used. The ox was the first draft animal of the Pimas. The plow was made of ironwood or mesquite, with a cottonwood tongue. It merely scratched the surface of the soil but prepared an adequate seed bed for the planting of crops. With the establishment of a stage line through the Indian country, late in the 1850's, supplies and tools were made available to them.

## *Pima-Maricopa Alliance*

ANY HISTORICAL facts regarding the Pima Indians in most cases involve the Maricopas as well. The Maricopas are a branch of the Yuma tribe, who seceded from that tribe more than a century ago. They came up the Gila River and lived for a time near what is known now as Gila Bend. The Yumas followed them and many bloody battles were fought, but the Yumas were not able to force the seceding group back to the mother tribe.

Finally, couriers brought news that the Yumas and the Cocopas, who were a neighboring tribe, were coming up the Gila to attack the seceding group, whereupon the secessionists moved farther up the river to the Pima villages. The old Pimas tell how their council debated for four days as to whether they would drive these people back down the Gila or allow them to stay. The latter course might invite trouble from the Yuma tribe, but, in the end, the council agreed to let the Maricopas stay and assigned them certain lands at the junction of the Salt and Gila rivers, where they are living today. Also, they told the Maricopas they must subsist by farming as the Pimas did, and that they must not go to the mountains to hunt, and become embroiled in trouble with the Apaches; that if they were attacked the Pimas would send warriors to their aid, and in like manner the Maricopas should send help to the Pimas if they were attacked by an enemy. It may be said of the Maricopas that they never broke their word and always have lived in peace with the Pimas. They have kept their identity as a tribe and have intermarried little with the Pimas or any other Indian tribe, and with the white man not at all. It seems that these people have the understanding and spirit of neighborly tolerance for which so much of the world is seeking today.

A grand old man of the Maricopas, Cyrus Sun, told me the following story of how the tribe got its name: It seems that after his people arrived at the Pima villages one of their warriors, who was in full war paint, met a Spaniard. The Spaniard asked the warrior what tribe he belonged to, and the Indian replied, "I don't know." This was literally true, for his group no longer claimed any allegiance to the Yumas, from whom they had broken away. Looking at the bright yellow paint of the warrior, the Spaniard said, "Maybe you are a mariposa." The mariposa lily is a bright yellow flower which comes up on the desert after the winter rains and closely resembles the yellow poppy.

The Indian went back to his camp and told his people what the Spaniard had said. They changed the name to Maricop and adopted it, thereafter calling themselves Maricop, the white man's version being Maricopa. This, in later years, became the name of the county in which they live and in which Phoenix and a large portion of the population of Arizona is found. That is Cyrus' story, but, in Spanish, "mariposa" is the word for butterfly, and perhaps the Spaniard merely thought the painted warrior looked like a butterfly.

The Maricopas live in two groups, one on the Salt River Reservation, and one on the Gila River Reservation. The main body, however, still lives at the junction of the Salt and Gila rivers, on the land their Pima benefactors gave them long ago. They are tall, broad-framed people, and the term "big" could be applied to them without reservation. They are taller than the Pimas, who themselves are not small men.

Lest their type might be misinterpreted from the origin of their name, let us say that, if you ever sat in one of their meetings and watched the men enter the door, noting how nearly they filled the opening from top to bottom, you would not associate the Maricopas with the lilies or the butterflies.

## *Sacaton—1871*

THE PIMA AGENCY headquarters was established at Sacaton in 1871. The first government buildings were erected and the Indian agent, whose offices were in Tucson until that time, moved to the new station on the Gila River. Sacaton is well situated with respect to the Pima villages, which extend both east and west along the river. It is about forty-two miles southeast of Phoenix and almost twice that distance northwest of Tucson. The establishment of the Pima agency in the Indian country brought with it the white man's law and order, which by that time was sorely needed.

Of the period immediately preceding, Russell has the following to say: "With the advent of the stage, the immigrant and the military trains, began the breaking down of the best that was old and the building up of the worst that was new. For a period of thirty years, or from 1850 to 1880, the Pimas were visited by some of the vilest specimens of humanity that the white race has produced. Until 1871, the tribe was without a teacher, missionary or, to judge from their own story and the records of the government, a competent agent."[6]

With the coming of the Indian agency to Sacaton, the first Indian police force was organized. From the stories which their descendants have told, the reputation of the Northwest Mounties might well be applied to these Pima police. It is said of them, "They always brought in their man." Sometimes he was bound and sitting upright in the saddle, and at other times he was slung limply across its pommel, but they did establish law and order on the reservation.

It should be said to the credit of the Pimas that, regardless of the hardships which the white man has brought upon them, there is no case on record where a Pima has taken the life of a white man. They have lived at peace with their neighbors and probably have assimilated the white man's ways and customs to a greater degree than any other tribe in Arizona. Their schools, their churches, even their language show the white man's influence, for today about 92 per cent of the Pimas speak English, and those who do not are all in the older age group.

6. Russell, *op. cit.*

## *Pima Baskets*

HISTORICAL INTEREST in the Pimas has centered chiefly about their irrigated agriculture and their contribution to the development of the Southwest through their friendly acceptance of the white man. In both these matters the men of the tribe were given the greater prominence, but the Pima women hold a place of honor and distinction in their own right. They are the artists of their people and their baskets are famous. Dr. J. F. Breazeale has said, "For strength and usefulness, for practical indestructibility, for gracefulness of shape and beauty and diversity of pattern, in my opinion, the Pima basket excels anything of its kind in the world."[7] With this statement I am in full agreement.

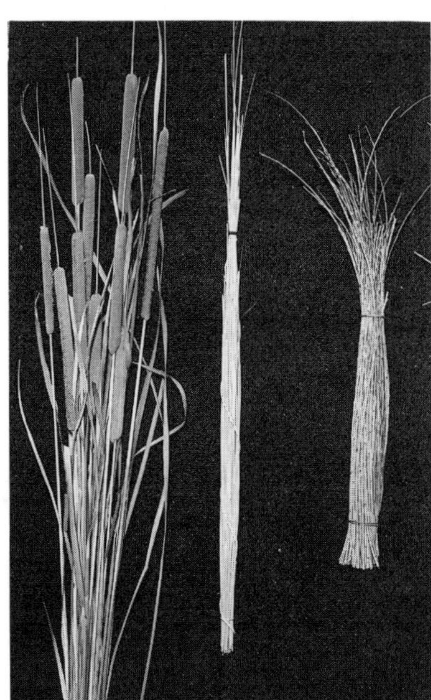

*Left, cattail; center, split sections of cattail stems; right, bundle of willow twigs* *PLATE II*

Pima baskets are made from three native materials: willow (mainly *Salix Gooddingii*), *Martynia* or devil's claw (*Martynia parviflora*), and the cattail or tule (*Typha angustifolia*). These materials are harvested by the weavers when they are ready and stored away just as a farmer harvests his wheat and corn. The willow twigs are gathered about the middle of August, at which time the buds which came out in the spring have matured into twigs twelve to eighteen inches in length and somewhat less in diameter than a lead pencil. They are tough and flexible and do not have the brittleness of the older stems when dried. The Indian women go to the river banks and cut the twigs, from which they immediately peel off the bark before it dries or withers. This is done by starting at the cut end of the stem, holding the bark in the teeth and running the thumb between it and the twig. Then they split the twig into three or four thin strips in much the

7. J. F. Breazeale, *The Pima and His Basket,* Arizona Archaeological and Historical Society, Tucson, Ariz., 1923.

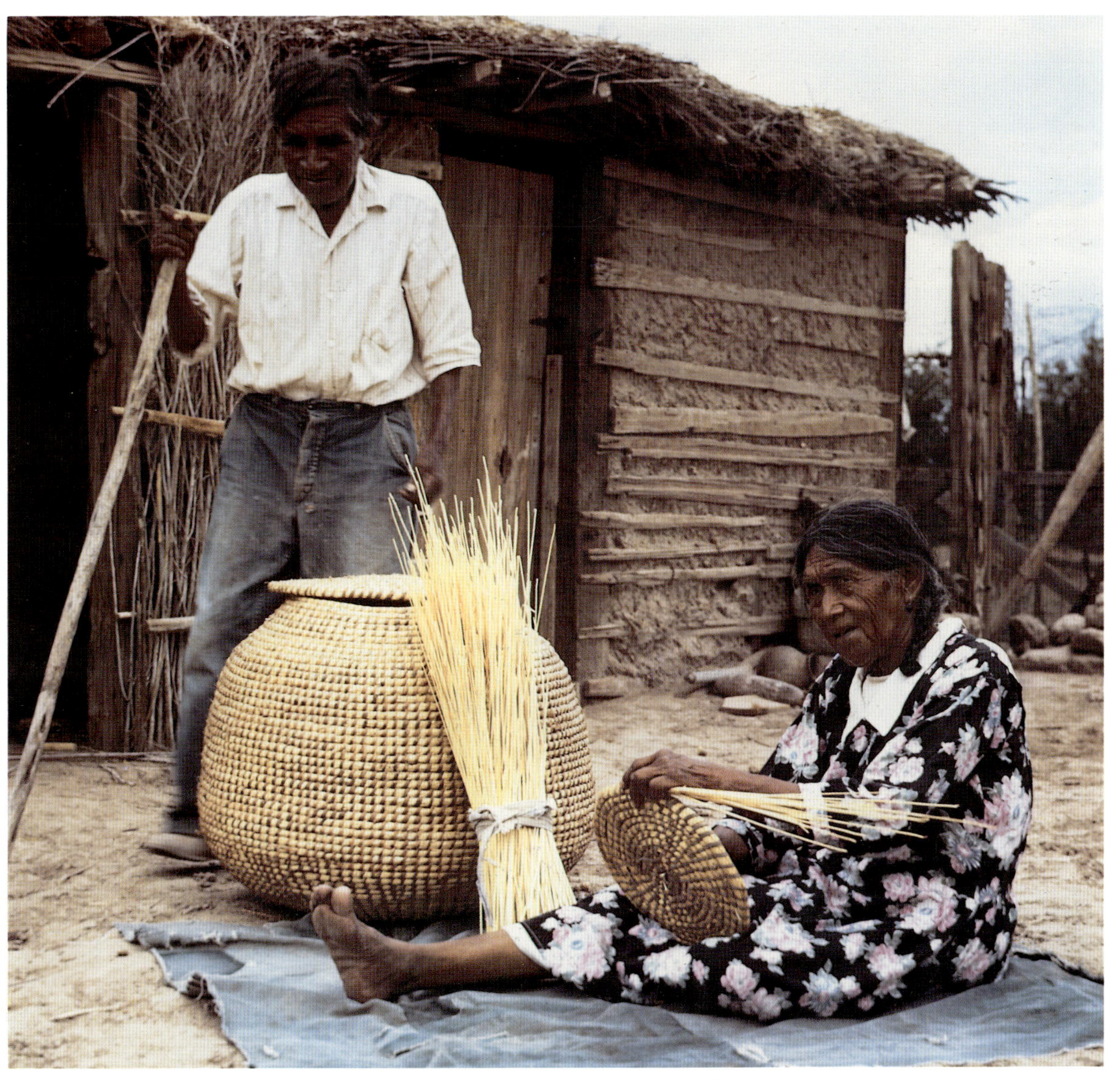

*Anastasia Harvey weaving a storage basket. Only two Pima weavers continue this almost forgotten art. The largest of these baskets will hold about twelve bushels of wheat, but many of the old storage baskets would hold forty to fifty bushels.* *(See pages 30-31.)*

*PLATE A*

*Location of the eight basket-weaving tribes of Arizona. Reservations where baskets actually are woven are shown in red.*

*MAP*

1. The Salt River and Gila River reservations both are occupied by the Pimas. Note that the Salt River Reservation joins the Fort McDowell Reservation on the north.
2. The Papago Reservation includes San Xavier, to the east. The Gila Bend and the Maricopa reservations to the northwest and north, respectively, are Papago also, but no baskets are made there.
3. The Apaches weave baskets in both the Fort Apache and the San Carlos reservations.
4. Most Yavapai baskets are made at the Fort McDowell Reservation. The reservations at Camp Verde and Prescott, to the north, are occupied by the Yavapais, but few, if any, baskets are made there.
5. The Walapais occupy the Truxton Canyon and the Big Sandy reservations, to the south, and baskets are woven at all three locations. Note variations in spelling between map and text.
6. The Havasupais occupy only the small area shown.
7. The Chemehuevi Reservation was inundated by water impounded by Parker Dam. This tribe now occupies land on the Colorado River Reservation.
8. The Hopi Reservation is entirely surrounded by the Navajo Reservation, the boundaries of which are shown.

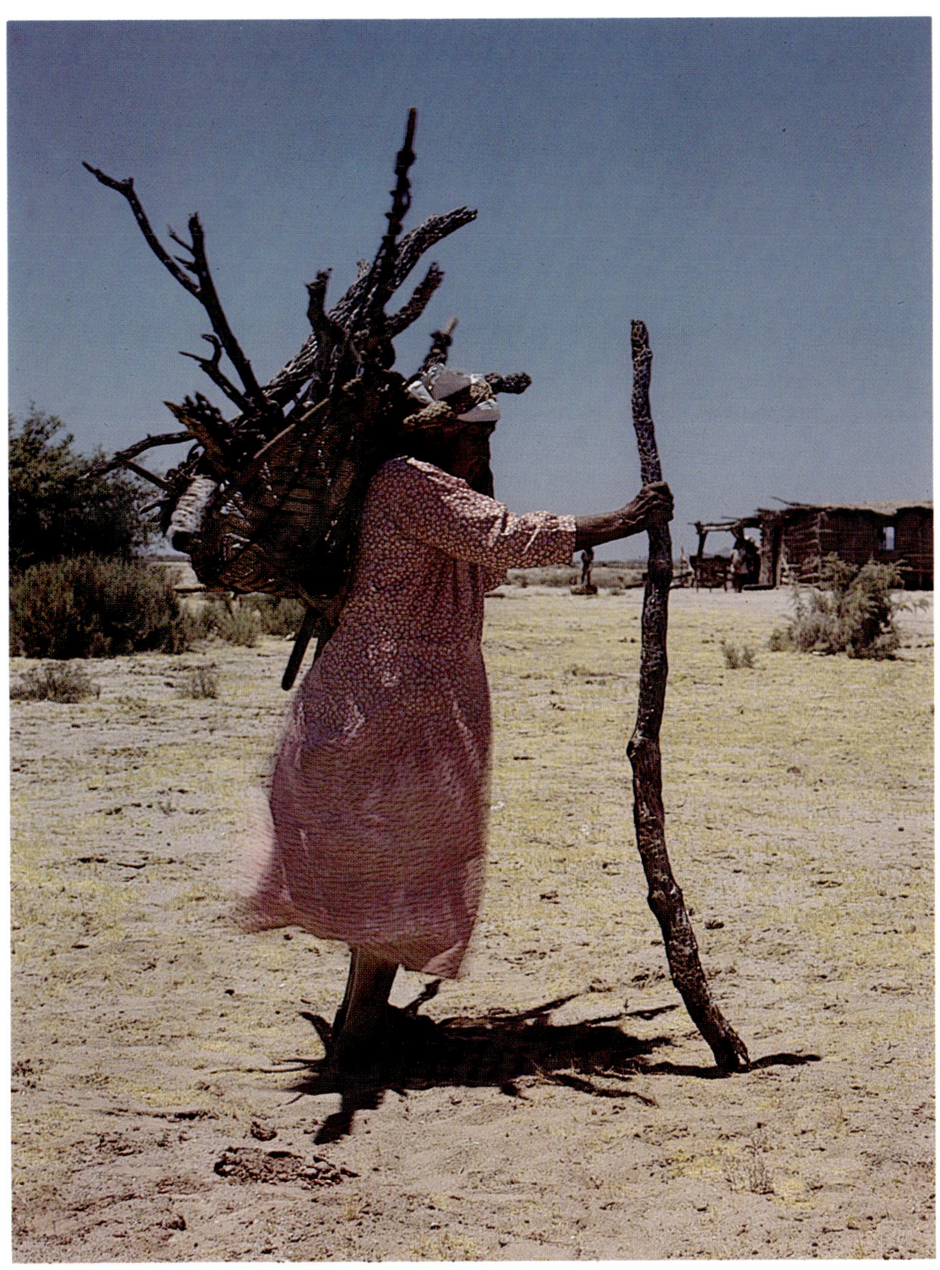

*Giho, or burden basket, laden with cholla cactus wood for fuel. This basket was used by both the Pimas and the Papagos. (See pages 51-52.)*

PLATE B

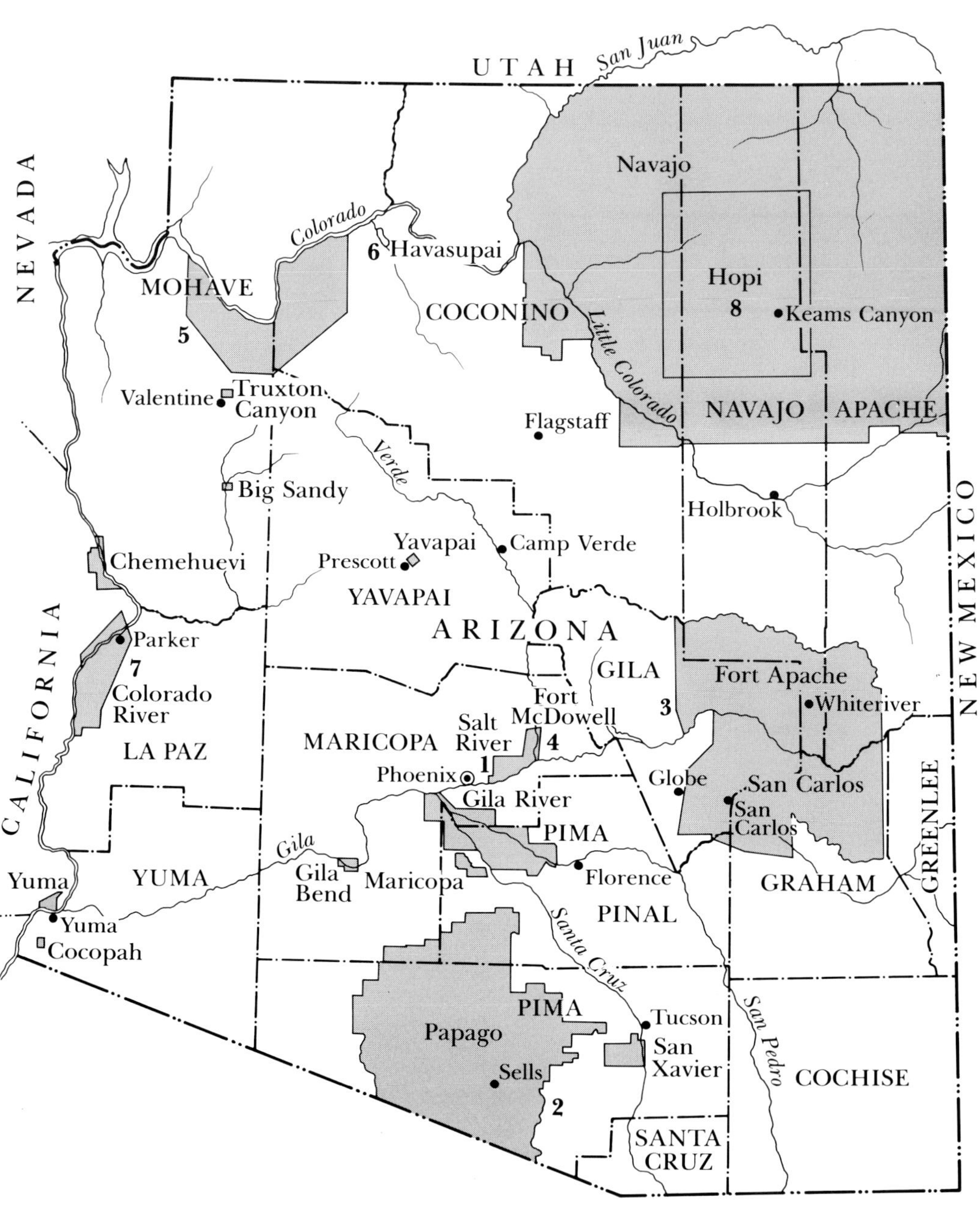
UTAH
San Juan
NEVADA
Colorado
6 Havasupai
Navajo
Hopi
8
Keams Canyon
MOHAVE
5
COCONINO
Little Colorado
Valentine
Truxton Canyon
Flagstaff
NAVAJO
APACHE
Verde
Big Sandy
Holbrook
NEW MEXICO
Chemehuevi
Yavapai
Prescott
Camp Verde
YAVAPAI
ARIZONA
CALIFORNIA
Parker
7
Colorado River
GILA
Fort Apache
Whiteriver
3
Fort McDowell
Salt River
4
MARICOPA
LA PAZ
1
Phoenix
Globe
San Carlos
San Carlos
Gila River
PIMA
GREENLEE
Gila
Gila Bend
Maricopa
Florence
Yuma
YUMA
GRAHAM
Yuma
Cocopah
Santa Cruz
PINAL
San Pedro
PIMA
Tucson
Papago
San Xavier
Sells
COCHISE
2
SANTA CRUZ

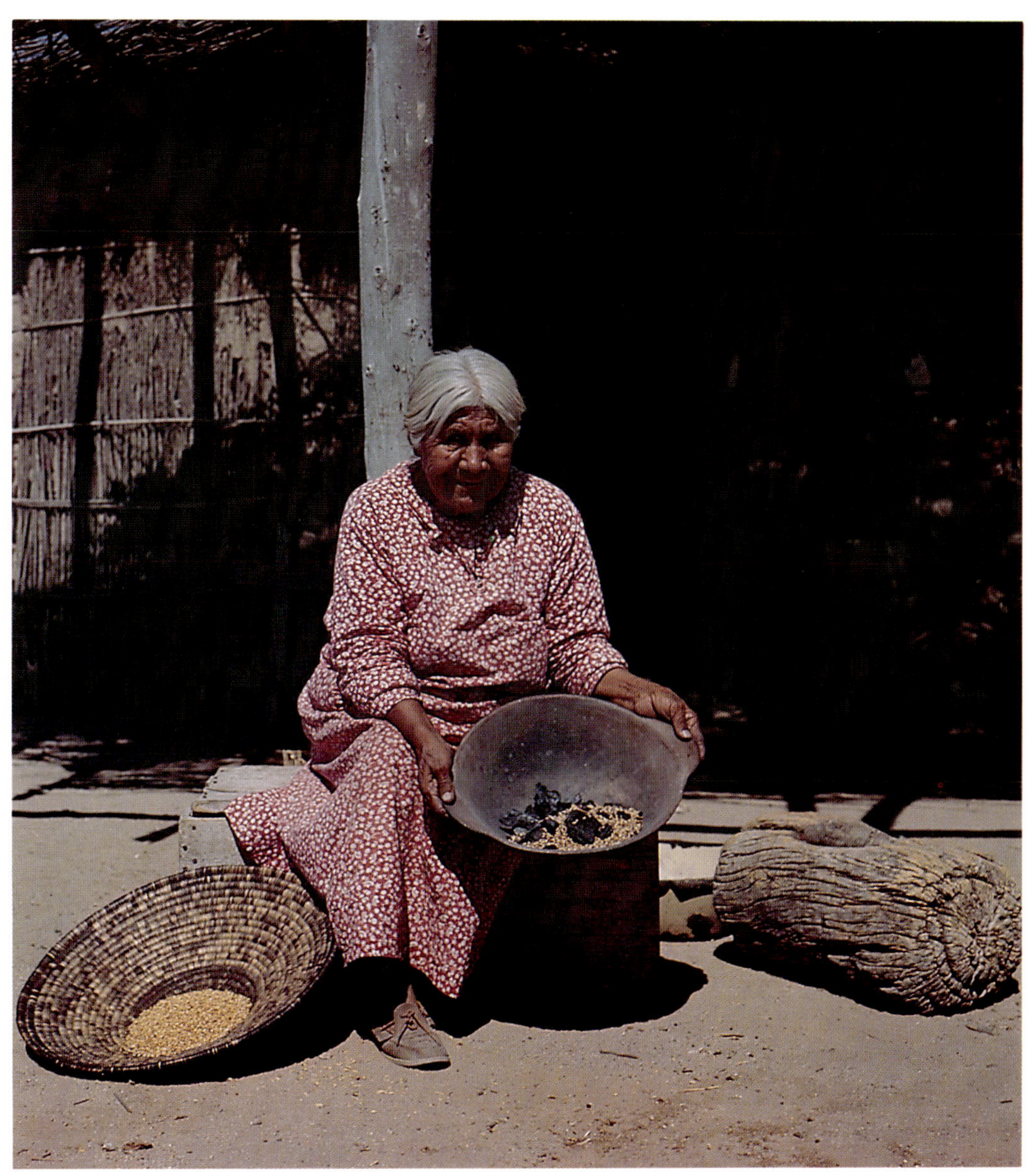

*Lucy Enos, a Pima, using a wheat-parching basket. The live coals may be seen in the bowl. Lucy and the three Pimas shown in Plate D represent four generations of Pima basket weavers (we hope).*

*PLATE C*

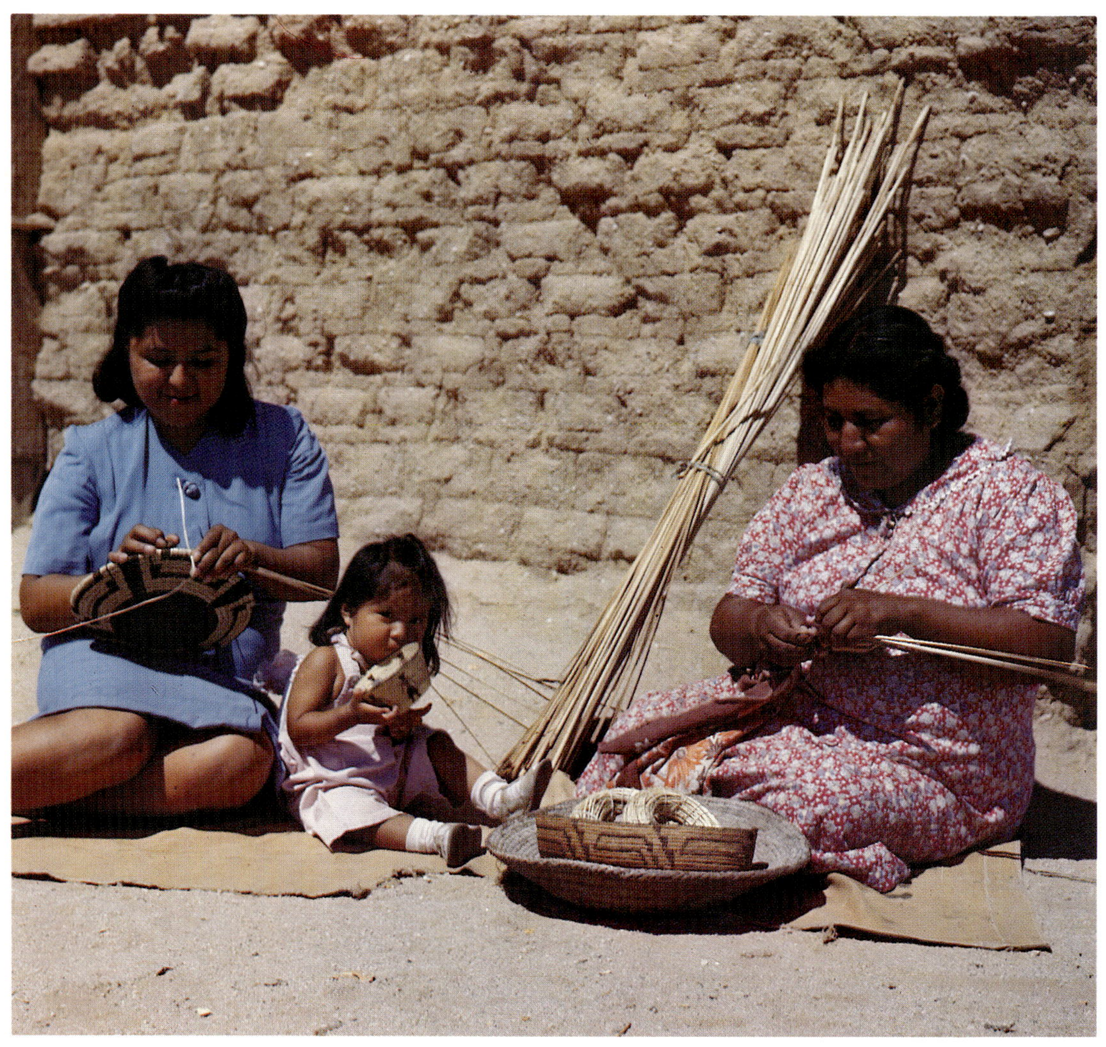

*Pima weavers have handed down their art from one generation to the next through many centuries. Shown here are Isobell Juan Jay, daughter; Louise Kuyiyesva, granddaughter; and Donna Kuyiyesva, great-granddaughter of Lucy Enos, shown in Plate C.*

*PLATE D*

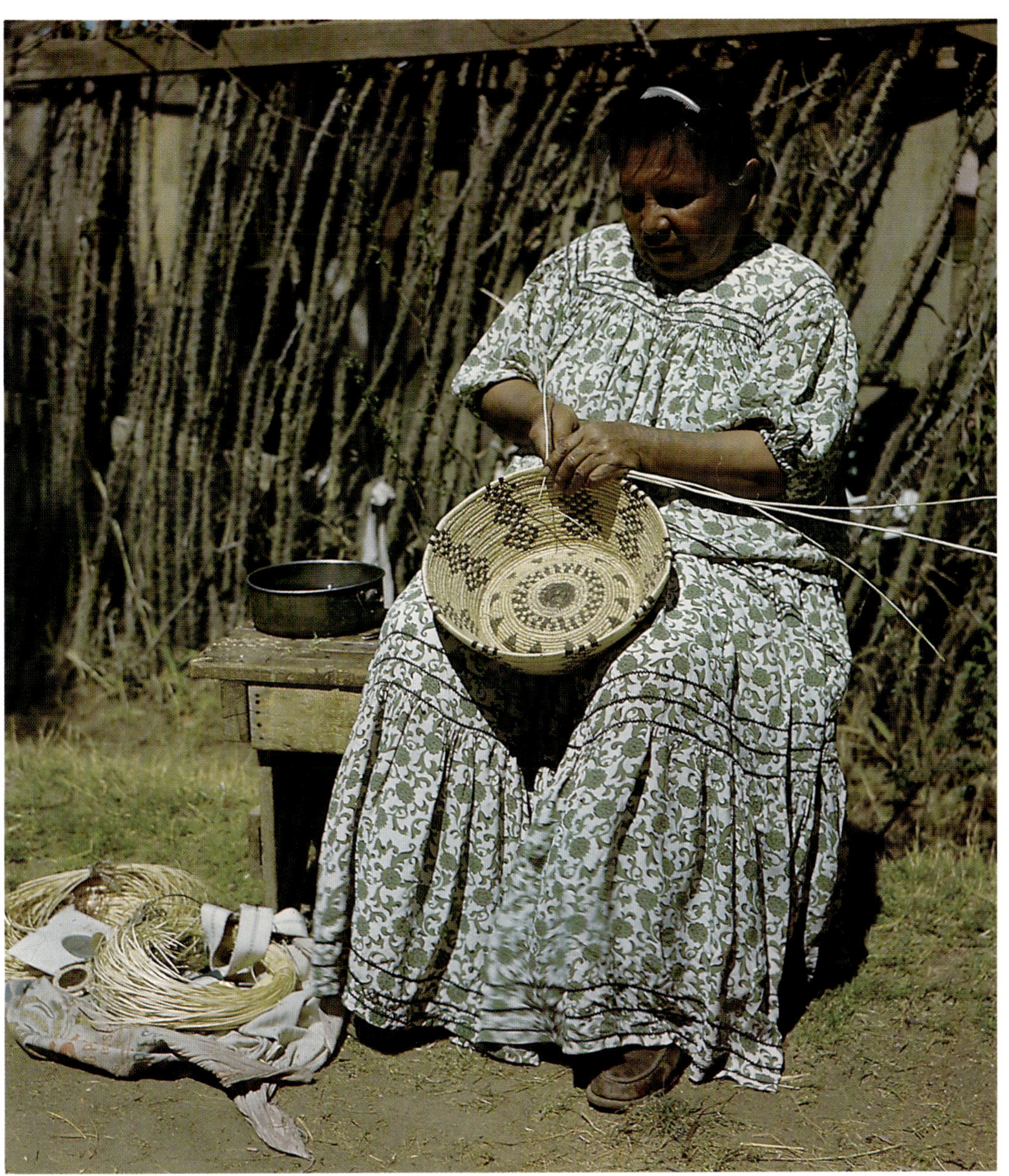

*The devil's-claw-and-cottonwood coiled baskets from San Carlos are the Apaches' greatest contribution to Indian art. Lizette Phillips, shown here, says the Apaches have "always made these baskets."*

*PLATE E*

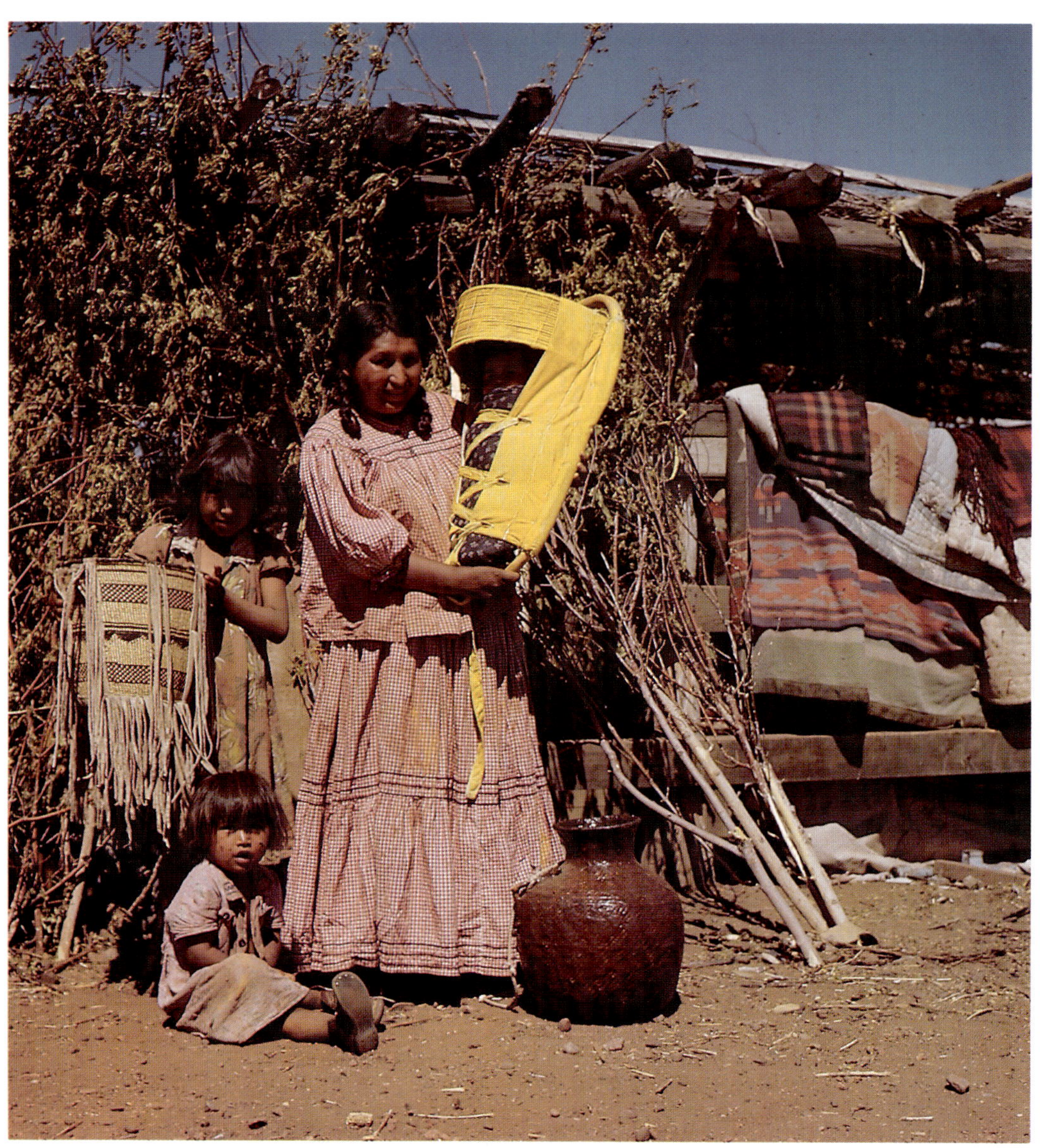

*A White Mountain Apache weaver and her three children. One of the children is carrying a burden basket. A tus is at the weaver's feet.*

PLATE F

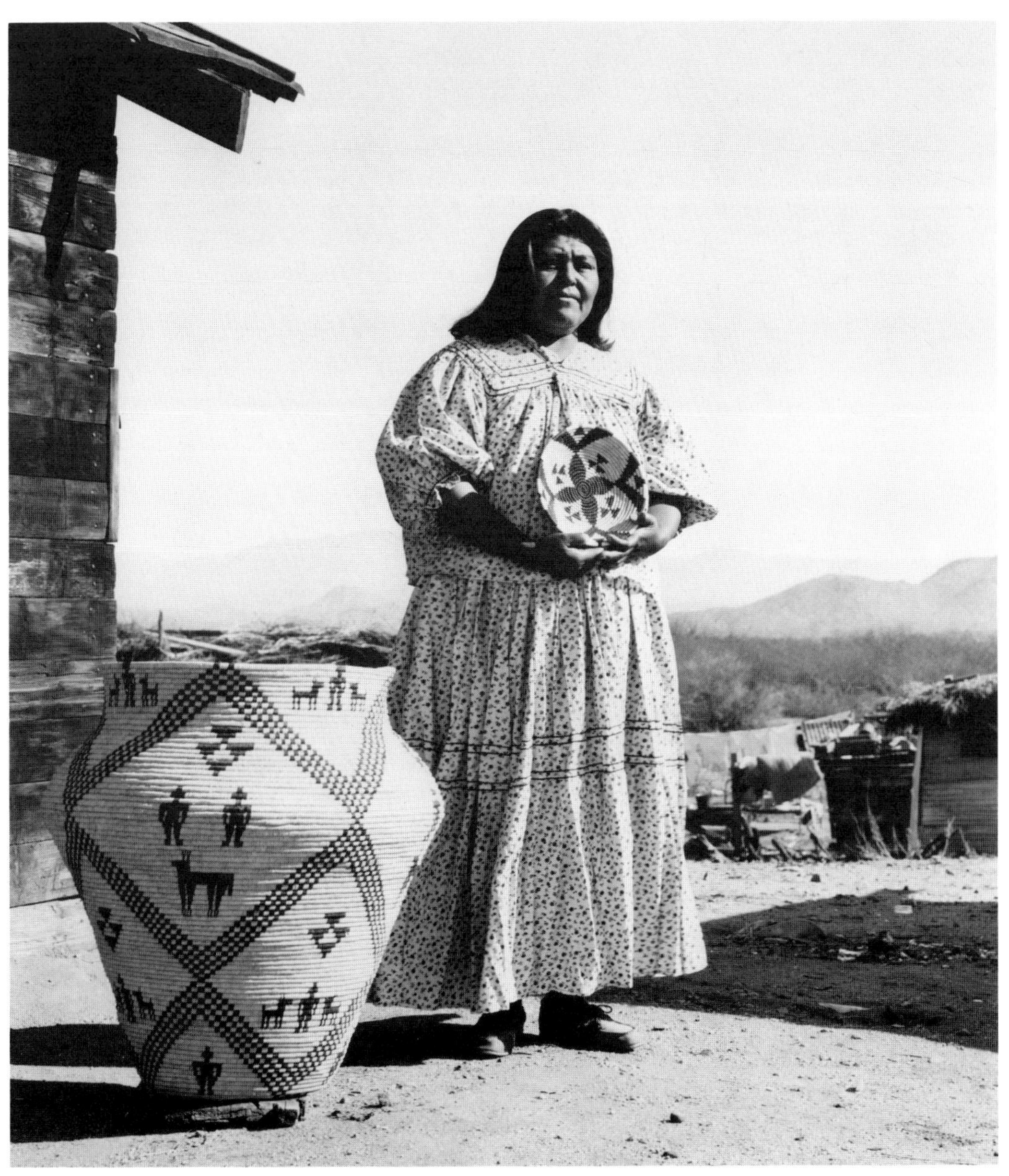

*Mabel Osife is the only Yavapai weaver who continues to make these large ollas.* *(See page 94.)*

PLATE G

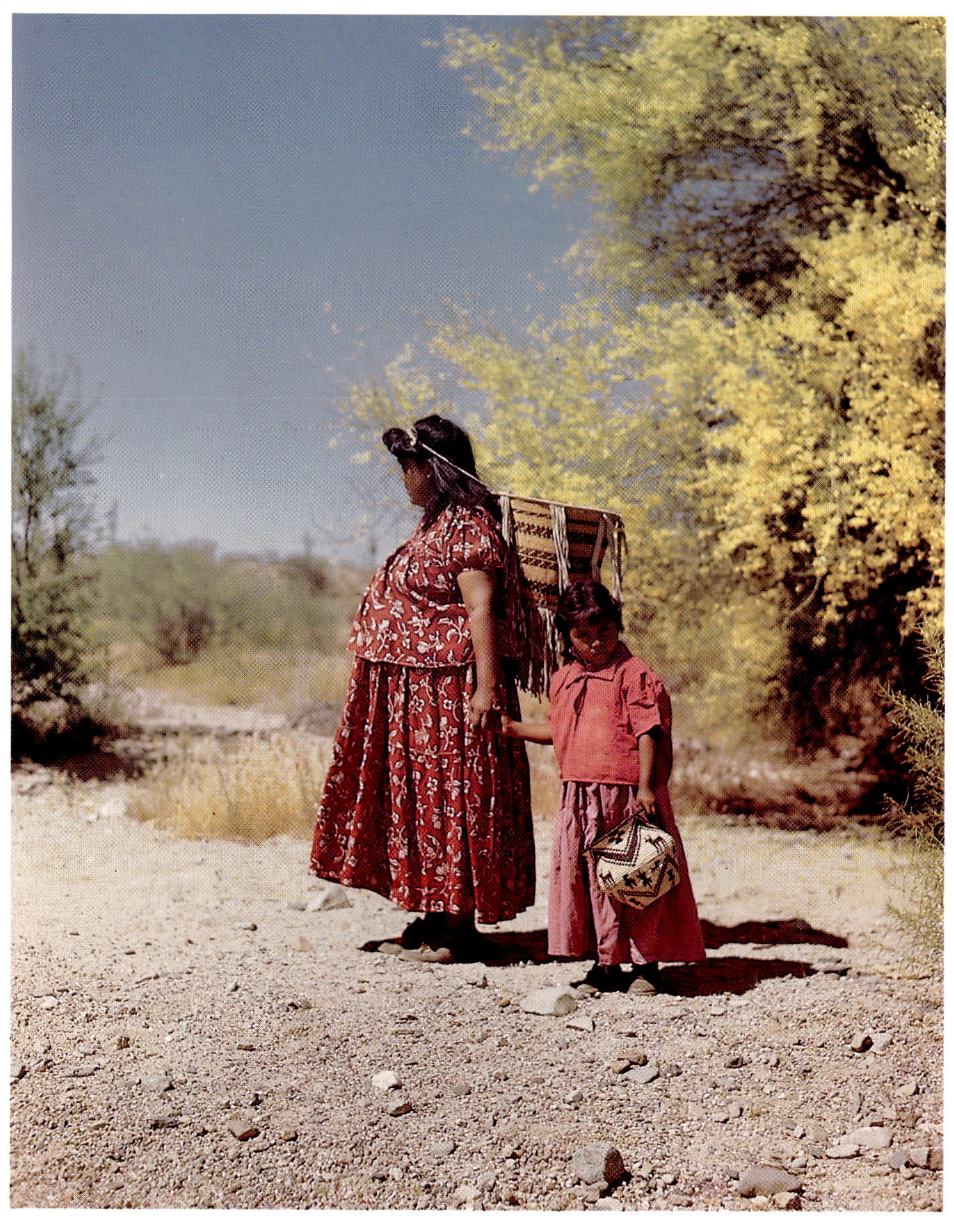

*In April the palo verdes bloom along the washes of the low country, and the squawberries are ripe.* PLATE H

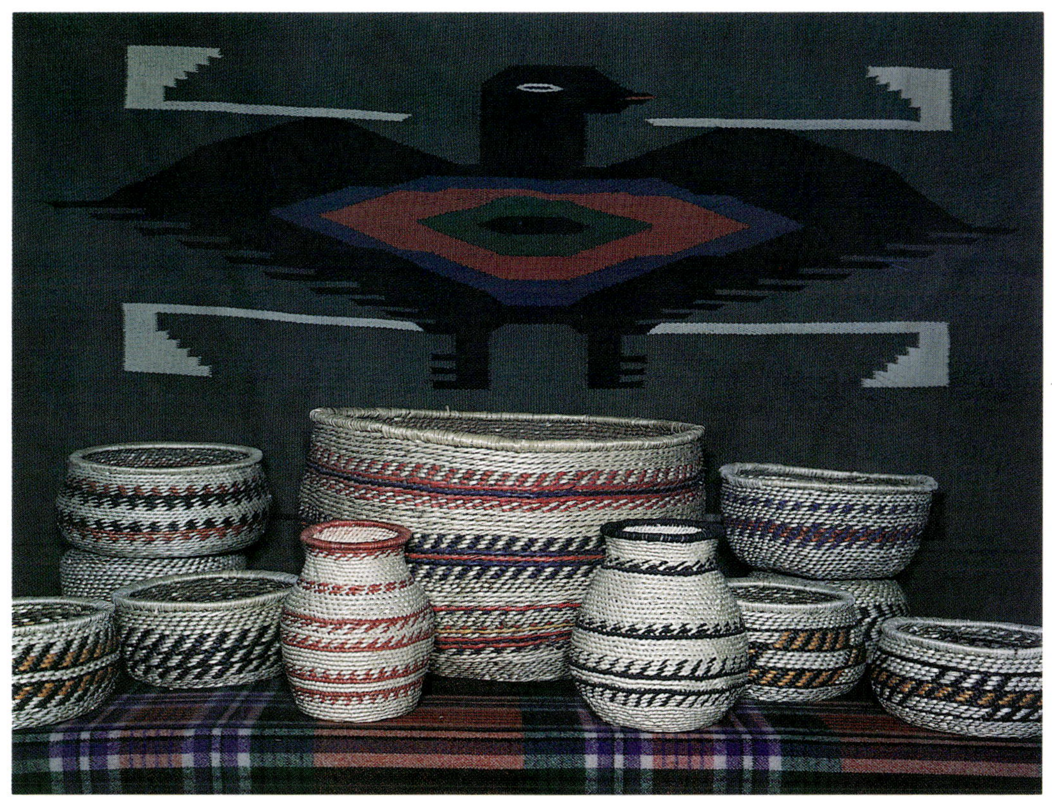

*Walapai baskets in the author's collection. The largest basket was obtained in 1926. (See page 122.)*

PLATE I

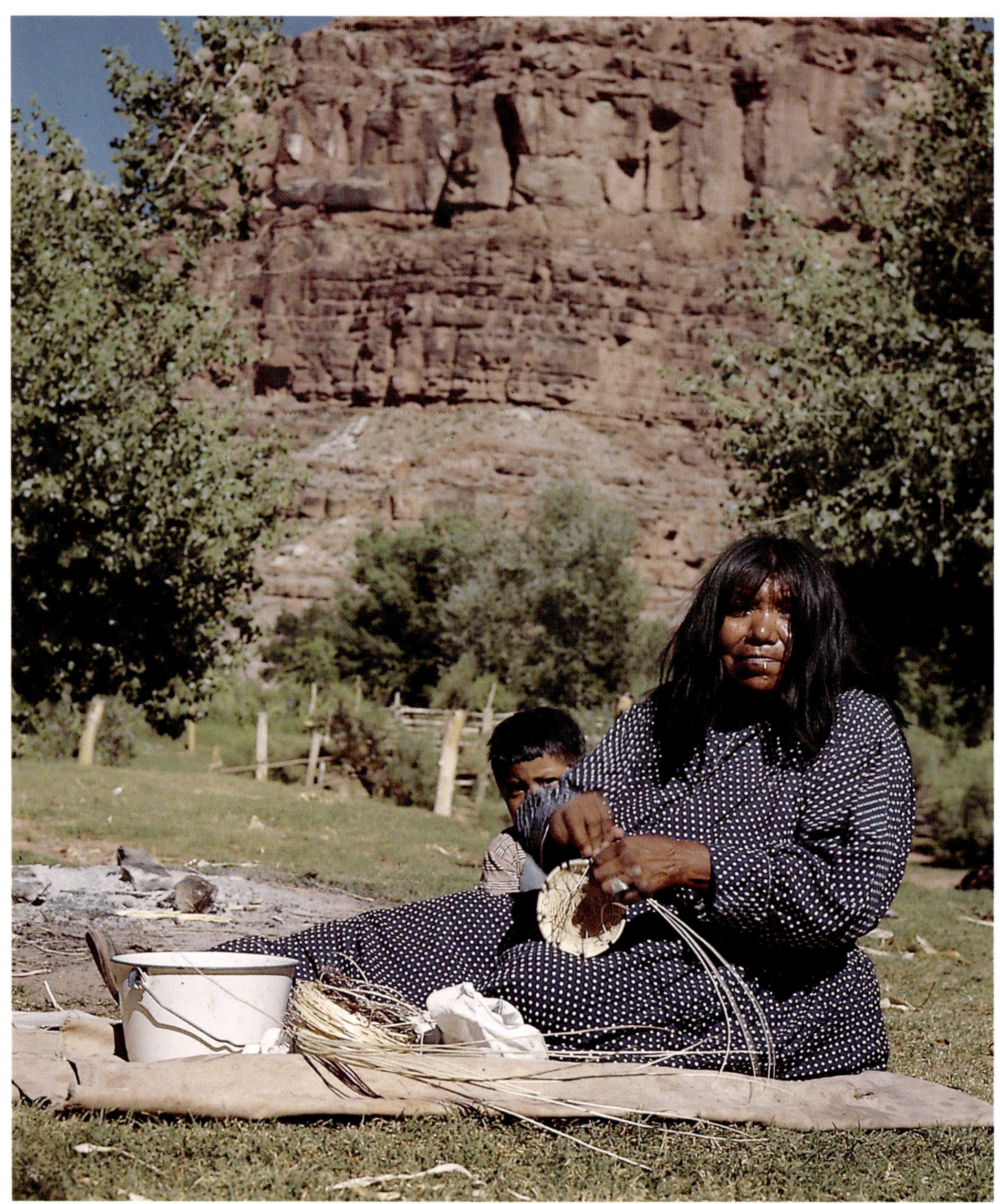

*A Havasupai weaver from the "Land of the Willows."* PLATE J

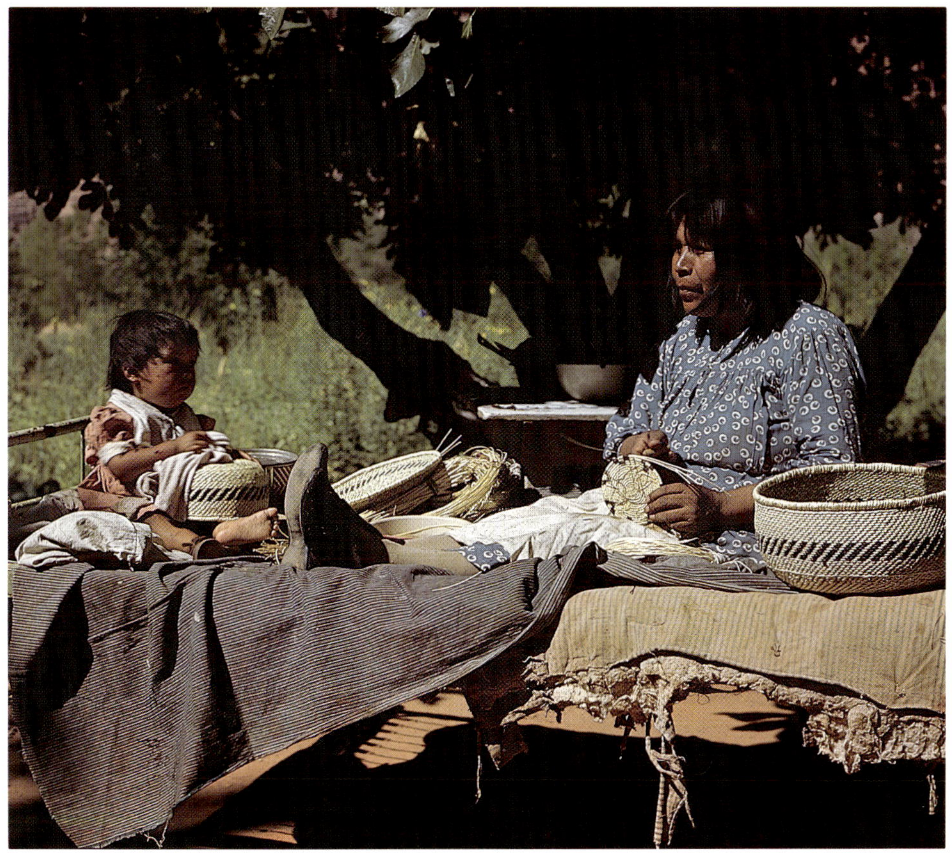

*When this Havasupai weaver finishes her basket it must be carried by a pack animal 7½ miles up the narrow trail along the canyon walls before it reaches the outside world.* *(See page 131.)*

*PLATE K*

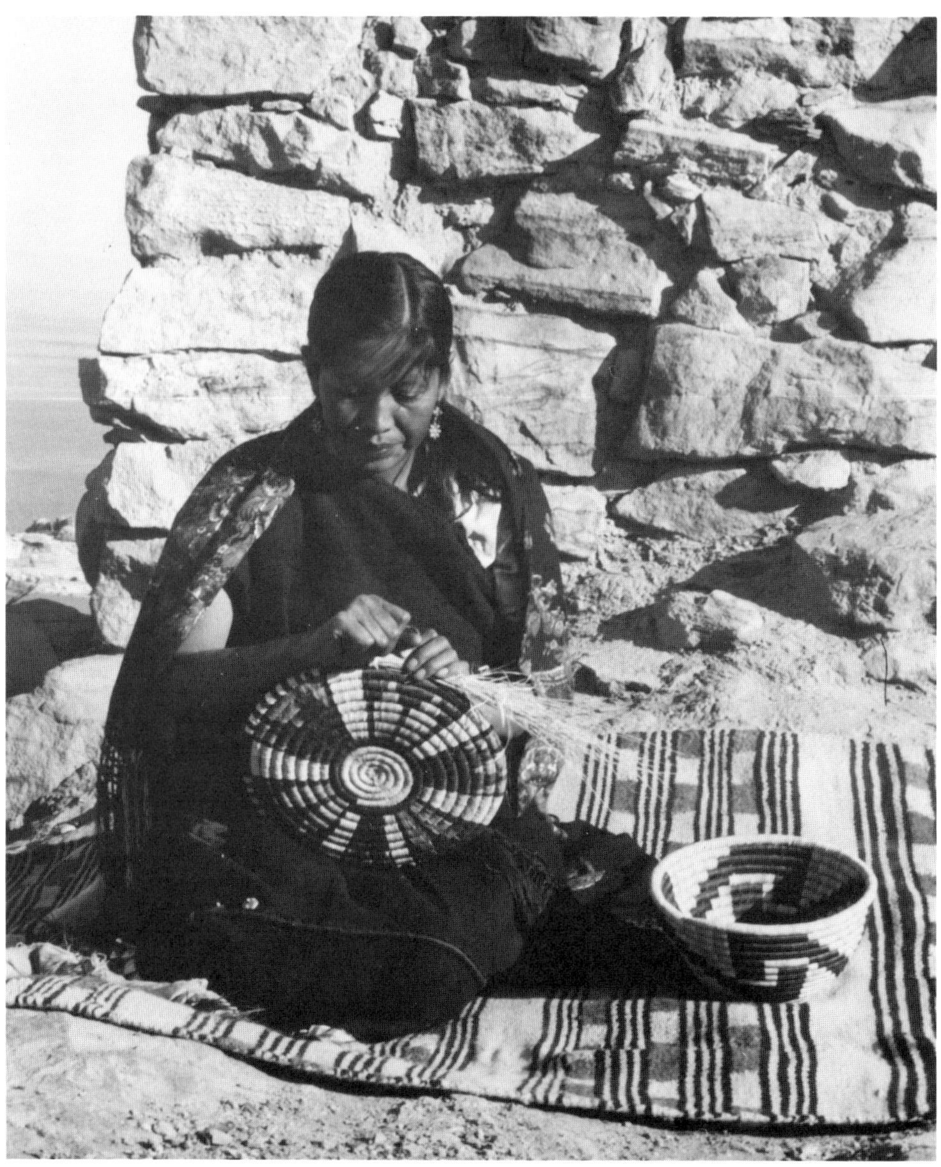

*A Hopi weaver from Second Mesa. Originally Second Mesa baskets were made only for ceremonial or household use.* *(See pages 153-154.)*

*PLATE L*

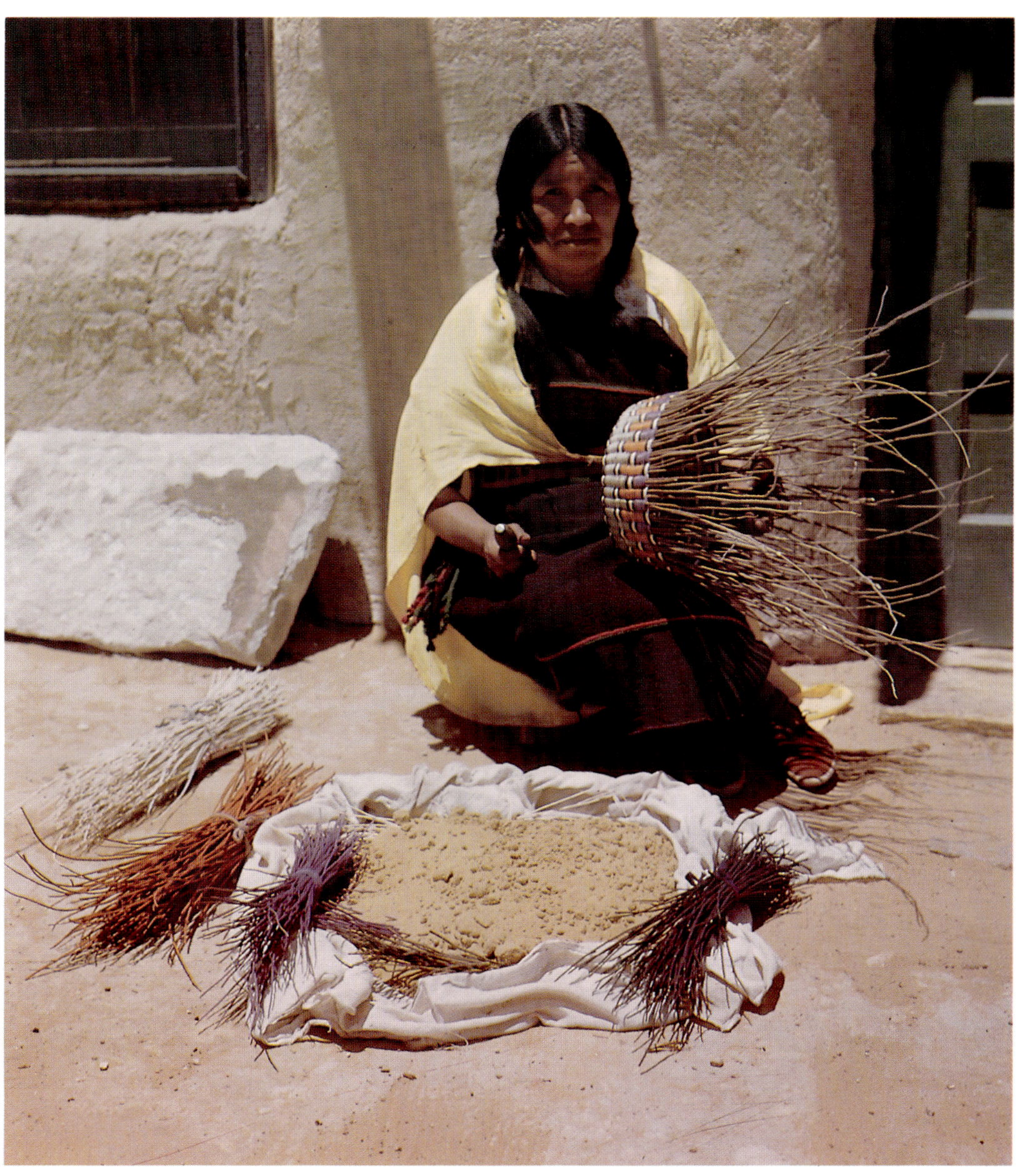

*A Third Mesa Hopi weaver. There is no similarity between baskets woven on Second and Third Mesas.* PLATE M

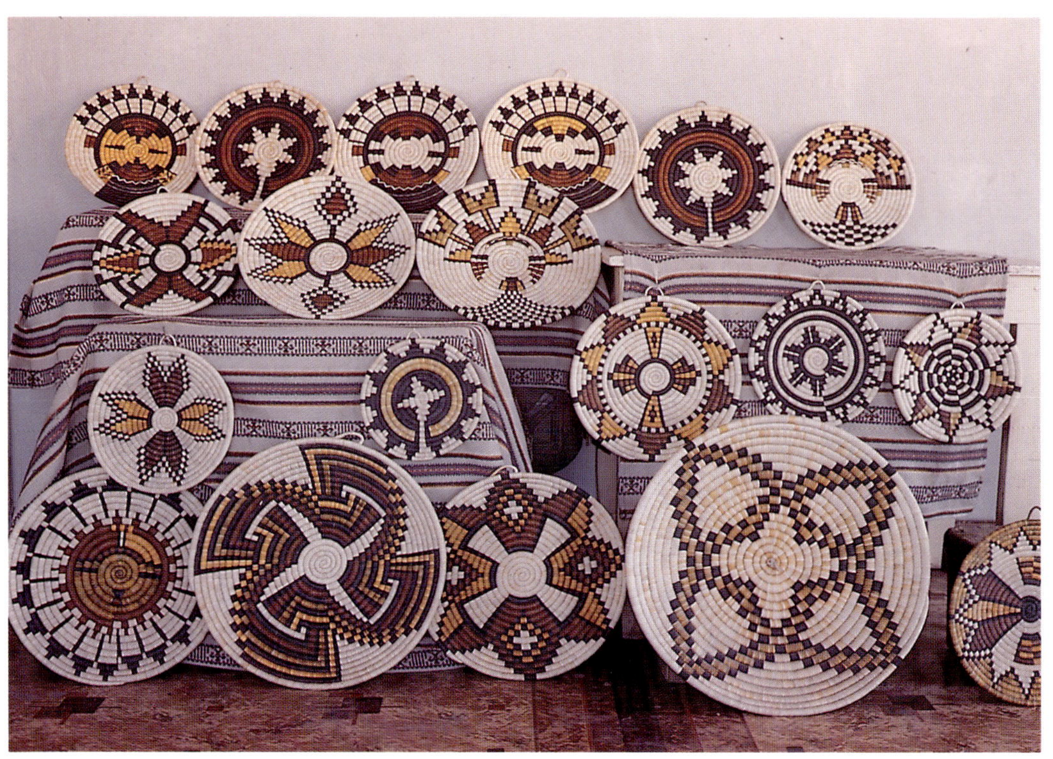

*Hopi wedding baskets. The presentation of these baskets, all laden with ground corn, to the groom's mother constitutes the last act of the wedding ceremony.* *(See pages 157-158.)*

*PLATE N*

same manner, holding the end of the thin section between their teeth and guiding the splitting process with the thumb down the full length of the twig. This is the material used in the basket, the bark being discarded. These thin strips dry almost immediately in the sun and have a tendency to coil up, which makes it possible to bind them together in circular rolls about six inches in diameter to be stored away.

The tule stems, which are used as the warp in weaving the baskets, are gathered at the same time as the willow. They are cut green and the heads and leaves removed from the stems. The stems are split in half, dried, and bound into straight bundles which may be two or three feet in length (Plate II) .

It must not be inferred that all of the Pima women weave baskets any more than all white women might do embroidery. In the olden times it is estimated that six out of ten women were basket weavers and, as in all other handicraft, some were more expert than others.

The *Martynia* is a weed similar to a cocklebur, and grows in the fields and along the ditches. It is not a true desert plant and is found only where the soil is rich and well supplied with moisture. The ripe seed pods of the plant are about one inch in diameter and two or more inches in length and have two tentacle-like horns six to ten inches long, terminating in a very sharp hook. The horns curve inward like the jaws of a pincer and the sharp, vicious hooks readily attach themselves to the feet of animals, clinging tenaciously and scattering their seeds as the animals walk along. This probably gives them their name, "devil's claw." To the Pimas they are "ehuk."

In October or November the seed pods, which grow profusely on the plant, ripen and drop off. The women gather them, and store them away in large clusters. The pod is black and the outer coat of the horn is used in basketry. When it is to be prepared for weaving, the pods are pulled apart and soaked in water or buried in wet sand to soften the fiber. Then two strips are peeled from each horn by splitting it at the hook and stripping the section back to the seed pod. In some instances, it would seem that the larger pods would afford more than two strips, but for some reason the Indian takes only two and discards the rest. These strips coil slightly when drying and are bound into small, curved bundles for storing (Plate III) , instead of being worked into a round coil like the willow. It should be remembered that the preparation of these materials, as described here, is only the preliminary step and much more work must be done before they are ready to weave into a basket. They might be compared to the rough boards coming from the sawmill, that must be surfaced and sized before being in a fit condition to be used in a structure.

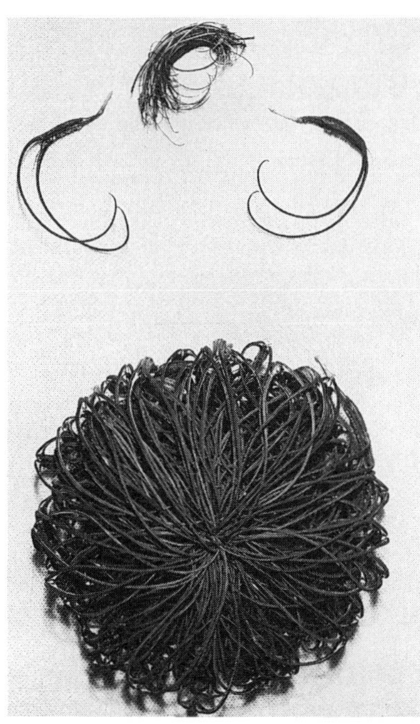

*Weaving material—Top center, split sections of devil's claw; top left and right, devil's claw pods; bottom, devil's claw in cluster* *PLATE III*

Pima baskets are of the coil type construction and are always started from the center of the bottom of the basket, and, as the weaving progresses, each coil is bound to the preceding coil in a counterclockwise coiling. The center of the bottom of the basket, as well as the finish of the edge of the basket, is always of devil's claw. The reason for this is that the devil's claw is much tougher and more wear resistant than the willow. In all probability, the first baskets made by the Pimas were woven entirely of willow or cottonwood, but the sharp sand around the cooking fire soon cut out the stitches on the surface exposed to the ground, especially if the basket was heavily laden. It is possible the ancient basket weaver, seeking something that would withstand more wear, found that the devil's claw, which fastened itself about her ankle as she walked through the fields, possessed the strength and toughness she was looking for. Also, its jet-black color gave her the contrast with which to execute her decorative designs. The devil's claw does not fade or change color; and, when worked into a background of the white willow, produces a very pleasing effect in contrast.

Until a few years ago, cottonwood twigs were used sometimes instead of willow. They were gathered in the spring when the sap begins to flow and the bark peels readily. But now I do not know of a single weaver who uses cottonwood. There are, probably, two reasons for this. First, the thin cottonwood fiber does not wear as well as the willow, and soon the stitches break where the coils are bound together. The other reason is that the cottonwood usually darkens with age, while the willow takes on a more mellow ivory color, which adds to the beauty of the basket.

When the Pima weaver starts to weave a basket she takes her material, which has been stored away in bundles, and begins to work it into final condition for use. First, she must soak it in water so that it will be flexible. Then she begins sizing the different materials for the type of basket she is going to weave. For the larger and heavier baskets the material will be coarser than for the smaller baskets of finer weave. In most cases, the size of the basket and the use for which it is made are the governing factors in the size of the materials used, but sometimes one will find coarse baskets in all sizes, which indicate the work of a beginner. The perfection found in many of our old Pima baskets has been achieved only after years of patient and devoted labor.

In the final preparation of the willow and devil's claw, the material is split into strands of the approximate size desired and then scraped with a knife until it is smooth and regular. The tule stems are split into fine sections and a number of these are taken together to form the warp around which the willow and devil's claw will be coiled. The number of sections of the tule stems used is governed by the size or fineness of the weave, and may vary from three or four fine sections in the small baskets to twenty or more sections in some of the larger baskets.

To start the basket, one end of the bundle of split tule stems is wrapped firmly with a strip of devil's claw for the distance of one-half inch, more or less, depending on the size of the basket. Then the tules are bent around this start and the coiling begins. Each stitch passes around the warp of tule, and, with the aid of an awl, passes through the coil below and is drawn tight. This binds the basket firmly together as the coiling progresses. The sections of tule stems are of various lengths, and overlap, and as one section is covered by the weaving a new section is inserted into the bundle. In this manner the coiling is kept uniform and any joints in the warp which might weaken the basket are avoided. When one strand of the willow or devil's claw is used up, a new strand is inserted through the completed coil and the protruding ends are carefully cut away. These cut ends are so well hidden between the coils that the surface of the basket is left perfectly smooth. A knife and an awl are the only tools used (Plate IV) . In olden times this awl was the spine from a cactus, but a steel awl like that used by a shoemaker is used now.

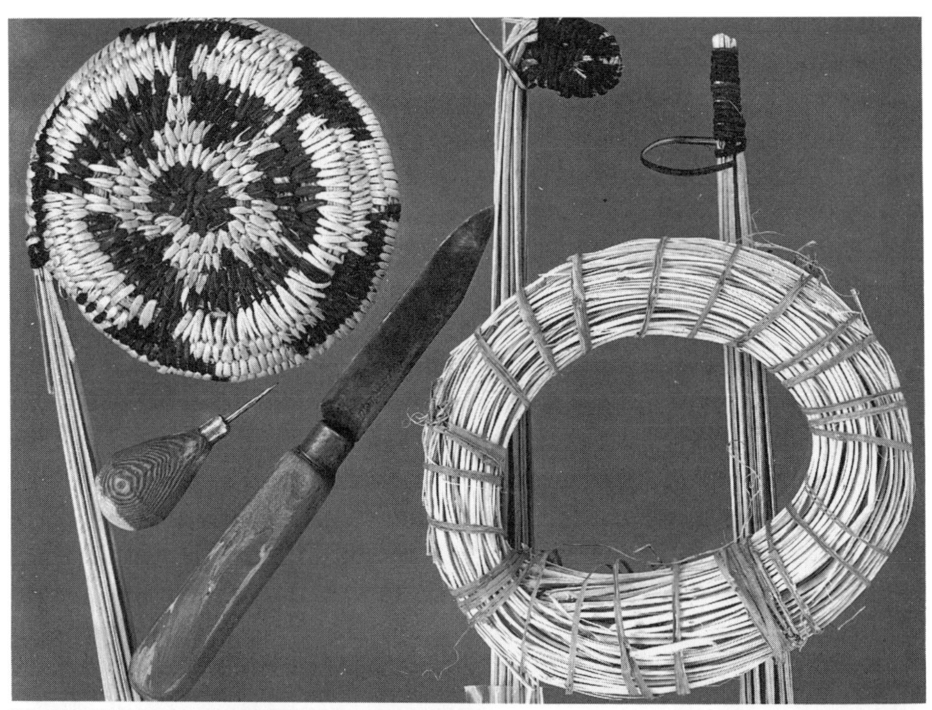

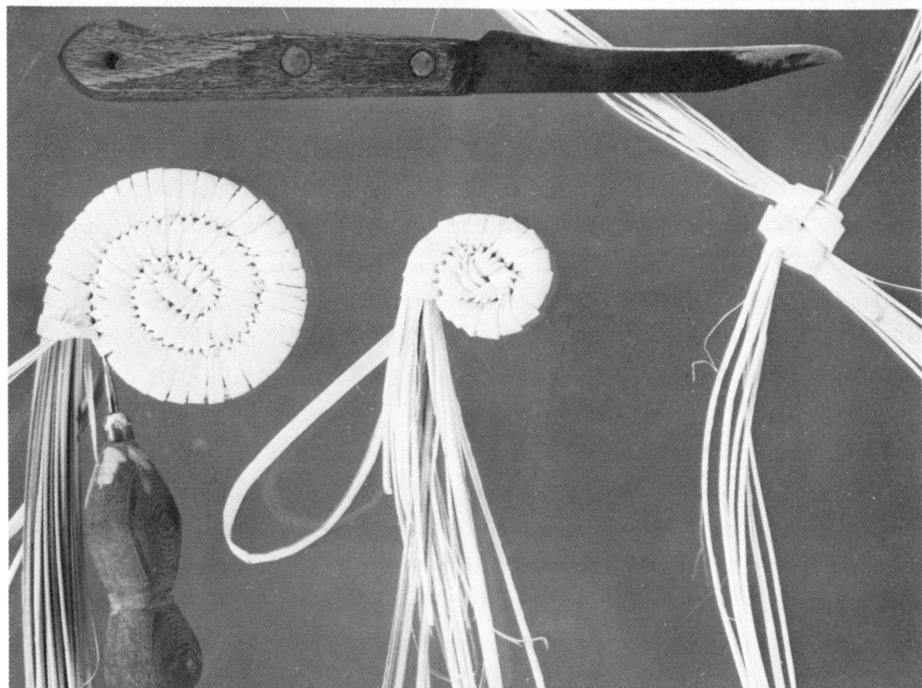

*The starting of a Pima* (above) *and a Papago* (below) *basket—An awl and a knife are the tools used. Note that the coiling always is counterclockwise*

PLATE IV

In a shallow bowl, which is the most common type of Pima basket, the black circle in the center usually is three to four inches in diameter, and, from there on, the willow makes up the background, with the devil's claw being used only to carry out the decorative design. The same would be true if a deep basket were being woven. The design of the basket always is worked from this black center outward. When the basket is completed, the devil's claw is worked into the edge in a cross stitch which gives the edge a very durable and attractive finish.

A painter may take a canvas of certain dimensions and fit his picture to the canvas, giving attention to proper balance, relative dimensions, and proper spacing so that the finished picture will fit properly into the space. With the Indian weaver, the space used is that which will permit her to execute properly her design, yet the balance and the relation of one section of the design to any other will be just as carefully and beautifully done as may be found in the painting. This is the reason why one seldom, if ever, can get a basket made to dimensions which he might give to the weaver. She will tell you that she does not know exactly what the diameter of the basket will be, because the size of the coil and the completion of the design will determine the size.

### *Basket Designs*

The Pimas use three classes of basket designs: geometric, symbolized, and original, in this order of frequency. Of the geometric designs, the Pima fret which is similar to patterns originating in Grecian art, is the most common (Plate V). If we look back into the history of the Pimas we find that their first contact with the white man was late in the seventeenth century, and fret designs had been in common use by the Greeks and, no doubt, the Pimas centuries before. Therefore, it would be only reasonable to believe that they originated independently of each other and that the Pima fret is as distinctly Pima in origin as the Grecian fret is the product of ancient Grecian sculptors. The Pimas know nothing about the origin of these designs. I have consulted a group of over fifty weavers and have shown them numerous baskets of different fret designs, but none of them could offer any information.

Very often one may ask a Pima weaver the name of the design of her basket and she will look confused and say, "I don't know." This does not mean that she has no name for the design but rather that she cannot interpret it into English. The name of the design might be like the name an artist gives to his painting. Probably the artists who created these basket designs gave them a name, but, the Pima language not being a written language, the name would have been lost in antiquity. The Pima weaver has learned her art from her mother or grandmother, who received her training from her parents, and so on back through a hundred generations or more.

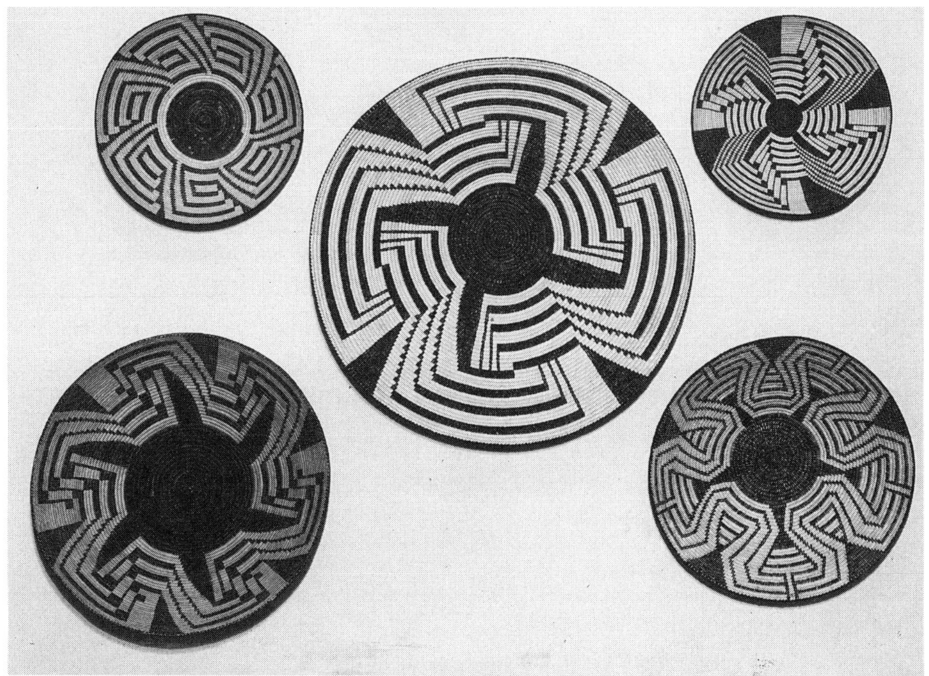

*The Pima fret, the oldest and most commonly used basket design. Many variations of this beautiful design are used. It is unlikely that it was copied from the Greek fret* *PLATE V*

Strange as it may seem, the Indian women never draw patterns of the countless designs which they use. The weaver carries the picture in her mind and, through one tiny strand after another, the picture unfolds until it stands out in all its perfection and beauty. In my collection, there are more than one hundred different patterns of the fret design, but I constantly find others to add. No doubt originally there were only a few basic fret designs, but the genius of the weavers who created them extended to the generations that followed, and their talent found expression in not only adding new designs but in modifications and combinations of designs already in use. Many of the designs are similar, but rarely does one find two baskets of identical pattern. Visitors sometimes have asked to have a certain basket duplicated, and a weaver might promise to do so. But the finished product, although a beautiful work of art, never has been an exact copy.

This is why Indian traders cannot have catalogues or stock numbers on their pieces of Indian art. Sometimes we find visitors who are criti-

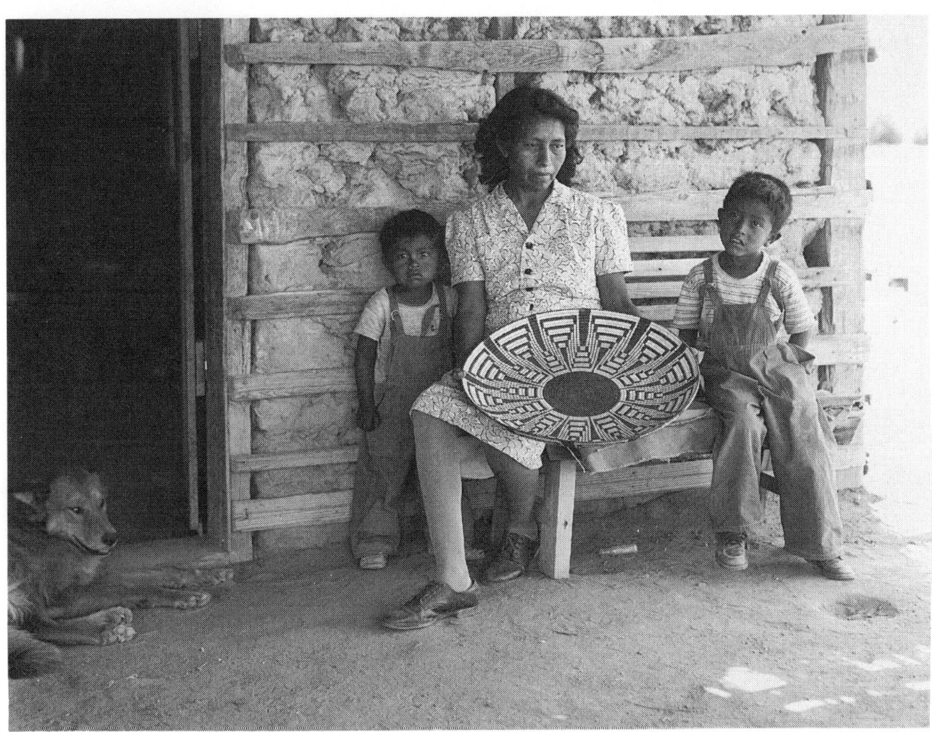

*Isabella Johns spent three months weaving this beautiful twelve-petal squash blossom basket. The four-petal design has been selected as the most representative of Pima art* *PLATE VI*

cal of what they consider the Indians' inability to follow a pattern, but an art as old as that of the Pimas is surely beyond the power of the tenderfoot critic to evaluate.

Next to the fret designs, those most popular with the weavers are the squash blossom (Plates VI, VII). The name indicates that these designs symbolize the flower of the squash plant, which grew in the fields of the ancient Pima farmers; therefore, they are classified as symbolized designs. Actually, they are also geometric designs and vary in the number of sections or petals from three to twelve or more. The four- and three-petal designs are the ones used most frequently. The Pima Basket Makers Guild has selected the four-petal squash blossom as the most representative design of Pima art and has adopted it as the symbol of the guild.

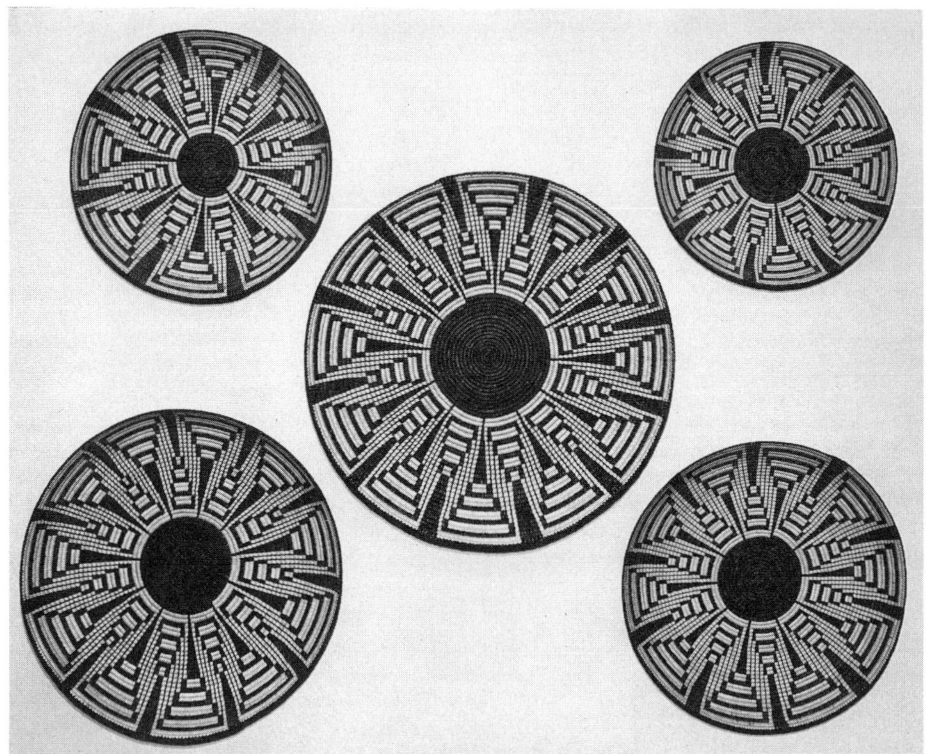

*Here are shown Pima baskets with squash blossom designs in which the petals number from eight to twelve. Note the even spacing of the petals* — *PLATE VII*

The proper balance and perfect spacing of the sections or petals in the basket make this design stand out in a very striking manner. It is my opinion that this is the most beautiful design the Pimas have. Because of the numerous variations, one might wonder if the name "squash blossom" was given to the design by the Indians themselves or whether it originated with some Indian trader with a gift of good salesmanship. The folklore of the Indian country often is enriched by the virile imagination of such an individual. Be that as it may, the name is accepted generally and it probably is better known than any other Pima design. Another design in much the same category as the squash

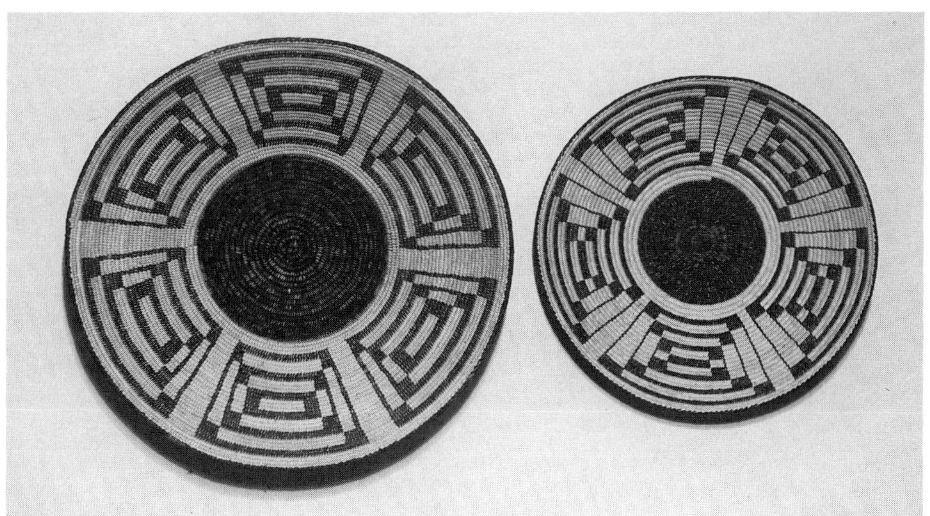

*Turtle's back—There are many variations of this design, also, but it has achieved less prominence than the fret or the squash blossom. It is an old design still in use* PLATE VIII

blossom, and similar, is the turtle back. However, this design (Plate VIII) appears much less frequently than the squash blossom and has achieved less prominence. Here again variations occur in the number of sections of the design, but no design has less than four sections, whereas the squash blossom starts with three sections.

Another beautiful design is the butterfly wings (Plate IX), with variations ranging from four to six sections. It is an old design and I have not seen one of these baskets made by any of the younger weavers.

Probably the most common of the symbolized designs is the whirlwind (Plate X). It appears in numerous variations, but the swirl of the design, sweeping from the center of the basket toward the outer edge, makes it easily recognized.

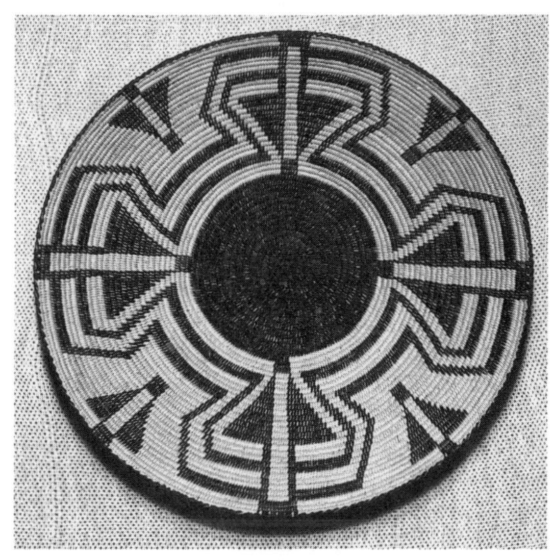

*Butterfly wings—This design is used rarely* PLATE IX

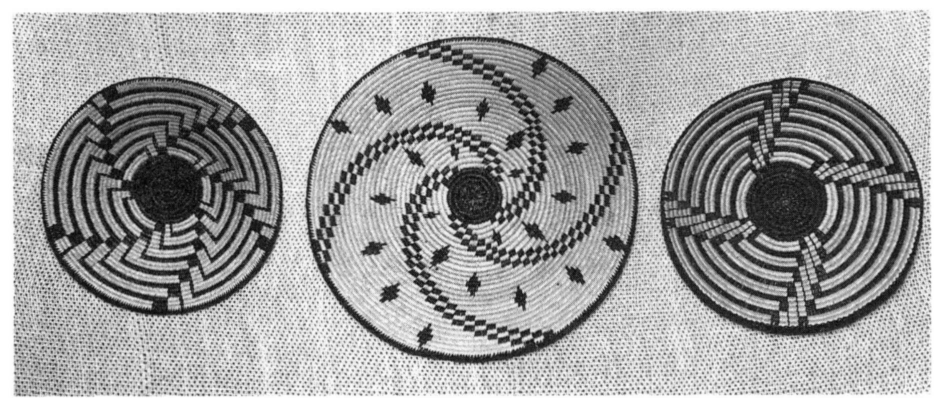

*Whirlwind—The most frequently used of the symbolized designs. It has many variations, but may always be recognized by the swirl sweeping from center to outer edge of the basket*

PLATE X

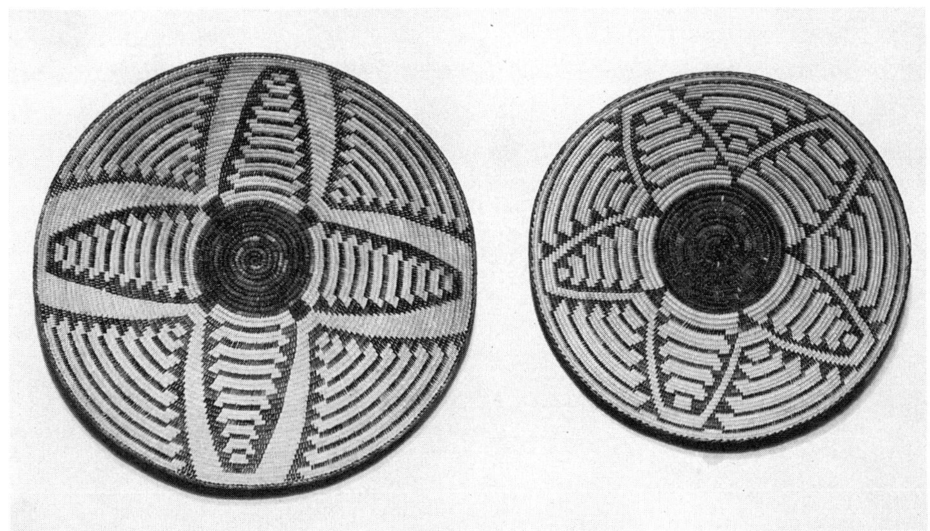

*Star—This design seems to have been discontinued by the weavers. It is the nearest to any celestial symbol used by the Pimas*

PLATE XI

The whirlwind is one of the most common phenomena by which Mother Nature disturbs the quiet of a hot summer day. It comes out of nowhere, picks up the dust, dead leaves, and twigs, whirls them skyward for a short distance, then disappears as quickly as it comes. I have, many times, looked across a dry stretch of desert or a freshly plowed field and seen literally dozens of these "dust devils." This design is not used so extensively in the larger baskets and appears more graceful in those ranging from eight to twelve inches in diameter.

The star design (Plate XI) is less common than any of those previously mentioned, and in my collection there are only two baskets of this design, both very old. The celestial bodies such as stars, moon, etc., have little part in the legends of the Pimas, and there are no signs or symbols used to represent these bodies. The nearest to it are the star designs of these baskets.

A design which occurs only occasionally is the maze. This, like the Pima fret, is sometimes associated with the Mediterranean, since ancient coins bearing this design were found on the Isle of Crete. Yet a definite connection between the two surely would be difficult to establish. A maze is carved into the mud walls of the Casa Grande ruins and possibly was there long before any white man visited the ancient structure. The black basket in Plate XII was exhibited at the Arizona State Fair in 1927. Although it was the best piece of Pima weaving exhibited, it was given second prize because it was not considered characteristically Pima, since the design had occurred in the Old World. I believe this was a mistake and that the Pimas have a right to this pattern as much as any other shown here. Their story, in connection with this design, is that it is "Siuu-hu Ki" ("Elder Brother's House").

Siuu-hu was the hero in many of the old legends of the Pimas. At first he was held in great esteem but later he lost his popularity and became more or less a vagabond, often being pursued after making some exploit into the villages. He would retreat to his home in the mountains, but the trails were so devious that his pursuers could never follow him. Yet if one will trace carefully the trail to his house in the center of the basket, you can follow him home without crossing any lines.

Designs which are used in combination with other designs for decorative purposes are swastika and coyote tracks (Plate XIII). The Indian's version, however, is the German swastika in reverse, and, of course, was used centuries before it was adopted as the emblem of the

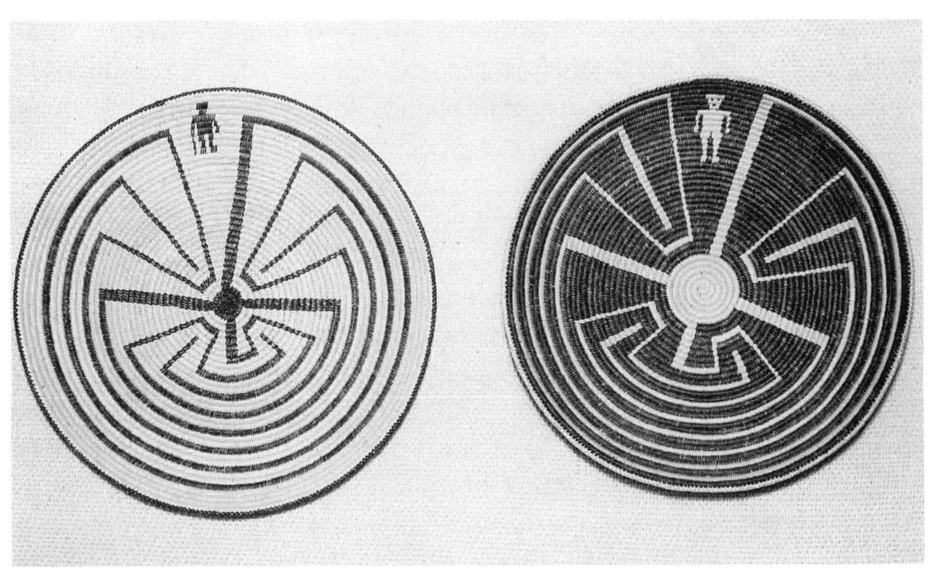

*Maze—A very old and rare design. Coins with this design were found on the Isle of Crete, but a connection between the two would be difficult to establish* PLATE XII

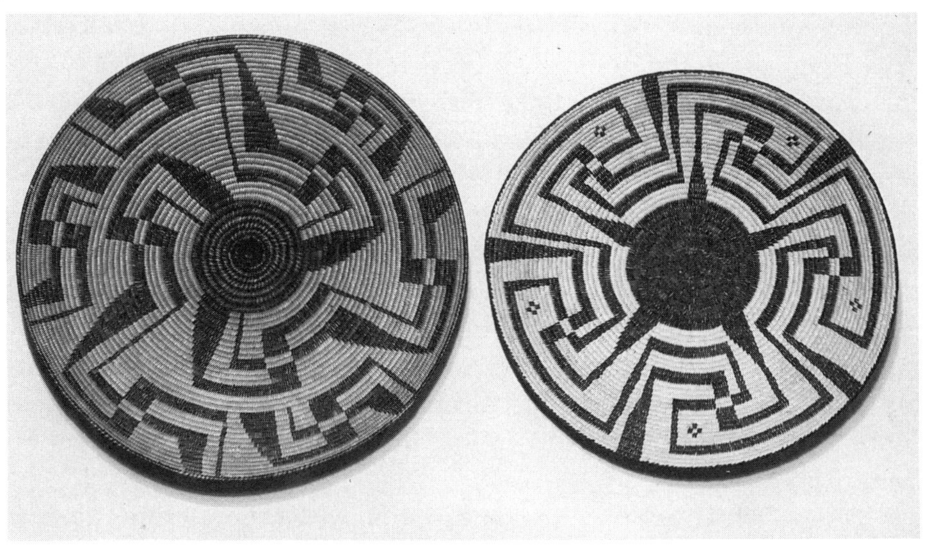

*Swastika and coyote tracks—These are symbols used frequently to fill space and give balance to the decorative design of a basket* PLATE XIII

Nazi party. It is not used exclusively by the Pimas, since it appears in the decorative work of many other tribes. Sometimes it is used as a complete design for a basket, as in Plate XIV. The coyote tracks design is four rectangular blocks of devil's claw set into the white background and symbolizes the tracks of one of the most common of desert animals. This design is used mostly in combination with other designs to fill in space in order to give the proper balance and finished appearance to the basket.

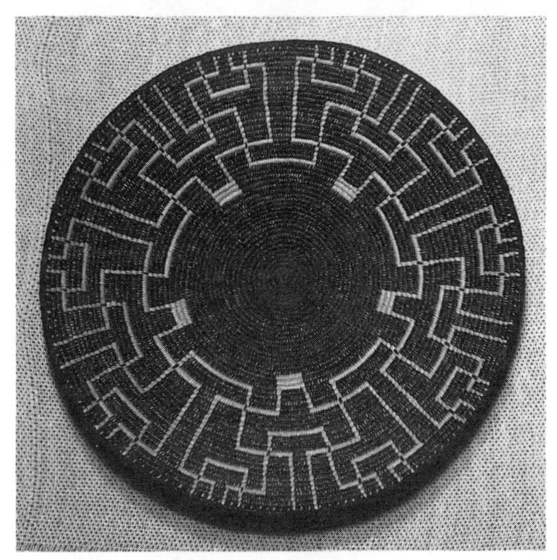

*Swastika design—The design and arrangement in this basket are unusual* *PLATE XIV*

Original designs, in the true sense of the word, are not common. Certain combinations of the fret or other designs mentioned here may be original as combined by the individual weaver, yet, basically, they should be considered as tribal designs. In Plate XV, however, we do find an original design that I have never seen duplicated. This basket was made about 1900 and sold to a pioneer family in Mesa, Arizona. The story told was that the design represented the Sacaton area at that time; the center representing the village, with trails radiating out through the mesquite trees, shown as small, peculiarly shaped figures. It has been shown to old weavers, but none can offer any confirmation or

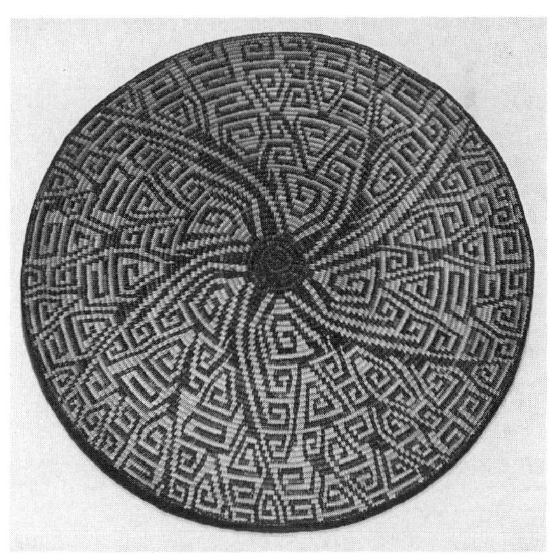

*Sacaton—An original design representing the Sacaton area* *PLATE XV*

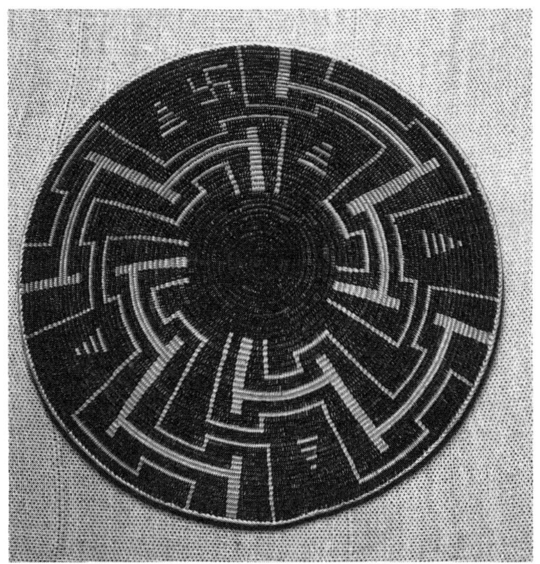

*Dream basket—An original design representing a dream, but the meaning is unknown* *PLATE XVI*

denial of the story. Although I have had them trace the old trails leading to Blackwater or to Santan or Casa Blanca from the Sacaton village, their only comment was, "Maybe so." Whatever the intent of the weaver might have been, it is interesting to note the wholly intentional lack of balance in the design. This was not the work of a beginner, for it is one of the finest pieces of craftsmanship in my collection.

The basket shown in Plate XVI was called a dream basket by the weaver. Her nephew, from whom I purchased it, explained that she had a dream one afternoon while taking her *siesta* out in the shade of the *ramada* near her house. From her dream she got the idea of this design, but what its meaning might have been was not known to the nephew. It must be remembered that Indian legends and Indian history all are handed down from one generation to another by word of mouth and that much of the historical background which would be so interesting to us has been irretrievably lost.

### *Basket Types and Their Uses*

The Pima baskets which have been shown here all are of the shallow-bowl type, and still are found in common use in many of the Indians' homes. Sometimes they are called wheat baskets, since they were used in winnowing the grain on the threshing floor (Plate XVIII) or for catching the ground wheat being prepared for pinole or to be made into tortillas.

The storage basket (Plate XIX) is made of wheat straw and the bark of the young mesquite tree *(Prosopis velutina)*. The straw is used for the warp, and around a bundle of it, which may be one inch or more in diameter, the mesquite bark is firmly bound, with the spacing in the stitches being an inch or more apart, there being no effort made to cover the warp completely as in the other types of Pima baskets. The storage basket is made for utility purposes only and has been the Indians' grain bin for many generations. When ripe, the wheat is cut with a hand sickle and processed in the crude Indian manner. It was stored in these large baskets for the next season's planting and for food for the

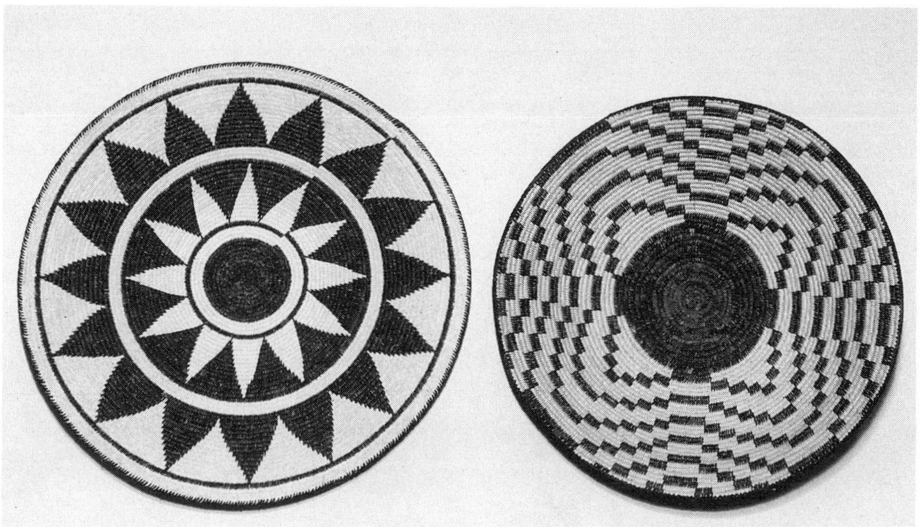

*Two old Pima basket designs that are now seldom used. Both of these beautiful baskets are in the author's collection* *PLATE XVII*

family. Grain baskets have almost vanished; only two weavers are known who continue to make them. They have been replaced by bins made of lumber, or empty oil drums, either of which are much more impervious to the gnawing teeth of the desert rodents than the soft wheat straw of these baskets. The largest of the storage baskets will hold five sacks of wheat, or about twelve bushels. Many of the old storage baskets would hold forty to fifty bushels. The lasting quality of the grain baskets is remarkable considering the materials used in their construction. The need for them no longer exists, since the Pima buys most of his flour at the trading post. A few of the old people still cling to the custom of grinding their wheat on the old stone metate. Bread made in this way may have some grit from the stone mill, but it has also all of the food value of the whole grain.

The Pimas make olla-shaped baskets in various sizes (Plates XX, XXI), but these are made almost exclusively for sale to the white trade. Under the white man's influence they have made wastepaper or scrap baskets of various sizes (Plate XXII), but in the Indian's home one will find only the flat bowl-shaped baskets, which serve many purposes in the everyday life of the family.

Another type of basket made exclusively for the trader's store is the miniature (Plate XXIII). The weaver who, probably, made minia-

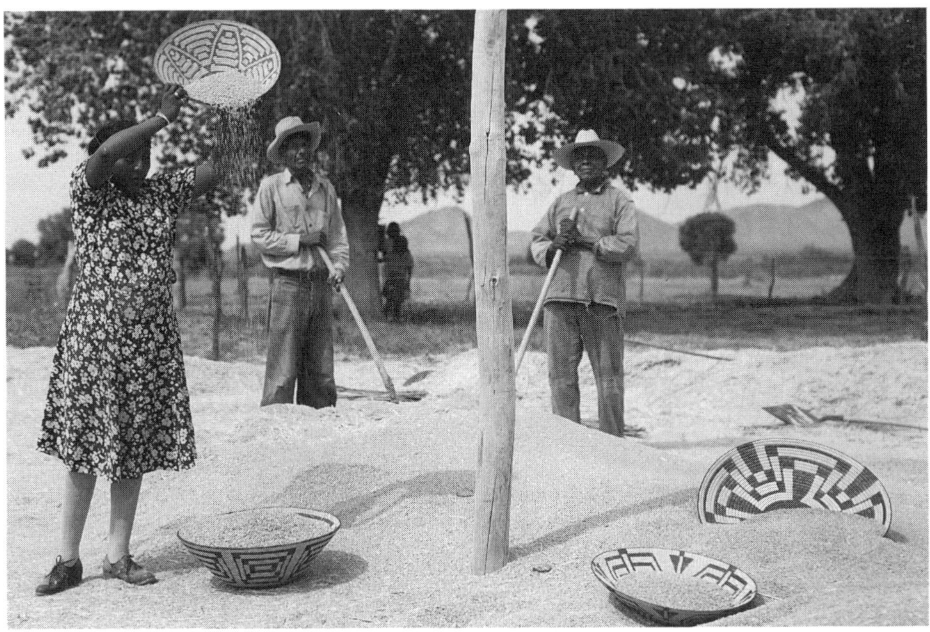

*Winnowing the wheat after it has been trampled from the straw by ponies hitched to the pole in the center and driven around and around* *PLATE XVIII*

tures more famous than anyone else is Susie White. There is no one on the reservation who can equal the beautiful workmanship she puts into these dainty little covered baskets; the design and contour are perfect. One will find some of the fret design, squash blossom, butterfly wings, and one which she calls "the dancers," showing a number of dancing figures circling the basket. Some weavers make miniature plaques and shallow bowls, which are replicas of the wheat baskets, but the market for miniatures is limited; likewise the ability to produce them, and as a result they are not plentiful.

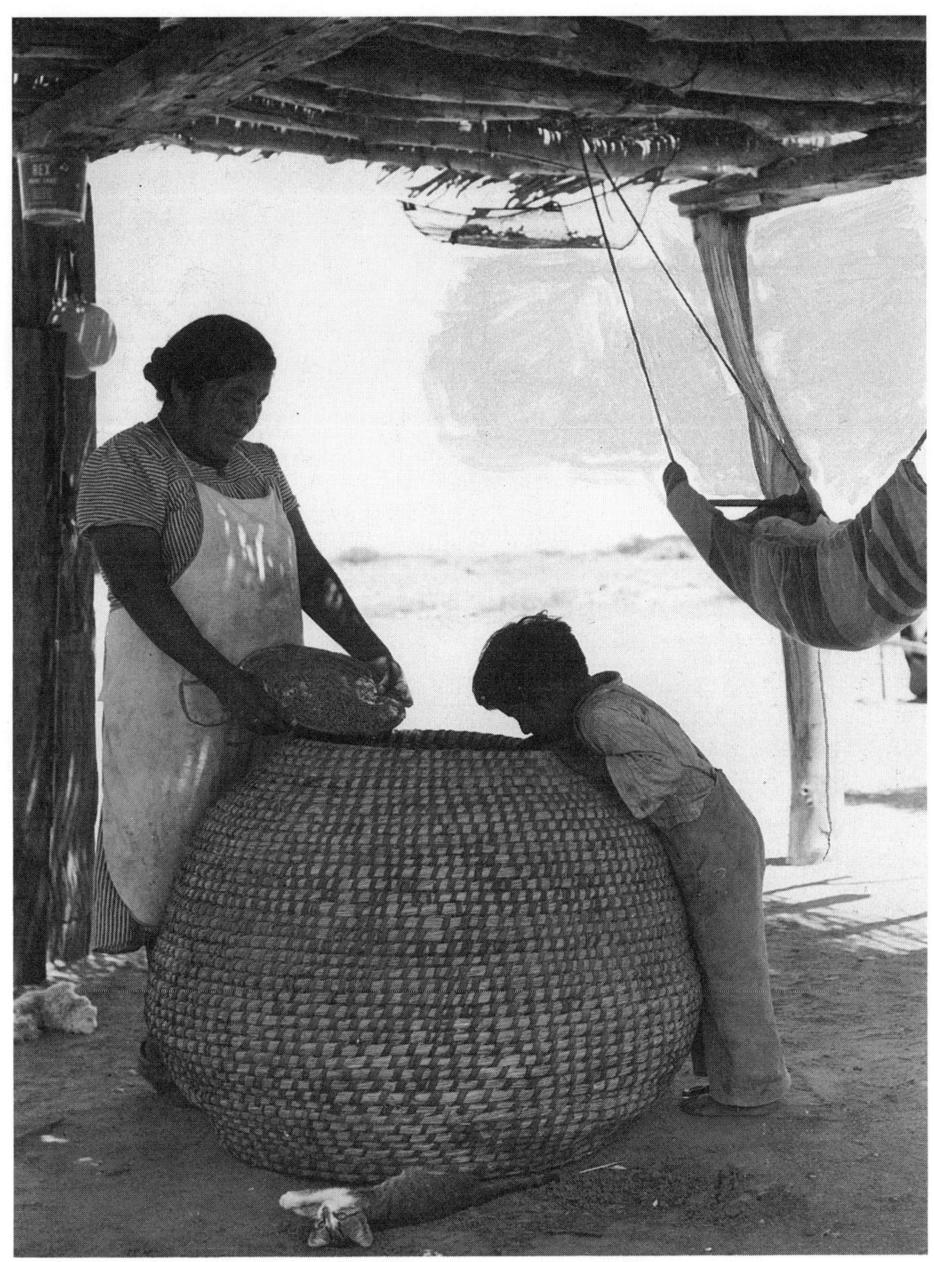

*Storage basket—In the Indian's home this basket was used to store wheat for the family's use. It is made of wheat straw and the bark of the young mesquite tree*

PLATE XIX

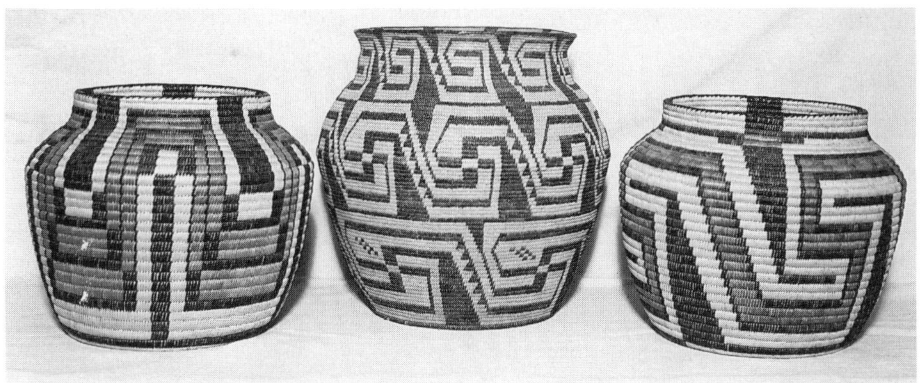

*Olla-shaped baskets made primarily for sale to the white trade. In many sizes, they make wonderful wastepaper or scrap baskets for home or office* PLATE XX

A few Pima weavers make baskets of horsehair. Like the miniatures, these baskets are made to sell to the white trade. They are constructed very much like the baskets made of willow and devil's claw, but occur more frequently in the olla or bowl shape. The long strands from the horse's tail are carefully selected for this purpose. The background of the basket usually is white, with the design being executed with black, sorrel, or red hair. The hair used is in natural color, and is used also for the warp over which the weft of the basket is coiled. The cut ends of the hair are so dexterously hidden between the coils that the

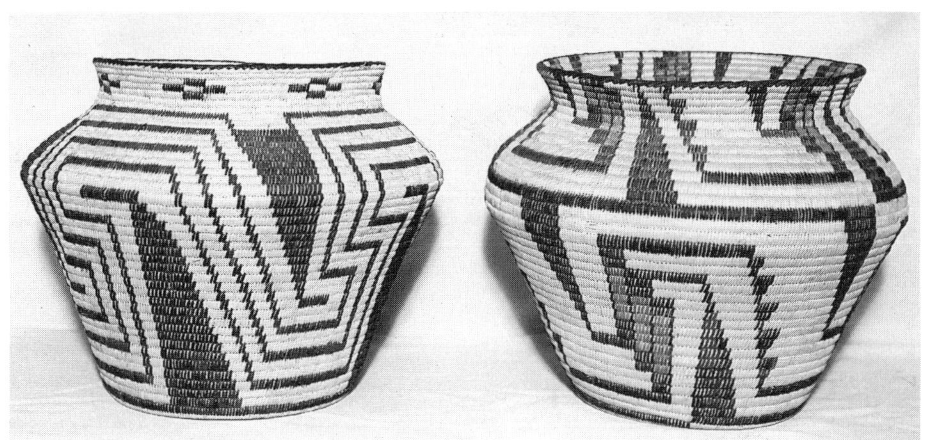

*An unusual type of distinctive Pima design in olla baskets. This type of basket is not found in the Indian's home, where only flat, bowl-shaped baskets are used* PLATE XXI

surface of the basket has the smoothness of a piece of china. These baskets are very scarce and are eagerly sought by collectors of Pima art. Ordinarily, they are not more than four or five inches in diameter.

The last, and possibly the oldest, of the Pima baskets to be mentioned here is the *giho,* or burden basket (Plate I) . It is the most picturesque of all Pima baskets and was made exclusively for utility purposes. The older members of the tribe say that it has not been made for the past forty or fifty years. It was the only basket made by the men and for the past several years I have tried without success to find some old man who could weave a *giho.* The framework is made of saguaro ribs,

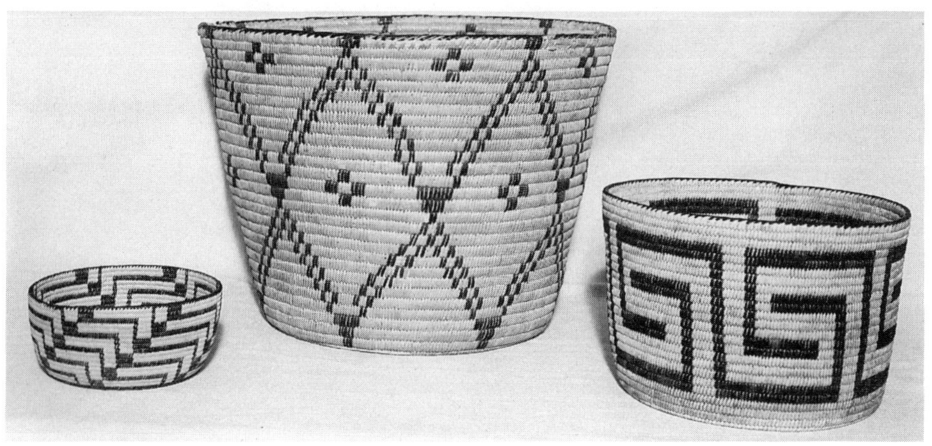

*Deep baskets, made to meet the tourist demand. Many uses may be found for these beautiful baskets, but the Indian, himself, never uses them* *PLATE XXII*

which extend high above the basket. The basket is woven of yucca fiber and is net-like in construction and flexibility. Back of this basket, and acting like a cushion to protect the carrier's back, is a mat woven of yucca leaves. Attached to the main uprights of the frame and in back of the basket are two short loops of yucca rope fastened to either end of a narrow yucca mat, making a loop which fits about the head of the carrier when the basket is in use. This headband helps balance the laden basket on the shoulders of the woman as she walks along, and small horsehair ropes bind the load in place. These baskets were used to carry wheat, beans, and other grain to the threshing floor; cactus fruits from the desert during the saguaro harvest; and were used also to carry wood to the Indian's home. Today, the only *gihos* to be found are in collections or museums.

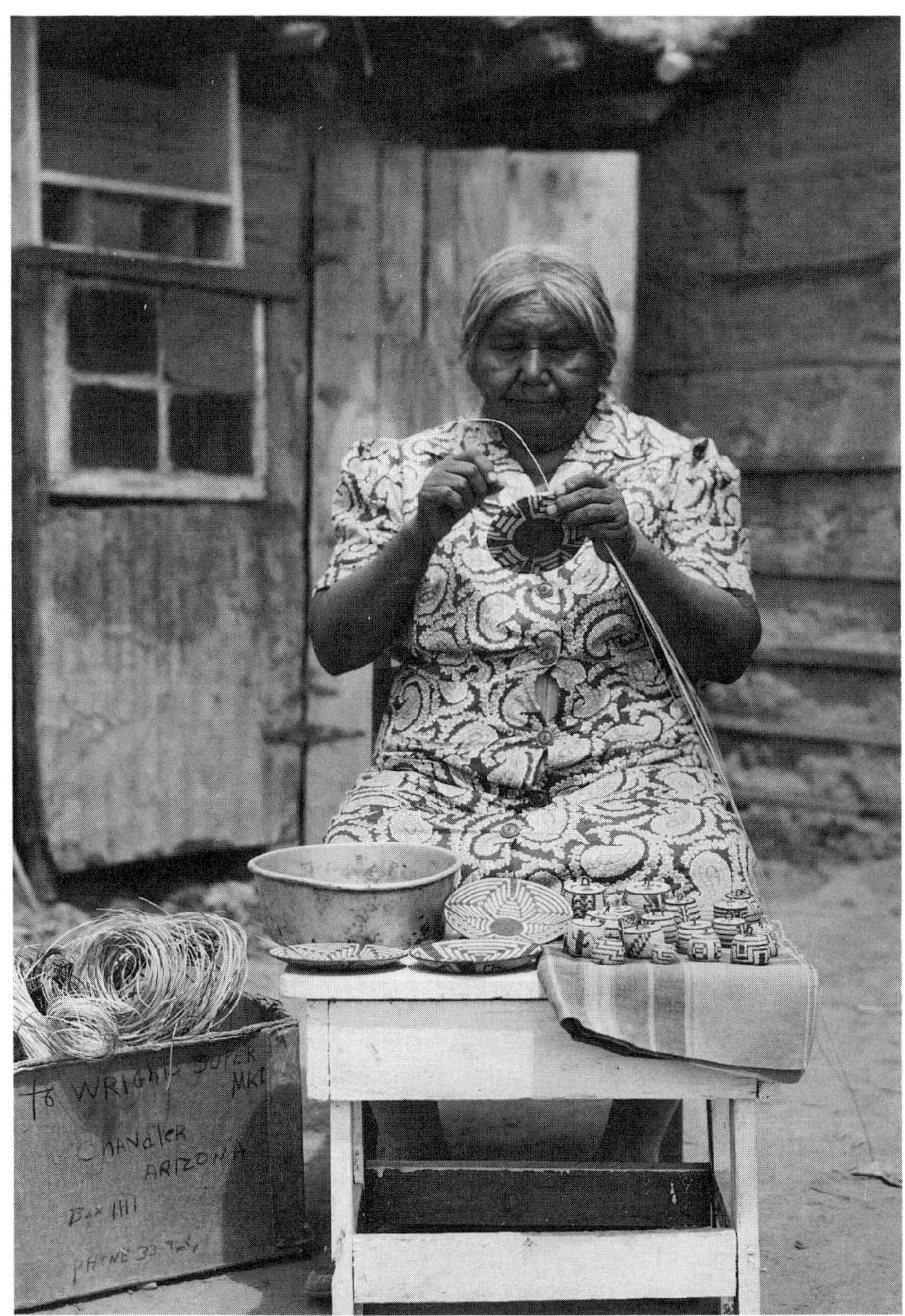


*Susie White is the most famous weaver of Pima miniature baskets. Most of the designs found in the larger baskets are woven into the miniatures also*

PLATE XXIII

# *The Desert People*

THE SOUTHERN portion of Pimería, which was mentioned previously as being occupied by the To-ho-no Aw-aw-tam, is now called the Papago country, and its people are the Papago Indians. The name comes from the Pima word "Papavi-ootam," meaning "Bean People," which was converted to "Papago" by the Spaniards.

The Papagos depend on the flash floods in the arroyos during the summer rains for their irrigation water. When these rains come late or in insufficient quantity to produce corn and other crops, the faster-growing bean plant produces the only crop to be harvested. Hence the term "Bean People" ("Papavi-ootam") frequently was ascribed to these desert farmers.

The first contact the Papagos had with the Spaniards occurred when Marcos de Niza came into their country on April 15, 1539. Incidentally, De Niza was the first white man to enter Arizona. He crossed over from Mexico at Lochiel, which lies about twenty miles east of Nogales. His visit was of no consequence to the Papagos, and their first contact of any significance with the Spaniards did not occur until Fr. Kino's visit, in 1687. Livestock was introduced to the Papagos by Fr. Kino and other early Spanish explorers. Only horses and the long-horned Spanish cattle were of importance from an economic standpoint. Sheep never were successful with either the Papagos or the Pimas because of climatic, as well as forage, conditions prevailing on their ranges.

## *Ancient Shrines*

WHENEVER MENTION is made of the old padres in the Papago country, the picture of San Xavier del Bac immediately comes into our minds. It has been called the "Queen of the Missions" of the Southwest, and from a standpoint of stately beauty this name would seem well deserved. Unlike so many of the other missions, San Xavier never was completely abandoned and was not permitted to fall into ruins. The Arizona Archaeological Society has credited Fr. Kino with establishing the first mission on the site of San Xavier del Bac, in 1700, although ruins of another culture already were there, a culture which these archaeologists say existed at the same time as that of Casa Grande ruins,

Possibly an old ruin was incorporated in the first adobe mission erected. The word "Bac" means marshland or wet ground. The spring at San Xavier is one of the very few to be found in an area of one hundred miles or more of that desert country.

During the next century the mission was destroyed and rebuilt at least two or more times, until the present edifice finally was completed in 1797, after being in the process of construction for a period of fourteen years. Few people ever view this gem of mission architecture who do not wonder why the east tower does not have a cupola like the tower on the west. There are several stories offered in explanation. One, which is credited to the Indians and probably told for local color, is that when a workman started to lay the first brick of the cupola he fell from the tower and was killed; thereafter, the work was never resumed. Another explanation is that, during the long process of construction, enthusiasm waned, and, like many cathedrals of Europe, the structure never was finished. Another less romantic story is that the tower was purposely left uncompleted to avoid taxation. In olden times the church property was taxed after the church was completed. Whatever may have been the cause, the tower stands unfinished and probably will remain so until it joins the ruins of the ancient shrine upon which it rests.

The Papago people have many customs similar to those of their Mexican neighbors below the border, and among them is the preservation of many sacred shrines scattered over their vast reservation. One of the most interesting of these is the Shrine of the Four Children. The legend dates back to A. D. 1300 or 1400, or during the time the Pueblo people occupied this area. There has been some confusion about this story, but the version quoted here, as given by Fr. Ventura Bonaventure, is fully reliable and authentic:

"During the quarter century or more that I spent among the Papagos, I gleaned the following version of the event. During the Great Pueblo Period (XIII-XIV-XV Centuries A. D.) there occurred an extremely heavy flood in the Altar Valley around Oquitoa which destroyed the entire village of Vamuri, barring four children who had been playing in the higher reaches adjoining. The ruins of the place are still shown and are called 'Tepelcates,' from the great number of pottery sherds covering the site.

"These orphaned children were picked up by a salt expedition from Santa Rosa and taken back with them. The expedition had barely reached Achi (Santa Rosa) when a copious spring burst forth out of a badger hole. The Piman tradition has it that the Great Flood was caused by a similar occurrence. Fearing a recurrence of the flood and laying the blame on the four children who had survived the Altar Valley flood, and taking the sudden appearance of the spring at the unlikely location as a sign that the relatives in the underworld demanded the presence of their children, it was decided to send the children to them. When the children had been sunk in the spring to the accompaniment of great ceremony, the water ceased to flow. To commemorate this event and to show their gratitude, the Wiikita is celebrated at intervals to renew the monument of ocotillo. The Wiikita was celebrated at other places too, as it is still at Quitovac, Sonora. But these celebrations have no reference to the children. That is local to Santa Rosa. The Wiikita antedates the Sacrifice of the Children."

I visited this spot more than twenty-five years ago, and on a recent visit the photograph shown in Plate XXIV was taken, showing the ocotillo fence about the shrine and the stacks of ocotillo branches on either side. A circular fence with openings facing each of the four directions is built about the shrine, and at the ceremony of the Wiikita,

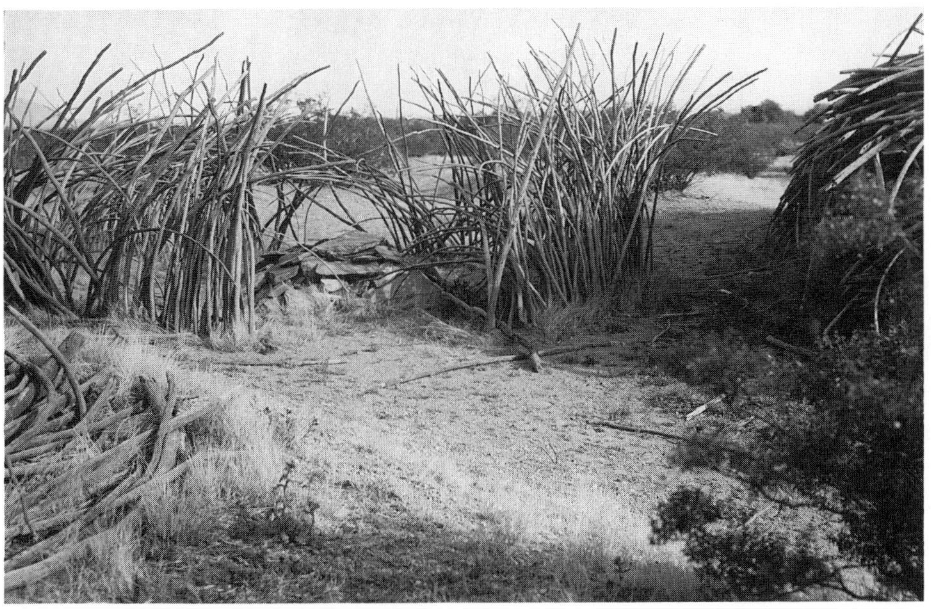

*The Shrine of the Four Children—Notice the stack of discarded ocotillo stems on the extreme right, next to the opening*

*PLATE XXIV*

approximately every four years, the fence is replaced and the old discarded ocotillo stems are piled on top of the stacks on either side of the enclosure. It is interesting to note that in a quarter of a century there has been very little increase in the height of these stacks. The ocotillo is a heavy tough wood and on top of the stacks the branches are firm and well seasoned from the desert sun, but downward they are found in all stages of decay and on the bottom the wood is again becoming a part of the dust of the desert. It is remarkable, in a desert country where wood is so scarce, that none of the ideal campfire wood in those stacks was ever known to have been removed.

A Papago gave me the following supplement to Fr. Ventura's story. There is supposed to be a subterranean room below the flat stones that cover the shrine, and in this room children's voices are sometimes heard as they run and play. In olden times, the people frequently would find pumpkin, corn, or beans by the side of the shrine. When this happened the old chief would have the people prepare their fields for the next planting season, and those particular crops would be planted, for it was an omen from the children that they would produce the most bountiful harvest for the ensuing year.

## *Papago Economy*

ALL OF the nearly seven thousand Papago Indians do not live in their desert home all of the time, for some take employment on the nearby ranches and in the towns, but always there remain the ties that eventually take them back. Sooner or later one will find them again living in a manner far removed from what is considered the necessities of our modern way of living. Their devotion to their desert homeland is beyond the understanding of their more migratory white brothers. When on the reservation, their main subsistence is by farming and stock raising.

Before the coming of the Spaniards, their only source of food was from their farms and the desert. There are no streams or lakes in the 2,700,000 acres of the Papago country. The rainfall varies, in different parts of the reservation, from four to twelve and one-half inches per year. There are two rainy seasons, and, at best, these are separated by long dry periods. One period of rains usually occurs during July and August, and the other during the winter. The summer rains are irregular, and often torrential. The drainage areas on the reservation collect these downpours in arroyos or washes, as they are commonly called, and these often are converted into raging torrents in a matter of an hour or two. Sometimes the rains do not come at all and then intense suffering occurs both to the livestock and to the people.

While the elevation of this vast desert varies from 1,400 to 3,000 feet, the greater portion of the land is a flat plain, and the short mountain ranges or peaks rise rather abruptly from this plain. Because of the flat character of the desert and the absence of any definite drainage system, these washes, in many instances, carry their floods only a comparatively short distance and then empty out onto a flood plain. Such a place is known to the Papagos as "Ak Chin," meaning "mouth of the wash," and until recent times these were the only places where farming could be carried on to any extent. Even now, in all of the Papago Reservation, only seven thousand acres are irrigable. Two thousand acres of the irrigable land are supplied with a stable water supply by means of pumps. The remaining acreage still is dependent on the flood water from the washes.

When the crops fail, about one year in five, the Papagos look to the desert for support, and it is remarkable how much food the desert can give to its people. In the spiny vegetation, which, to the casual observer, looks anything but palatable, the Papagos find dozens of plants that provide food. Cactus fruits of various kinds and in unlimited quantities form the greater portion of the wild food supply. Some are cooked, some are dried, and some are eaten fresh from the plant. It might be noted here that the most beautiful cactus country in Arizona, both from the standpoint of variety and vigorous growth, is found on the Papago Reservation.

In the olden times the Papagos had two separate homes, one in which they lived during the winter and the other near the Ak Chin where they planted their crops. Several districts or villages became known as Ak Chin, and it was necessary, a few years ago, for the government to change their nomenclature so that only one village would be so named. This village, which is south of the Maricopa station on the Southern Pacific railroad, resulted from the migration, more than seventy years ago, of a band of Papagos over a distance of seventy miles to take advantage of the flood waters from the Vecol Wash. In 1911, the government set aside about 21,000 acres surrounding their village, of which only 600 acres were irrigable.

The chief cash income of most of the Papagos now comes from outside labor. However, in recent years, the cattle industry has been greatly expanded. The reservation was fenced into grazing districts, and water holes were dug in all sections of the reservation. This permitted a fuller utilization of the range than ever before was possible, and the Papagos have contributed thousands of beef cattle to the national meat supply.

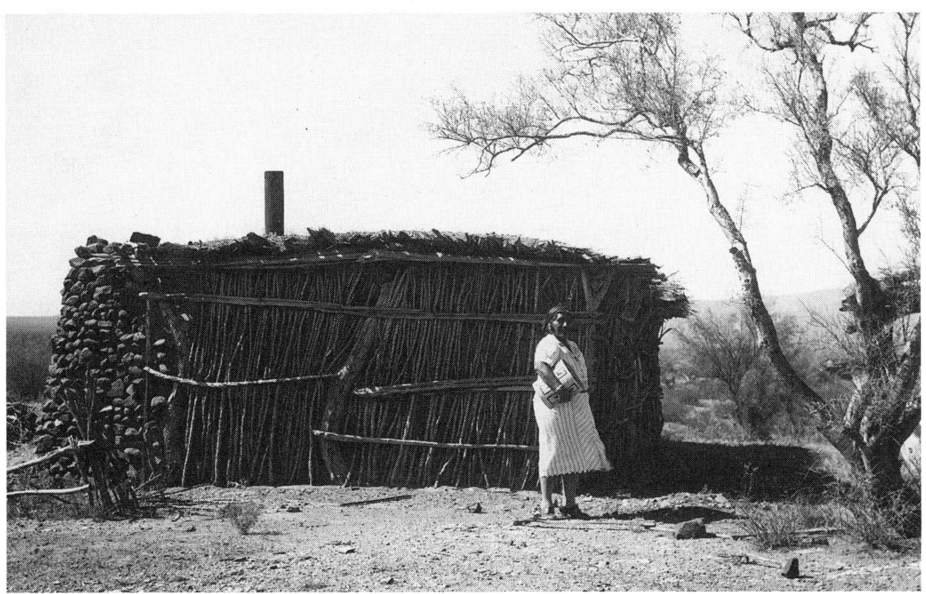

*Old type Papago home—The tough, strong ocotillo stalks form the walls of this house, while the roof consists of the same material, covered with brush* *PLATE XXV*

Another source of income to the Papagos is their arts and crafts work, especially baskets. They weave more baskets on a commercial basis than any other tribe in the Southwest. During the year preceding the second world war these Indians marketed $10,000 worth of craft work, the greater portion of which was baskets; $6,000 worth of these products was sold through a tribal enterprise located at Sells, which is their tribal headquarters.

In the Papago household, different members of the family have definite responsibilities toward the maintenance of the home. If a woman needs a new dress or some article for the house, it is her responsibility to provide the money for its purchase. Likewise, the man must purchase his overalls or his harness or farm implements with *his* earnings. This attitude toward a division of communal earnings and property extends even down through inheritance rights. The parents or the brother of the husband feel that, upon his death, their right to his farm implements or livestock supersedes that of his wife, and it is only through the application of the white man's inheritance laws that justice is achieved in such cases. In the case of death of the wife, her mother or sister may make claim to personal or household articles which she had made or purchased.

Among some Indians, baskets have a part in the rituals or religious ceremonies of the tribe, but there are no records of this having been true among the Papagos. Baskets did have an important place in the economy and, to some extent, in the social order of the tribe. They were used rather extensively as gifts and were much prized as such, for the Indians know the amount of time and labor that such a gift represents. Often such a basket would remain in a family for generations.

While visiting in a Papago home several years ago, I noticed that the grandmother was preparing cactus fruits from a very fine old basket. Through her son as interpreter, she was asked if she would sell the basket. She replied that it was too old to sell, that it had been a present to her when she was a girl, and she had kept it all these many years, but that she would make a new one for me. Finally, however, she sold me the old basket. When it was taken home and the stains of many cactus harvests were carefully washed away, the design was found to be an old tarantula pattern which I never have seen elsewhere (Plate XXVI). I was most fortunate to secure it, for frequently the old people request gift baskets to be buried with them.

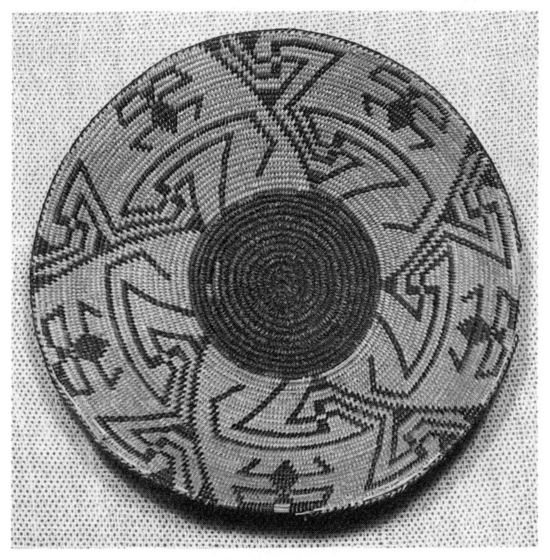

*The tarantula design—This basket is about seventy years old and was in use in the Indian's home for nearly half a century* *PLATE XXVI*

## *Yucca Baskets*

DYES ARE NOT used in the making of Papago baskets. The materials are prepared and woven in their natural colors. The background of the baskets is white, the decorative designs being worked in black or green or with both, and sometimes some red. The white and green materials are the thin, flexible leaves of the narrow-leaved yucca *(Yucca elata)* and the black is the devil's claw, the same as used in Pima baskets. The principal source of the red material is the root of the narrow-leaved yucca. Other materials utilized for this purpose are the root of the Spanish dagger *(Yucca arizonica)* and the root of desert willow *(Chilopsis linearis).*

The gathering and preparing of these materials is carried on as follows: In the spring or early summer the women go to the foothills to gather yucca. The tip of the yucca plant actually is a large terminal bud. By pushing aside the outside leaves, the whole bud can be pulled from the center of the plant. The longer, outside leaves of the bud are the ones selected for use, and the shorter, inside leaves are discarded. The leaves are of an eggshell shade when gathered and must be bleached and dried in the sun to obtain the clear white that is found in Papago baskets.

When the leaves of the yucca are gathered, the edges are removed by inserting a sharp instrument into the leaf and pulling away the narrow margin, which separates readily from the main body. The leaves are split, laid in the sun, and occasionally turned so they will be uniformly bleached. This bleaching process occurs immediately after the leaves are gathered, to prevent mildew or discoloration. They are then bound into small bundles and stored away. The green outer leaves are cut from the yucca plant, and after the edges are removed they are split and dried in the shade to prevent bleaching, and stored in the same manner as the white leaves.

The yucca plant grows on only a small portion of Papago country. In fact, it would be a two-day journey for many of the women of the north or west villages of the reservation to gather their material. This has brought about an industry for some of the Indians living near the areas where the yucca grows abundantly. They go in their wagons and gather large quantities of yucca leaves, then trade or sell them in other parts of the reservation.

The Papagos follow the same procedure as the Pimas in collecting the devil's claw, but there is some difference in the way the plant grows on the two reservations. Along the Gila River it grows wild on the canal banks, along the fences, or in abandoned fields where there is plenty of moisture. In the Papago country it is raised as any other field crop and must be irrigated and cultivated with the summer crops.

The red material forms a rather insignificant part in the weaving of baskets, its use being more or less confined to certain areas on the reservation. There is no definite season or time at which the yucca roots are dug except that usually it is in the spring when the ground is soft and moist from the winter rains. While the root of the yucca is, probably, the least stable of the red materials used, it is abundant and, consequently, most extensively used. When the roots are dug, the outer layer is removed and the woody part of the root is split into thin strips. The strips are coiled very much in the same manner as those of the willow. Care must be taken not to have the red material too damp, for then the color is likely to run and stain the white background and thus ruin the basket.

All the materials described are used in the coiling or woof of the baskets, and the warp or bundle about which they are coiled may be either bear grass, tule stems, or, occasionally in small baskets, shredded yucca leaves. The bear grass *(Nolina microcarpa)* is used almost exclusively except in the extreme northern portion of the reservation. It is a grass-like plant with leaves three to five feet in length and grows in the hills in the general locality of the yucca. The edges of the leaf blades are very sharp, resembling a fine saw, and may readily cut the hands.

In gathering bear grass, the women bend the long outside blades over and chop them off near the ground. They then carefully gather the tips of the longer blades in their hands and shake them, allowing the shorter ones to fall out. One clump of bear grass may be several feet in diameter and will furnish sufficient material for several baskets. After the blades are cut, the saw-like edges are scraped away with a knife. Then they are split from the base toward the tip into two or more sections and stored in bundles about two inches in diameter. Like the gathering of the yucca leaves, the gathering of bear grass is carried on by some of the Indians on a commercial basis because it also grows far from the northern and western villages. In some of the northern villages, especially at Chiu Chuschu, tule stems are used instead of bear grass, no doubt because the tule grows in the irrigation ditches, providing a convenient source of supply. The stems are gathered in the summer, split in half, and dried.

The techniques in the weaving of Papago coil baskets are the same as those of the Pimas, with, possibly, the exception of the starting method. The Pimas almost always start by wrapping approximately one-half inch of the tule stems, then bending the bundle over this wrapped section and sewing the coil to it. The Papagos usually start their baskets by taking two bundles of several strands each of the coiling material and tying them into a knot from which the loose ends extend like the points of a compass (Plate IV). The start is then made by bending one bundle of the loose ends to the left and the coiling is started by sewing this bundle to the knot. As the coiling progresses, another bundle is added until eventually all four bundles are bound around the knot. Then sections of bear grass are inserted and the weaving is under way.

The coiling always proceeds toward the left or counterclockwise, which is the practice of weavers of many tribes. One technique not commonly used by other tribes is the pounding of the coil with a hammer or smooth stone after each coil is completed. This accounts for the flat wall surface of the Papago basket instead of the corrugated surface common to most coil baskets.

Two types of stitching are used. In the finer baskets, the stitching appears on the surface as a narrow rectangular block of the yucca material. In coarser weaving, the hole made by the awl in piercing the lower coil may be smaller than the strand of the coiling material and, therefore, may constrict the material. When the finished coil of the coarsely woven basket is pounded flat, it takes on the shape of an elongated teardrop and for this reason is called the teardrop stitch. The pounding not only spreads the stitch but also causes some overlapping in the stitches. Nevertheless, the surface of the basket remains extremely smooth and flat. The Papagos finish their baskets with approximately the same kind of cross stitch of devil's claw as is found in the Pima baskets. In some modern baskets an overstitch is used after the basket is completed. Overstitching may be used to outline the eye in an animal figure, the beak of a bird, or perhaps the long pole used in the saguaro fruit harvest.

## *White Man's Influence*

THE INFLUENCE of the white trade on Papago basketry is greater than on that of any other tribe in Arizona. This influence has extended to materials, technique, and even to decorative designs. We might even classify them as tribal designs and commercial designs.

It must be remembered that the Papagos weave willow baskets the same as the Pimas, and in their home one seldom finds yucca baskets. On the other hand, there are few Papago homes that do not have some willow baskets in daily use. It is not definitely known how long they have woven yucca baskets. Kissell made a rather comprehensive study of the Papagos and their culture about 1910 and tentatively fixed the beginning of the yucca craft at about 1890, or perhaps a little earlier.[8] It was not until the white man began to come into the Papago country that the craft flourished. The designs used in the willow baskets might be called universal designs, since they were used throughout Pimería, but the designs used in the newer craft also are new, much simpler, and, therefore, easier to make. The old designs seldom are used with the yucca material, for the time and labor required to execute a squash blossom or an intricate fret design would not be compensated with the price that a tourist usually is willing to pay for a souvenir.

The beauty of the intricate designs is lost with the use of the coarser yucca material. This, no doubt, helped bring about the types of design now commonly used. These types vary from straight or horizontal lines in contrasting colors to simple blocks, cross figures or "S" figures, birds, reptiles, animals, cacti, and human figures. The size and shape of the basket often determines the type or kind of design employed. For example, the tall scrap, or wastepaper, basket may be decorated with a saguaro cactus or gila monster in vertical position, or perhaps an owl, while the bowl-shaped baskets may be decorated with lines or blocks of contrasting color. The trays may have birds, snakes, turtles, or geometric designs. The number of figures used to decorate a basket may vary from three to six, or even eight in the deep or bowl-shaped baskets. The number most frequently used is four. We know that four is the perfect number in the Indian legends of this area, and no doubt the Indian trader would tell the tourist that is the reason why so many baskets have designs repeated four times or made in four

8. Mary Lois Kissell, "Basketry of the Papago and Pima," *Anthropological Papers,* Vol. XVII, Pt. IV, American Museum of Natural History, New York, 1916.

sections. The Indian weavers would laugh at this story and say it was easier to space four designs around a basket than any other number, which is quite understandable.

Papago weavers develop original designs with great frequency, as compared to Pima weavers. This is because the Papago designs are newer. There is a certain code of ethics observed among the Papago weavers which does not permit one weaver to use another weaver's design.

It is interesting to observe the various ways in which the white man's influence affected Papago weaving and the apparent effort on the part of the weavers to satisfy the tourist desires. For instance, they weave novelty baskets, as shown in Plate XXVII. Dolls are more com-

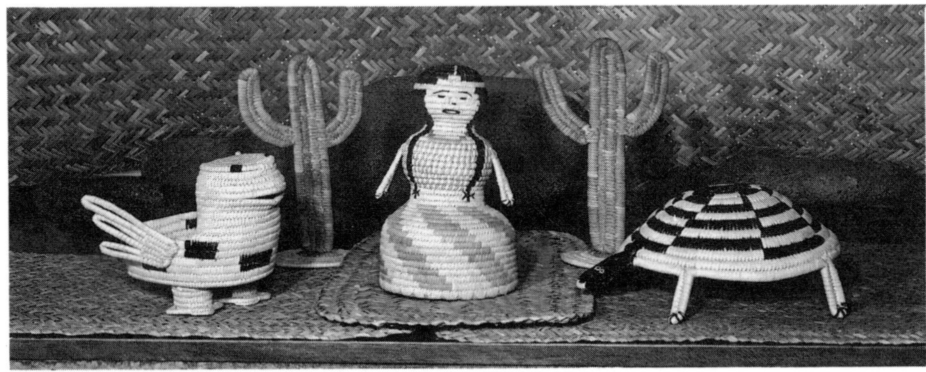

*Novelty baskets—The Papagos do more of this type of weaving than other Arizona tribes. The saguaro, turtle, and bird figures shown above are not made by any other tribe* *PLATE XXVII*

mon than other figure baskets and are sometimes found in baskets made by Pimas and other tribes of the Southwest. The saguaro, turtle, and the bird figures are individual to the Papago weavers and do not appear anywhere else. Other baskets that might come under this general classification of novelty types are shown in Plate XXVIII.

Trays or shallow bowls are sometimes finished with openwork, not found in any of the older designs or types of Papago baskets. I have never seen a willow basket of this type, so the natural deduction is that openwork baskets are woven exclusively for commercial purposes. The lace effect is accomplished by wrapping the bundle of warp instead of stitching it to the coil below, except at intervals, and the

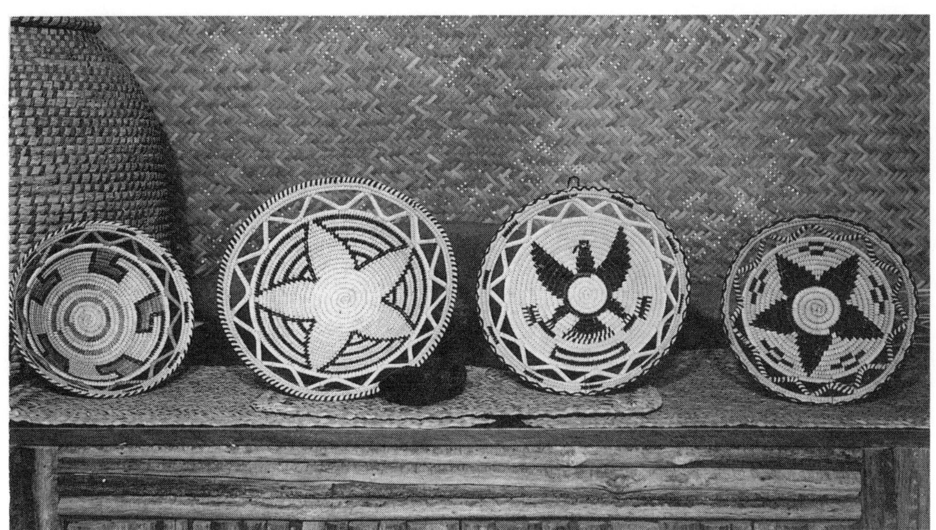

*Openwork novelty baskets—These baskets are woven exclusively for the commercial trade. The Papagos are the only Arizona tribe to make this type of basket* PLATE XXVIII

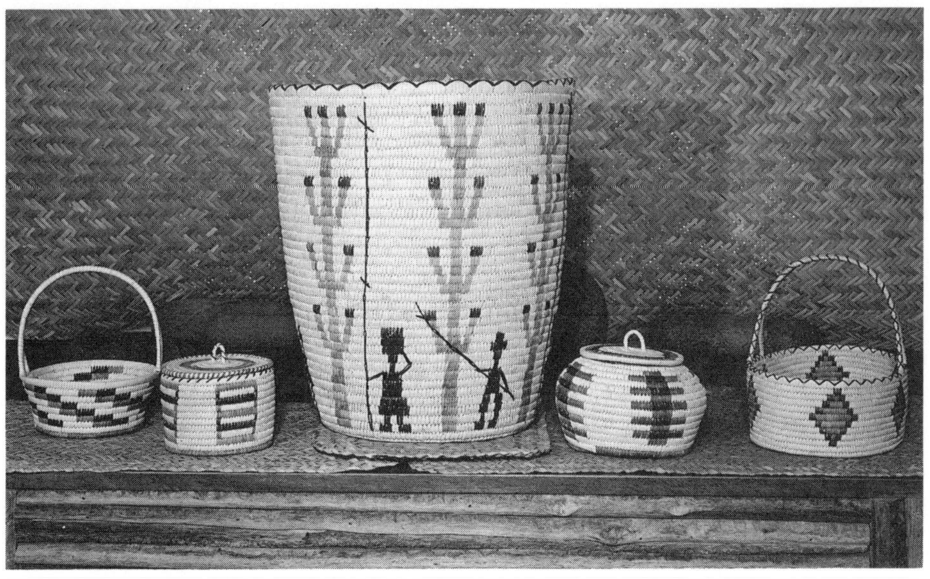

*The design of the large basket represents the harvesting of saguaro fruit. In all these Papago baskets, green yucca and black devil's claw are used in the decorative design* PLATE XXIX

wrapped portion can be formed into a loop or a point like a scollop, all of which is designed for decorative purposes only.

The saguaro fruit harvest design is illustrated in Plate XXIX. The saguaro plant is woven of green yucca material, with the ripened fruit in red, and the pole used for pushing off the fruit is an overstitch of devil's claw put on after the basket is completed. In all the baskets in the group shown in Plate XXIX, the green yucca is used in combination with the black devil's claw in the decorative design.

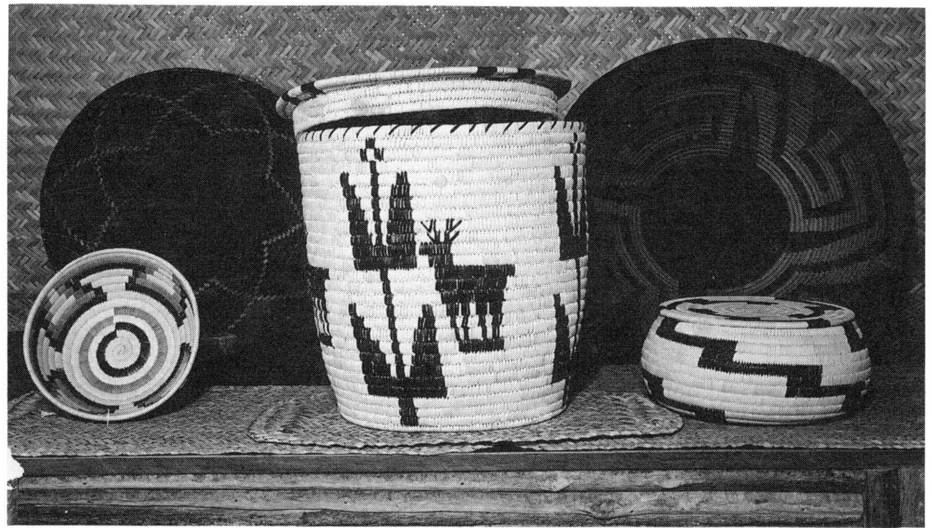

*Papago baskets—Old willow and devil's claw wheat baskets in background. The lids of these covered baskets will not come off even if they are turned upside down* *PLATE XXX*

Another type of yucca basket that is popular with the white trade is the covered basket (Plate XXX). The lids of these baskets fit so snugly that even though the basket be turned over, the lid will remain in place. The smaller ones frequently are used for holding trinkets or as sewing baskets. In most cases the lid fits into the top of the basket but occasionally the lid fits over the top. It may be finished with either a knob or a loop (Plate XXXI). This type of basket may vary in size from five or six inches in height up to a large hamper. While most of the baskets shown here might be classified as commercial types, it must always be borne in mind that the Papagos also make finer weaves that are used primarily in their own homes.

With the adoption of the white man's civilization much of the older culture, including not only their old customs but certain utensils and implements, was discarded. Certain pottery and basket specimens that at one time were in common use are now museum pieces. This is true of the tiswin baskets and wheat-parching baskets shown in Plate XXXIII. These tiswin baskets were so closely woven as to be water tight and were actually used in making tiswin, which was the only intoxicating beverage made by either the Papagos or the Pimas.

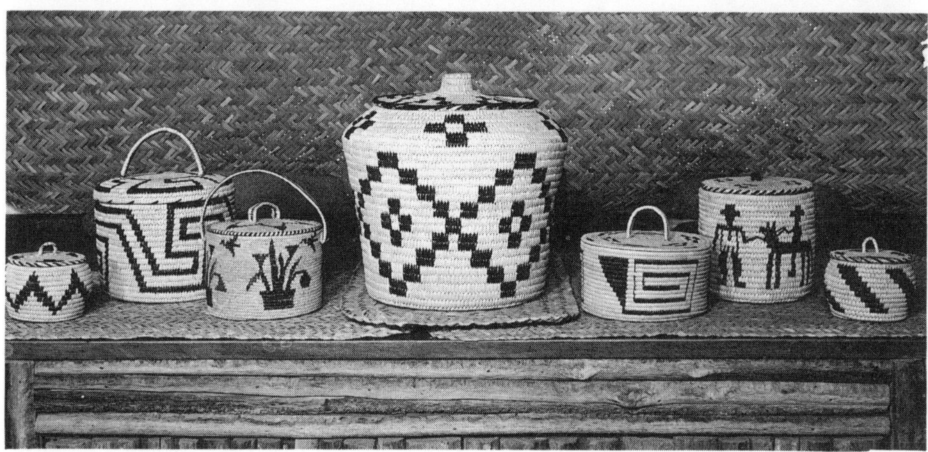

*Papago weavers excel in making covered baskets such as these. Most of them are commercial, although some are used in the homes* *PLATE XXXI*

The wheat-parching basket is made mostly of devil's claw because of its greater strength and its resistance to fire. It is used in the following manner: Live coals are placed in a large shallow pottery bowl made especially for this purpose and over these coals a thin layer of wheat is poured. When the grain is parched, the bowl is emptied quickly into the basket. By rapidly agitating the contents, the grain settles to the bottom and the lighter coals come to the surface where they can be brushed away. The ashes are then winnowed from the grain and it is ready to be ground into pinole on a stone metate. Care is always taken to keep the coals away from the basket as much as possible, and it is remarkable how long these wheat-parching baskets last, some having served for many years. Papago weavers still can make these baskets.

In olden times the *giho,* or burden basket, was in common use by both the Papago and Pima tribes, but now weaving of the giho is a lost

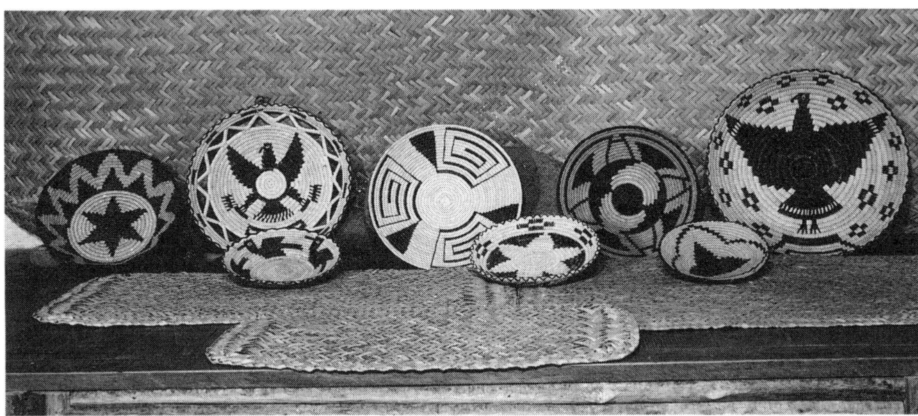

*A selection of fine specimens of Papago tribal designs and craftsmanship* PLATE XXXII

art among the Pimas. Although one Papago continues to make them, I have never seen one of recent make. They no longer have any utility value, having long since been replaced by the white man's pail or gunny sack. The labor involved in the selection, preparation, and assembling of the material for a giho, as well as the weaving, is so great as to make them expensive. This fact, together with the size and peculiar shape, which presents difficulty in packing for shipment, prevents the gihos from being popular with tourists. Actually, about the

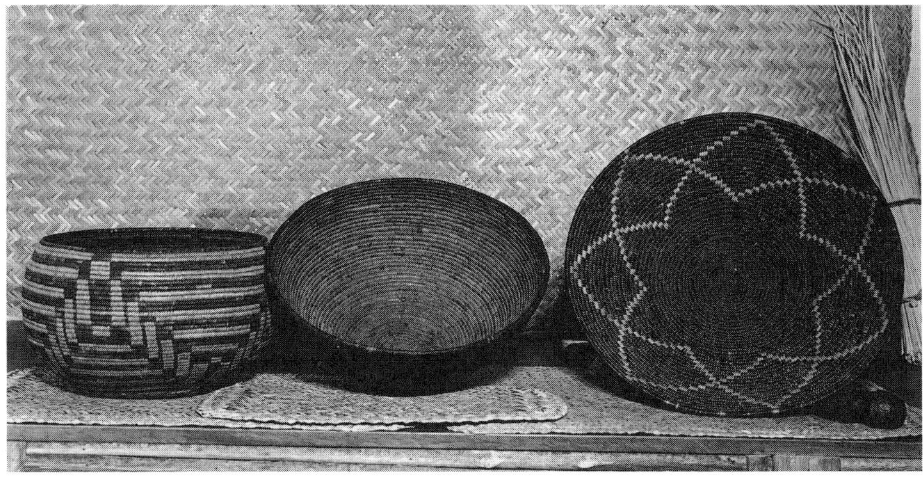

*Papago utility basket—Right, wheat parching basket; center, tiswin basket; left, deep bowl. The tiswin basket is watertight and was actually used in making tiswin* PLATE XXXIII

only purchasers of gihos are collectors, but even with them the supply does not equal the demand.

Through the efforts of the weavers and their tribal arts and crafts board, Papago yucca baskets have been given wider distribution than any other baskets in the Southwest. They may be found in Los Angeles, Kansas City, Chicago, Washington, D. C., and in all way stations along the line. The Papagos have recognized the tourists' demands and have adjusted their craft to meet those demands. This adjustment has included not only size and shape but material as well, although the weavers have retained the distinctive Indian characteristics. Their baskets seem to hold within themselves an intangible part of the desert from whence they came and of the Papago women who wove them. The public has responded by purchasing as much as $10,000 worth of their baskets in one year. Many of these baskets sold for less than one dollar each. It is not to be inferred, however, that all Papago baskets are cheap, for they are not.

# *Weavers of*
# *The Mountain Country*

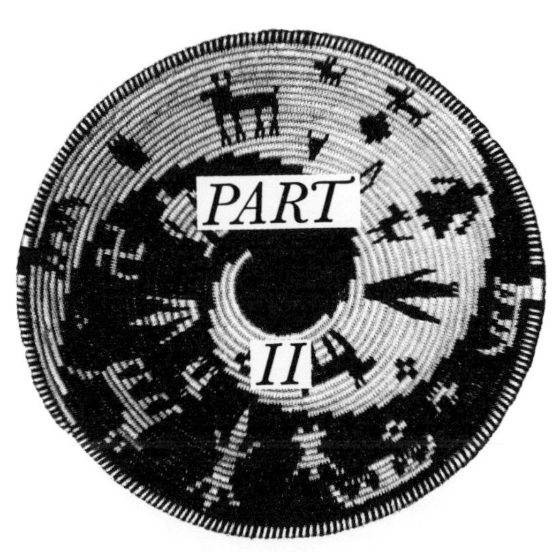

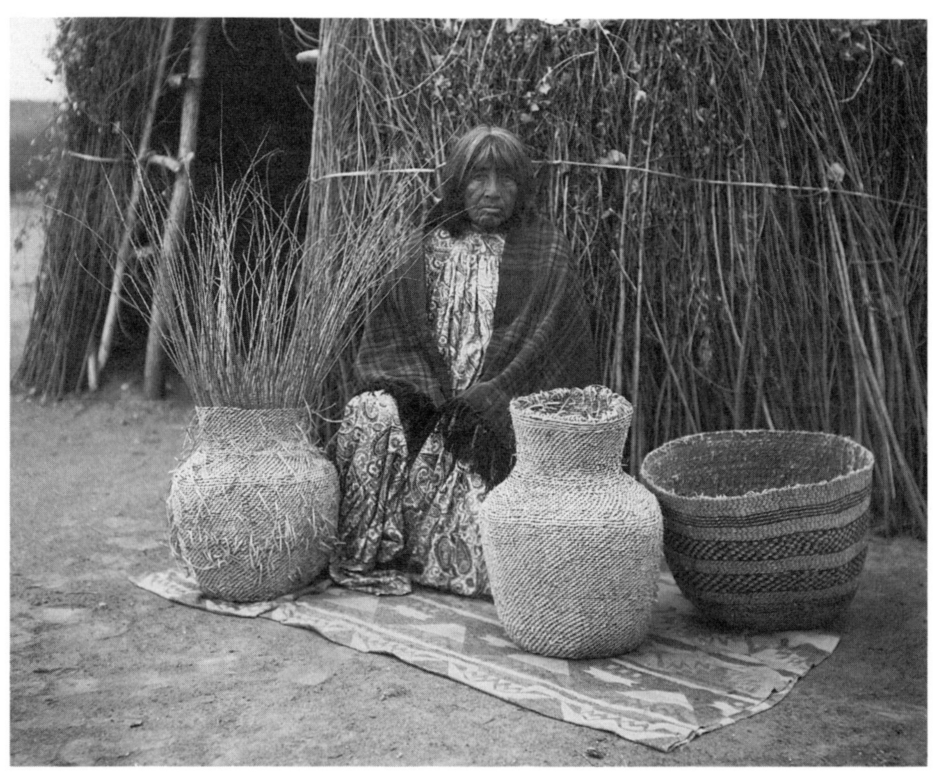

*Whole willow twigs are used for the warp, and split twigs for the weft in weaving both water jars and burden baskets at San Carlos*

*PLATE XXXIV*

# *The Athabascan Apache*

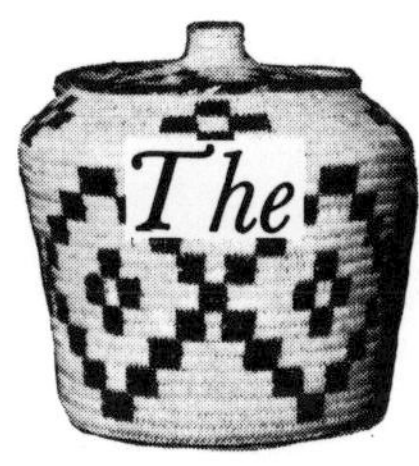


APACHE BELONGS to the great Athabascan family, which is the largest linguistic group of the Indians of North America. Branches of this family extend down the Yukon River, of Alaska; the Mackenzie River, of Canada; down the West Coast; and across the Southwest into Mexico. The Apache, or southern, branch of the family formerly took in southern Colorado, southern Utah, Arizona, New Mexico, and northwest Texas, down into the Sierra Madre Mountains, of Mexico.

In Arizona, there are two tribes of Athabascan origin, the Navajo and the Apache. Evidently the same thing happened here that occurred in the Pima country, for the two tribes speak the same language, are of the same physical type, and are, unquestionably, the same people. At some time prior to the coming of the white man there was a division into two tribal groups, possibly because of economic and social trends. The Navajos were more inclined toward agriculture.

When sheep were introduced into this country by the early Spaniards, the Navajos became expert herdsmen and, with the wool from their flocks, they wove beautiful blankets which they used to trade with other tribes. They continue to weave commercially today. On the other hand, the Apaches were nomads and warriors, who subsisted by hunting, raiding, and pillaging.

Coronado probably was the first of his race to come in contact with the Apaches. However, his chronicler, Castañeda, did not mention any such contacts. This may have been due to one of two reasons. First, the Pima Indian guides who were leading the Coronado expedition to the Zuñi country in 1540 may have avoided encountering Apache bands; or they may have been encountered and mentioned under a different name, since they were first called Apaches by Oñate later in the century, after Coronado's expedition. The name comes from the Zuñi word "Apachu," meaning "enemy." Use of the name in combination with other tribal names, such as Yuman-Apache, Kiowa-Apache, Mojave-Apache, etc., none of which belongs to the Apache group, has caused some confusion. The question often is asked, "Were the Apache Indians named after the French Apaches or was the order reversed?" The vicious underworld gangsters of Paris, France, that were called Apaches did not make their appearance until late in the eighteenth century, which was long after the American Indian tribe had acquired its name.

The Apaches are divided into numerous tribes or bands. In early times, several Apache tribes ranged over New Mexico and some below the border into Mexico, while an even greater number of tribes occupied eastern Arizona. This group generally has been called the Western Apaches, and it is with these bands that we are primarily interested. The principal bands or tribes which made up the group were about as follows: In the north, the White Mountain band, and included with them were the Cibicu and Coyoteros. To the west of these bands were the Northern and Southern Tonto, which were separate groups. The central section of the Apache country was occupied by the San Carlos group, together with the Pinals and Aravaipas, and the southern part of the area, extending down to the Mexican border and beyond, was the home of the dreaded Chiricahua. This latter group has contributed more than any of the other bands to the ill fame of the Apache people.

The Apache was traditionally a warrior and his ambition in life was to improve his technique as such. He was conquered only after forty years of warfare against the American soldiers, whose supremacy in numbers, equipment, and supplies brought about his defeat. A warrior's training began almost in infancy and continued until he was fifteen or sixteen years old, when he was considered ready to go on his first raid. This training was severe to the point of being cruel. As a child there was no kindness or tenderness in his life, for such an attitude would have been a mark of weakness under the code of his wild people. He saw his mother do all the drudgery around the camp and saw her repaid with kicks and blows for her labor. When he grew up he treated his wife in like manner and if she proved unfaithful he cut off her nose, which he was allowed to do according to tribal custom.

To excel as a warrior was to be able to kill without undue exposure and to steal or plunder without being caught. A part of his training was not only the use of his weapons but also how to make them. They consisted of a lance, war club, or short belt-knife, and bow and arrow. The arrowhead was fastened to a short piece of wood, which was inserted into a hollow cane shaft. In withdrawing the arrow from a wound the arrowhead and foreshaft remained embedded in the flesh.

The white man probably furnished the Apache with his most valuable asset, for what he needed most was transportation in making a swift getaway after a raid. The horse, introduced into the Southwest by the Spaniards, furnished such transportation. While the Apaches could travel thirty to forty miles in a day on foot, they could travel twice the distance on horses. Women and children often accompanied the men when on a raiding party but usually were hidden away at a safe distance in a spot to which the warriors would return after a raid.

The estate of a wife in the Apache family was comparatively low, but there were certain prerogatives which were reserved to her. The care of the children and the collecting of wild fruits, as well as all other work about the camp, was her responsibility. The family unit of the Apaches differed from our own in that it was a family group rather than an individual household. Apaches did not like to live alone; in fact, one writer has said that they were afraid to be alone, and this fear may account for their always living, hunting, and gathering food in groups.

When a young man married he went to live in the family group of his wife's parents, and thereafter their welfare and care in their old age were his responsibility. His connection with his own family was completely severed. Marriage occurred at a younger age among the Apaches than it normally does among our own people. Soon after puberty a girl was given what we might call a coming-out party. This was an elaborate affair to which a large number of friends and relatives were invited. It lasted four days and was not only a social affair but a religious ceremony as well. The primitive Apache was, in his weird belief, deeply religious. This statement may be difficult to accept in view of the savage atrocities that have been recorded against him.

In courtship the Apache girl was more aggressive than the boy, but the proposal of marriage was made by the young man. When he found the lady of his choice, he would take some of his horses and tie them near her home during the night as a gift to her father. The number of horses would depend upon the boy's wealth or his ardor and might vary from one to all that he possessed. If the girl fed and cared for these horses it would indicate her acceptance of him. If, after four days, the horses were left starving and uncared for, he could only take his livestock and, like the Arab, steal silently away into the night.

After acceptance, preparations were made for the wedding ceremony, which lasted for three days and was accompanied by many weird dances and rituals. In the end, the young couple stole away into the woods to a hideout previously arranged, where they remained for several days. When they returned to the camp they built their wickiup near that of the girl's mother but facing in the opposite direction, for the husband must never speak to his mother-in-law or even, in fact, look at her.

Usually several families lived in close proximity and thus formed a local group. In such a group, outstanding ability as a hunter or successful leadership in conducting raids might gain for a man the position of headman or chief. This position, however, would be held only so long as his success continued and he could be replaced at any time by another who showed greater success or ability. Membership in the local group was not confined to blood relationship or other ties but was open to any who might wish to join. Such a community or unit fitted in perfectly with the Apache way of life, as it possessed great mobility, and the ease with which it could be maneuvered in warfare or in raids was an important asset. It could be dispersed quickly when pressed by an enemy, a baffling, elusive trick at which the Apache was a master.

Several such local groups, occupying a certain locality, might be called a band, but they maintained their own individuality, except when expediency or convenience dictated otherwise. This caused much confusion in their dealings with the American Army, and often caused the Apache to be accused of bad faith with regard to treaties, since one group or band might make peace today and another come along tomorrow and continue to fight.

Slight differences in dialect and customs existed between the tribes, but a friendship was maintained to the extent that there was no warfare between them. Sometimes there was intermarriage among the tribes but the man never lost his tribal identity with his wife's people. For instance, if a Tonto married a woman from the White Mountain tribe he would go to her family group to live but he would always remain a Tonto and an outsider to the family. The chief of the tribe attained his position in the same way as the chiefs of the local groups and bands. By a strict merit system the Apaches developed some of the most outstanding leaders among Indian people. Such men as Mangas Colorado, Cochise, Diablo, and others were great leaders in their native mountains. They were strategists of the highest order, perhaps possessing greater ability than any leaders opposing them, with the exception of General Crook. Geronimo gained great notoriety as a renegade and outlaw, but his cruel cunning did not compare with the brilliant ability of the other chiefs mentioned here. It is now believed that if these leaders had been dealt with by our government with patience and understanding, many pages of the lurid history of the Southwest would not have been written.

## *Early History*

WHEN THE SPANIARDS first encountered the Apaches they were rather impotent bands of nomadic raiders who preyed upon neighboring tribes but were rather ineffective against the white invaders. In time, they grew in power through their natural increase in numbers, and the taking of captives from other tribes. Although Oñate was the first to call them Apaches, it is assumed that the Querechos mentioned by earlier Spanish reports may have been the same people.

In Friar Alonzo Benavides' report, in 1630, he describes the Apaches as fierce raiders who preyed upon the Pueblo villages but who had not, as yet, made direct attack upon the Spaniards. A few years later, however, this did occur and, in raiding the Pueblos, priests were killed and churches and other property destroyed. By 1670, the Apaches were openly attacking rancherías and missions and killing all they encountered. Between 1670 and 1680, numerous attacks were made on the Spanish missions.

A typical raid, which occurred in 1698 on the lower San Pedro, involved a mission established by Fr. Kino, who had figured prominently in the early history of the Pimas. Most of the friendly Indians of the mission were away when the Apaches attacked, and after killing their chief and some of his warriors, the rest were driven into the mission building. The Apaches climbed to the roof and set it afire; then, thinking their victory complete, they slaughtered the horses and cattle of the mission and started feasting on the meat. Captain Coro, a Pima chief, lived at another of Fr. Kino's missions about three miles down the river, and, hearing the fight, came to the aid of his friends. When he arrived, the Apache chief, Capotcari, heaped insults on the Pimas and proposed that ten men from each tribe be chosen to oppose each other in a mass duel. Capotcari headed his own group, but the Pimas, with their bows and arrows, were too much for the Apaches and soon Capotcari was the only man of his group left in the fight. He was so quick that he could catch in his hand the arrows launched at him, which was an accomplishment frequently achieved by the Apaches. When his Pima opponent saw this he rushed Capotcari, threw him to the ground, and beat him to death with a rock. Undoubtedly the Apaches watched while this was being done but offered no assistance. This is characteristic of Indians and, even today, regardless of how unevenly matched two opponents may be in a fight, onlookers seldom interfere. In the general battle which ensued after Capotcari was killed, the Pimas pursued the Apaches into the hills, killing a large number of them. The duel or tournament between picked men from opposing tribes was a common practice in Indian warfare; and after this preliminary fight was over and one side was defeated the battle between the opposing forces became general.

During the first half of the eighteenth century the Spanish colonies suffered greatly at the hands of the Apaches, who carried on their depredations almost within sight of the presidios. By 1768, the situation had become so serious that the government in Spain realized that some remedial action must be taken. Accordingly, a full study of the problem was made, and, following this, General Don Hugo Oconor was sent to reorganize the entire border defense system. Presidios were located at intervals of one hundred miles all along the 1500-mile front, and each was equipped with mounted brigades that could operate swiftly within a radius of fifty miles. General Oconor then organized an expeditionary force to carry the fight to the Apaches. Each presidio contributed a number of men, and other forces were recruited from the ranches, villages, and friendly Indians of the district. An army of about two thousand men was placed in the field and the Apaches were pursued into their mountain retreats, and, for the first time, a major offense was carried on against them. As they retreated northward, their old enemies, the Comanches, struck from that direction and, between them and the Spaniards, the Apaches suffered the most crushing defeat they had, as yet, sustained.

So well beaten were the Apaches that for the next two decades the territory enjoyed the nearest semblance to peace that it had known for many years, but during the ten-year period of confusion, while the Spanish colonies were achieving their independence, the Apaches again became the menace they had been in former years. They were quick to recognize the mortal fear in which they were held by the Mexicans and their raids grew bolder and more frequent. When retaliatory action against them became too effective they offered to make peace, and the ready response of the Mexican military displayed such fear and weakness that the shrewd Apaches were quick to recognize it. Such a truce was used only as a convenience by the Apaches and when the livestock they had stolen was disposed of they would again start their raiding and murdering. Finally, recognizing the abject weakness of the garrisons, in morale as well as effectiveness, the settlements resorted to the practice of offering a bounty for the scalp of an Apache, either man, woman, or child. This resulted in a general season of head hunting and since the friendly Indians were easier to get than the warring Apaches, there was some question at times as to the tribal identity of the scalps. In retaliation, the Apaches raided and destroyed settlements with more fierceness than ever, and continued their raids until they were conquered by the Americans.

## *Apaches vs. Americans*

OF COURSE, the conflict with the Americans overlaps both the Mexican period and the latter part of the Spanish period, for Americans had begun to infiltrate into the Apache country early in the nineteenth century.

The first Americans to encounter the Apaches were trappers who had come in search of beaver pelts. Strangely enough a friendly relationship was established between these hardy woodsmen and the Indians, in spite of the bitter hatred which the Apaches held toward the Mexicans and Spaniards. They found in the Americans a new type of white man, who differed in many respects from those they had met previously. Their integrity and honesty were better, also their courage and marksmanship, and no doubt all four characteristics were factors in establishing the friendship and respect they had for these Americans.

But, as white immigration increased, the desperate characters that always appeared on our western frontiers came. An act of treachery on the part of an American named James Johnson brought about the first large-scale hostilities with the Apaches. Johnson had been in contact with the Mexicans in northern Sonora, who were continually subjected to raids from the Apaches and who were offering a bounty for scalps. One chief, Juan José, had terrorized the garrisons as well as the settlers for a long time and they were seeking means to destroy him. Finding that he and Johnson were on friendly terms, they bribed Johnson to lure José into his camp and kill him. This brought open hostilities toward the Americans, for, under the Apache code, José's followers would be bound to avenge his death, and no doubt many American lives were lost in payment for Johnson's treacherous act.

In 1849, James Calhoun was appointed first Indian agent to this district, with headquarters at Santa Fe, New Mexico, and was the first to advocate that the Indians be brought onto reservations and taught to subsist through agriculture and the other pursuits followed by white settlers.

Doctor Mitchell Steck, Apache Indian agent from 1855 to 1860, followed the lead set by Calhoun in recommending that the Apaches be placed on reservations and provided with food and clothing until they could develop in the white man's way to support themselves. The long struggle they had staged against the superior forces of the whites had taken a terrific toll, their strength was broken and, in many instances, their health, for among other things the white man had brought were diseases and vices which hitherto were unknown to them. Many of the tribal chiefs asked for peace and expressed a desire to settle down and live quietly on land provided for them. Had it been possible to put into effect the suggestions of Calhoun and Steck the great losses in life and property that occurred in the settlements during the next few years might have been avoided.

When the Civil War broke, in April, 1861, the garrisons from the three remaining forts on the Arizona frontier were withdrawn for service farther east, leaving the settlements at the mercy of hostile Indians. The Apaches mistook the withdrawal for capitulation and fell upon the settlements in a war of extermination. It so happened that the two greatest war chiefs of the Apache people were at the height of their power at this time and through their leadership the Indians were almost successful in their quest. In the north, Mangas Colorado led the Pinals and other bands of the Upper Gila basin in raids against the copper mines in the district. Farther south, Cochise, the great leader of the Chiricahuas, made savage raids against the settlements and gave special attention to the overland stage line that passed through the Chiricahua territory between El Paso and Tucson.

The Chiricahuas had long had a bitter hatred for the Mexicans, and through the blundering of a young American officer, Lieutenant Bascom, the full fury of that hatred now was turned upon the Americans.

Late in 1861, a troop under the Lieutenant was camped at Apache Pass, near the present site of Bowie, Arizona. Cochise, with his wife and some relatives, visited the camp to inquire the reason for the soldiers being in the area. He was told that his warriors had stolen some cattle and had taken a white boy captive about forty miles west of Apache Pass and that he must release them to the soldiers. Cochise denied that his people had perpetrated this raid and when he was told that he and his group would be held as hostages until the boy and the cattle were returned, he slashed the wall of the tent and escaped. He and his band went on the warpath and when three of his relatives, who were held as hostages, were hanged in retaliation for murders perpetrated by his band, he set out on a frightful campaign to avenge their death. It is said that he killed more than twenty-five white men with his own hands. Some he bound and dragged to death behind his pony; he cut chunks of flesh from the bodies of others until they died. Another fiendish act practiced by his band was capturing a wagon train and driving off the mules and oxen, then tying the men to the wagon wheels and setting wagons and contents on fire. The women and children were held as captives to await a worse fate. This continued for nearly a decade, for, in the rough, rugged Chiricahua country, these Indians were almost invulnerable. Later it was found that Cochise really had told the truth; that neither he nor his band were involved in the raid that precipitated the Chiricahua war, but a band of Pinal Apaches from up near the Gila River were the raiders.

As the Apache troubles continued, Arizona, on its own behalf, made a concerted effort to control them. In 1865, five companies of Arizona volunteers were organized. Three were composed of residents of the territory who, for the most part, were of Mexican extraction or birth; the other two companies were Maricopa and Pima Indians. This small force was wholly inadequate but it was, in proportion, more effective than any of the several others that had come into the territory, possibly because it was made up of men hardened and experienced on the Arizona frontier.

With the combination of all the forces sent against them the Apaches were finding it very hard to continue with their warfare. Their numbers were growing smaller and so were their food supplies, and their horses, and mules were decreasing in number. Several forts and army camps had been set up throughout the Indian country, and persecution and punishment followed almost every raid against the settlements. Some of the bands began to realize the futility of continuing their warfare and came to the forts to surrender and ask for peace.

Another problem now began to present itself. Others besides settlers and home seekers were causing trouble. Some of these have been characterized by historians as among the vilest and most desperate characters this country has produced. Members of the families of many of the settlers had been slain by the Indians. These men, whose hatred for the Apaches was understandable, sometimes joined with the desperados, and many Apache groups that were seeking to live at peace were murdered in a fashion comparable to the most vicious of the Indian marauders. The seriousness of this menace to the establishment of peace was brought to the attention of the nation by the Fort Grant massacre.

A large number of Pinal Indians had been told that if they would settle down near Fort Grant they would be protected and given food and other assistance. They did this, but raids on the settlements continued. The citizens charged that the raiding bands were from the Fort Grant camp and demanded that they be punished. But the Indians denied these accusations, and no doubt they were truthful in doing so. When the military officials did not act, the citizens took the matter into their own hands. They quietly gathered together a large number of Papagos and all of the available white members of the community and fell upon the unprotected Apache camp. Most of the Indian men were away on a hunting party and only the old people, women, and children remained in the camp. In the slaughter that followed, more than one hundred were killed and about forty children taken captive by the Papagos, few of whom were ever heard of again.

The whole nation was incensed at the brutality of this raid, but it brought the whole Apache problem squarely before the American people. It resulted in improvement in both the number and caliber of the military personnel sent to cope with the situation.

In 1871, General George A. Crook, the most colorful of all the soldiers of the Apache war, came into the military picture of the Southwest. He organized his forces, giving special attention to pack trains, which he developed to a high state of perfection. Then he called upon the Indians to surrender and go onto reservations, where they would be protected, supplied with food and implements, and taught to live peaceably according to the white man's way of life. He promised that if they refused he would destroy them. So well did he keep his word that their mountain retreats no longer provided sanctuary. They were followed to their winter camps, their food supplies destroyed, and their wickiups burned. For the first time the end of the long savage struggle was in sight.

Some of the old Apaches still remember the terrible hardships of that winter, and, strangely enough, they say their greatest privation came from being unable to build a fire. They were driven into the open and kept continually on the move by Crook's forces. A fire might have revealed their whereabouts to the scouts working with the troops. But the great difficulty came because of the rain and snow that kept the woods continually wet. They say they would sometimes try for days before they could start a fire, since they employed the friction method commonly used by Indians.

In 1871, General O. O. Howard was sent south to the mountain hideout of the aging Cochise to negotiate a treaty of peace with the Chiricahuas, and the following year a reservation fifty-five miles square was set aside for this tribe. The old chieftain and the remnants of his band lived there peaceably until his death, in 1874. Later this reservation was abandoned and the Chiricahuas were placed with other Apache bands on the San Carlos Reservation. It was from here that the notorious Geronimo launched his raids into Mexico and southern Arizona, and it was not until 1886 that he finally was forced to come in and surrender to General George A. Miles. Then his band and all the Chiricahua tribe were removed to Fort Mariam, Florida, to remain in military custody for two years and then brought to Fort Sill, Oklahoma. After being held for twenty-eight years they finally were released from Fort Sill in 1914, and the small remnants of the band now live on the Mescalero reservation, in New Mexico.

### *San Carlos*

In 1875, the government determined that their difficult problem could be handled more efficiently and economically on one reservation than from the various posts where the Indians were being held. Accordingly, all hostile bands were concentrated on the San Carlos Reservation, with John P. Clum as the first government agent assigned to this difficult administrative task.

To further complicate the situation, almost immediately, dissension sprang up between the civil administrative officers of the Indian Service and the officers of the garrisons maintaining military control. Charges of exceeding authority, inefficiency, and even corruption were hurled back and forth until the controversy became a national issue. This condition continued for more than a decade and the records of this period form a rather regrettable chapter in the history of Indian and government relationship.

## *The Modern Apache*

THE APACHE INDIANS of Arizona now live on two reservations that adjoin each other in the eastern central part of the state. They no longer depend on wild game or the gathering of wild foods for their subsistence, but have become industrious and successful stockmen. Their great mountain meadows are dotted with thousands of fine beef cattle, and the tribe as a whole is one of the most prosperous in the state. Their agriculture is rather negligible because the rainfall over this area is insufficient to produce crops without the aid of irrigation.

Originally, in 1872, the reservation was set up as a single unit, but later a dividing line on the Salt and Black rivers was agreed upon, separating the area into two reservations. The Fort Apache Reservation, in the north, is in the higher elevation of the area and is, for the most part, covered with pine and juniper forests. The juniper has little commercial value, but the pine is an important asset, for a good portion of the great ponderosa pine forests of northern Arizona lies within the reservation. In 1946, more than 38,000,000 board feet of lumber were cut on the reservation. The Indians operate a small sawmill at Whiteriver, but the greater portion of the lumber is cut at McNary, where a large mill is operated under lease from the government. The royalties from the lumber cut are deposited to the account of the tribal fund. It is estimated there are over four billion board feet of commercial lumber standing on the reservation. Under laws governing the use of this timber, the yearly cut cannot exceed the estimated reforestation; therefore, this will continue to be one of the most important resources of the tribe.

The San Carlos Reservation, which makes up the southern half of the Apache reserve, has a much greater variation in altitude and climate than the Fort Apache area. In the mountains of the northeastern part of the reservation elevations range up to 8,300 feet, with winter temperatures dropping as low as –20°, whereas in the southern part, along the Gila River, the elevation is only 2,200 feet and summer temperatures have been recorded up to 117°. Naturally, the vegetation varies with the elevation.

There is no lumbering industry on the reservation but it is estimated there are 250,000,000 board feet of timber, which probably will be sufficient for the needs of the tribe in any future home building program. There are some desposits of asbestos, iron, copper, and manganese that may in the future prove to be valuable resources, but to date only minor exploratory work in mining has been done.

The chief industry of the reservation is cattle raising, and the herds at San Carlos have been improved until they rank among the best in the state. Only small tracts in the remote districts of either reservation are leased to white men, and all the balance is operated by the Indians. There are 1,640,000 acres in the San Carlos Reservation and practically the whole area is devoted to this industry, since less than 1,000 acres are used for agricultural purposes. The cattle are all in individual ownership by members of the tribe. A small herd is operated for relief of old and indigent persons, and a third herd is operated to furnish purebred breeding stock for the different associations and individuals.

The Apaches still cling to some of the old customs, especially the type of dress worn by the women. Their dresses have voluminous

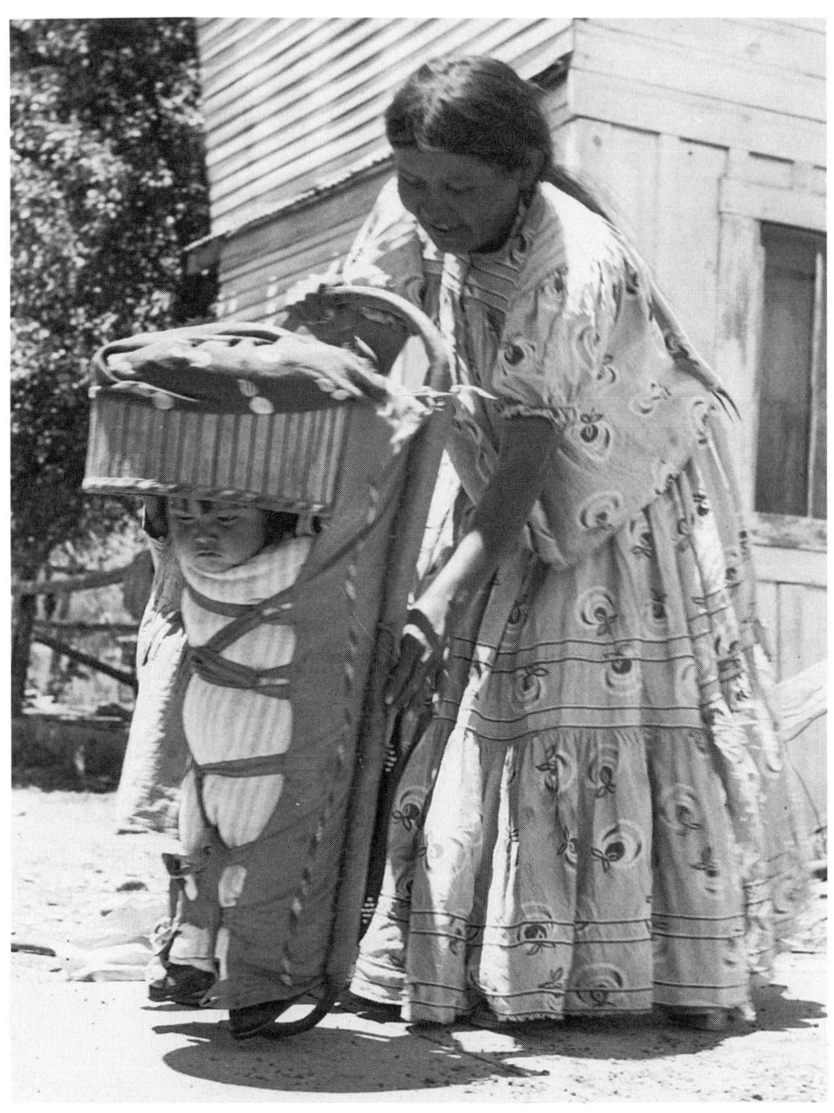

*Apache babies are securely strapped to the cradle board and apparently experience no discomfort*

PLATE XXXV

skirts of bright colored calico, and the brighter the color, especially if it is red, the more the garment is prized by the owner.

Many of them still live in their brush and grass wickiups, but there also are several hundred small cottages on the reservation. One of the reasons for the continued use of the wickiup is that these people still retain the old custom of burning the house and all its contents when a member of the family dies. I have been told that none of the frame houses has been burned, probably because a patient who is known to be dying is removed from the house before death occurs. The Navajos, who have the same custom, practice the same preventive measures, usually removing the afflicted person from the hogan when death is approaching.

There are now about seven thousand Apache Indians on the two reservations and their rate of increase is equal to or above the normal increase of white communities. This is in direct contrast to conditions which prevailed for many years after their surrender, for in the early period of their confinement their death rate was exceedingly high.

In summarizing the modern Apache, we should consider that seventy years ago his grandfather was a primitive warrior who opposed our government and all the institutions that it stood for. Geronimo had left the reservation and gone on the warpath and many of the Indians who remained at home were in full sympathy with him. Now, after two generations, we find that the Apache's adjustment to his new way of life has converted him into a successful and useful citizen. His grandfather had to be supplied with food, blankets, and clothing by the government, whereas today the Apache not only supports himself and cares for the dependent members of his tribe, but in one year he has produced $1,725,000 worth of beef to add to our nation's meat supply, and as his development continues this amount will increase.

In going back over the history of the Apache people, their nomadic unstable way of living would seem to leave little opportunity for the development of arts and crafts such as we find among many other Indian tribes. On the Fort Apache Reservation this is true to a certain extent, but at San Carlos we find that their weaving of baskets ranks high in the Indian art work of Arizona.

## *Apache Baskets*

IN SUCH CRAFTS as basketry, pottery, silverwork, and weaving, the early Apaches were surpassed by many other Indian tribes of Arizona. Of the crafts mentioned, basket weaving was practically the only one developed to any extent. Even in this craft there is some question as to its origin in the tribe. It is suggested that their art in basketry may have been borrowed from captives taken from other tribes.

The Apaches make three different types of baskets, namely, water jars *(tus),* burden baskets *(tuts-ah),* and devil's-claw-and-cottonwood coiled baskets *(tsah).* There is some variation in the distribution of these three basket types in the different sections of the Apache reserve. The water jar and burden basket are made and used on both the northern and southern reservations. The coiled baskets are made almost exclusively on the San Carlos Reservation. Apache baskets are made primarily for utility purposes about the home and camp. Especially is this true of the water jar.

The Apache country is a semiarid region where streams or springs are often long distances apart. There are no wells, so it is necessary for all domestic water to be carried to the home or camp. The *tus* is admirably adapted for such use. It is strong and durable and lacks the fragile characteristics of pottery, yet holds water equally well. It is made in various shapes and sizes to fit the many purposes it serves. Sometimes the larger sizes are slung on burros. Since the responsibility of furnishing water for the family rests upon the women, they often may be seen carrying the *tus* on their backs. When traveling, a water jar of a different type is used, as in Plate XXXVI. This double-necked *tus* can be carried on the back and under the belt or, with a strap or rope looped about its waistline, it can be hung over a saddle horn.

Only one kind of material is used in making each water jar. This differs in the northern and southern sections of the Apache country. On the San Carlos Reservation it is made entirely of willow, while in the higher elevations, around Fort Apache, the squawberry bush is sometimes used. Only the young shoots or sprouts of the squawberry can be used, because, as the plant matures, it branches into a heavy bush. In using either material the whole twig is used in the warp.

The twining material or weft is made by splitting the twig into three sections. The weaver does this by placing the large end of the twig in her mouth and starting the splitting process with her teeth.

Holding one section between her teeth and guiding the splitting with her hands, she separates the twig into three equal wedge-shaped sections. These sections are scraped with a knife and are ready for immediate use. The weavers say that they make their water jars at any time of the year. They do not dry or store their material, nor do they peel the bark from the twigs. Instead, they are gathered and woven into the basket fresh from the plant.

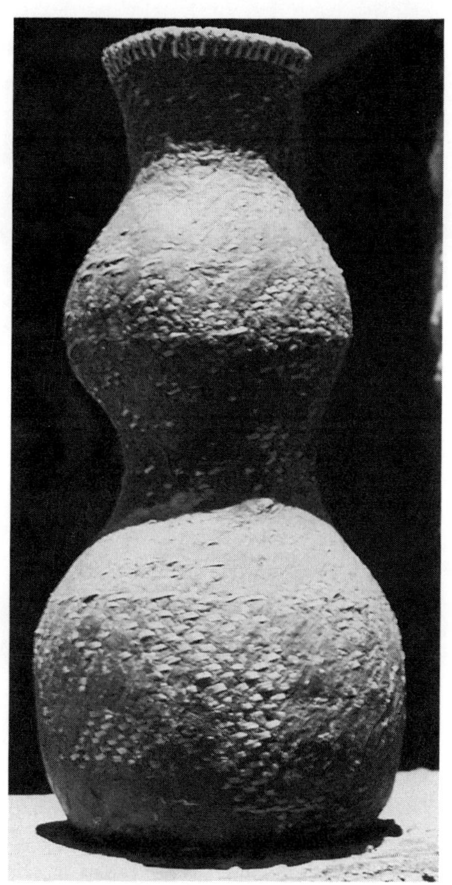

*The double-necked tus is used for carrying water when traveling* *PLATE XXXVI*

No apparent effort is made to make these baskets smooth or even, and when finished they are rather crude in shape and appearance. Two loops, used as carrying bands, are sewed about one foot apart near the top of the basket. In early times these loops were tough bent twigs, but Mrs. Cassadore, Plate XXXVII, now uses short leather straps. Cedar leaves are ground fine and rubbed into both the outer and inner surface of the basket until, as Mrs. Lewis, another Apache weaver, says, "You can't see daylight through the basket any more." After the cedar filling has set, a light coating of red ocher or clay is applied. Pitch from the piñon pine tree is heated and brushed on the outside of the jar with a piece of cowhide, the hair being the brush (Plate XXXVIII). When this has cooled and hardened more heated pitch is poured inside of the jar and distributed by rolling the jar around. Usually several baskets are coated at one time.

In making their burden baskets, the Apaches use a twining method of weaving quite similar to that used in making their water jars. On the San Carlos Reservation the same willow material is used and the same method of preparation employed for both, the main difference being the better craftsmanship and greater strength of the burden basket. These baskets formerly were used in gathering wild foods, such as acorns, berries, walnuts, and piñon nuts, and for carrying wood and other supplies to camp. The Apache now buys most of his food at the trading post, and a sack or metal pail serves to carry it home. Although

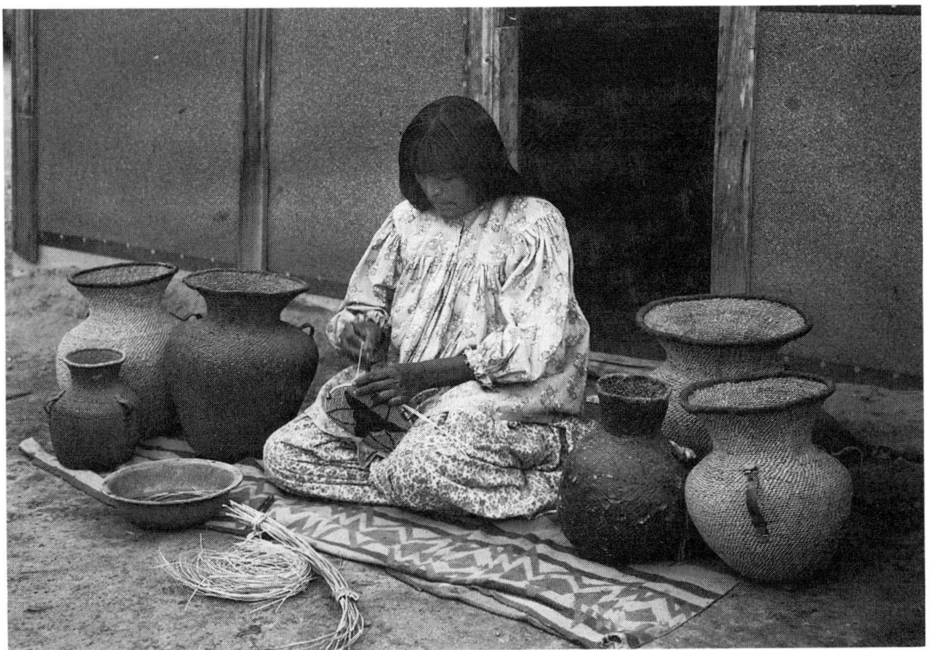

*Instead of bent twigs, Mrs. Casadore uses loops of leather, to which the carrying band is attached* *PLATE XXXVII*

the burden basket is no longer a necessity, it is highly prized and many fine old specimens can be found in the Indian homes. The greater strength of these baskets lies in the close formation of the willow twigs in the warp. These are all of a uniform size except four which are larger and are placed at equal distances apart to serve as reinforcing rods in the wall of the basket. A carrying band attached to two of these rods passes around the forehead and supports the basket on the woman's back just below her shoulders. Sometimes the weaver decorates her basket with colored bands of red or black material, the red being obtained from the root of the yucca plant and the black from the devil's claw. No significance is attached to such decorations and they are made for ornamentation only. The finished basket is further decorated with buckskin fringe and trappings. The bottom is covered with buckskin, and from the edge of this covering a buckskin fringe is attached. The top is bound with buckskin and, frequently, strips of buckskin are sewed from top to bottom on the outside of the basket with occasional tufts of buckskin fringe (Plate XXXIX).

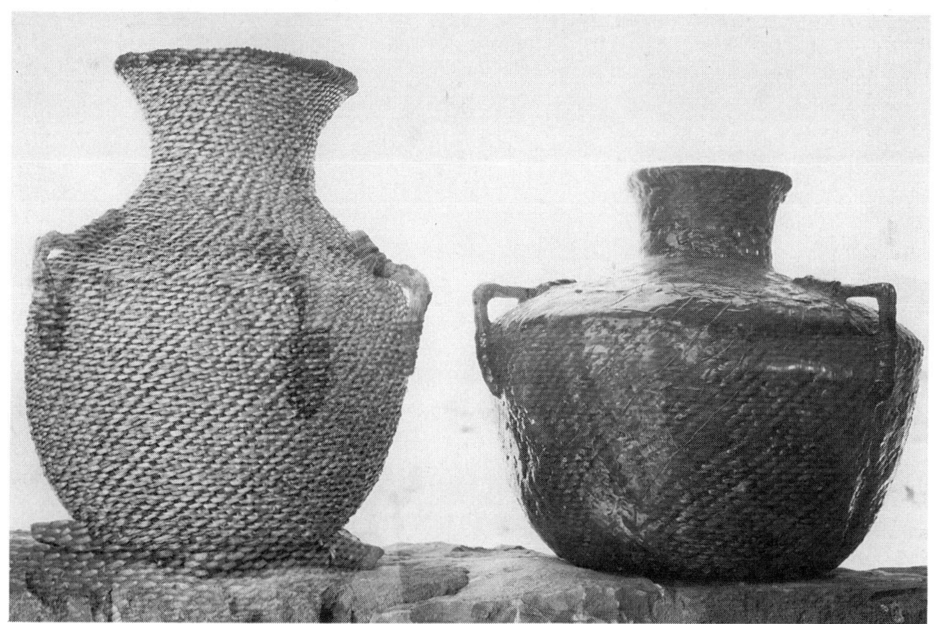

*The tus or water jar before and after the piñon pitch was applied. The carrying-band loops on these jars are tough twigs attached to the sides* *PLATE XXXVIII*

On the Fort Apache Reservation, wild mulberry twigs sometimes are substituted for the willow. Plate XL is a basket made of wild mulberry from the Fort Apache Reservation, but the two old baskets made of willow shown in Plate XXXIX are from San Carlos.

The devil's-claw-and-cottonwood coiled baskets from the San Carlos Reservation are unquestionably the Apache's greatest contribution to Indian art. Whatever the water jar and burden basket may lack in decorative design and craftsmanship is overcompensated for in the profusion of design in the ollas and trays made of this fine coil weave. This superiority is gained by the infinite amount of labor and patience which go into the weaving of such baskets. Sometimes a year or more is required to make a large olla.

No small amount of labor goes into the gathering and preparing of the material before the weaving begins (Plate XLI). The cottonwood twigs may be gathered at any time of the year, but preferably in the spring or summer when the bark peels easily. If gathered at any other

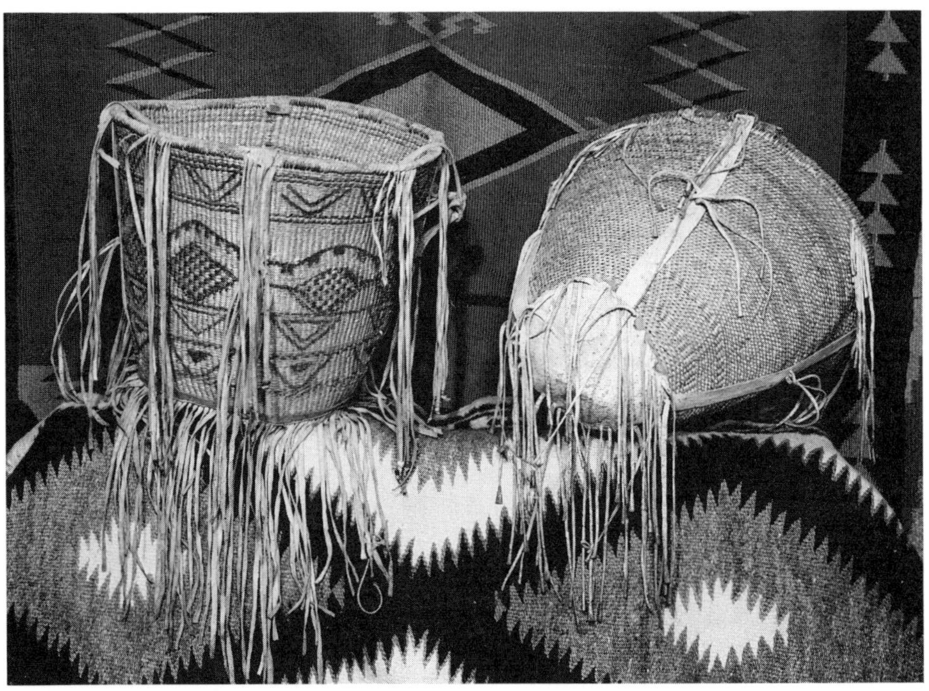

*Two old willow burden baskets from San Carlos. The burden basket is highly prized and fine specimens are still to be found in Indian homes* *PLATE XXXIX*

season, these long slender twigs, which are smaller than a lead pencil in size, are boiled in water to loosen the bark. After the bark is removed the twigs are split into small sections, bound in coiled bundles, and stored away. The devil's claw is gathered and prepared in the same manner as by the Pimas.

The willow twigs used in the warp of the basket may be gathered at any time but the bark must be removed as soon as gathered. They are dried whole and stored in small bundles. Three such twigs are used for the warp of the basket about which the cottonwood and devil's claw strips are coiled. By using one large and two smaller twigs, the contour of the wall of the basket is controlled. When the large twig is placed behind the two smaller twigs the wall curves inward, and with the

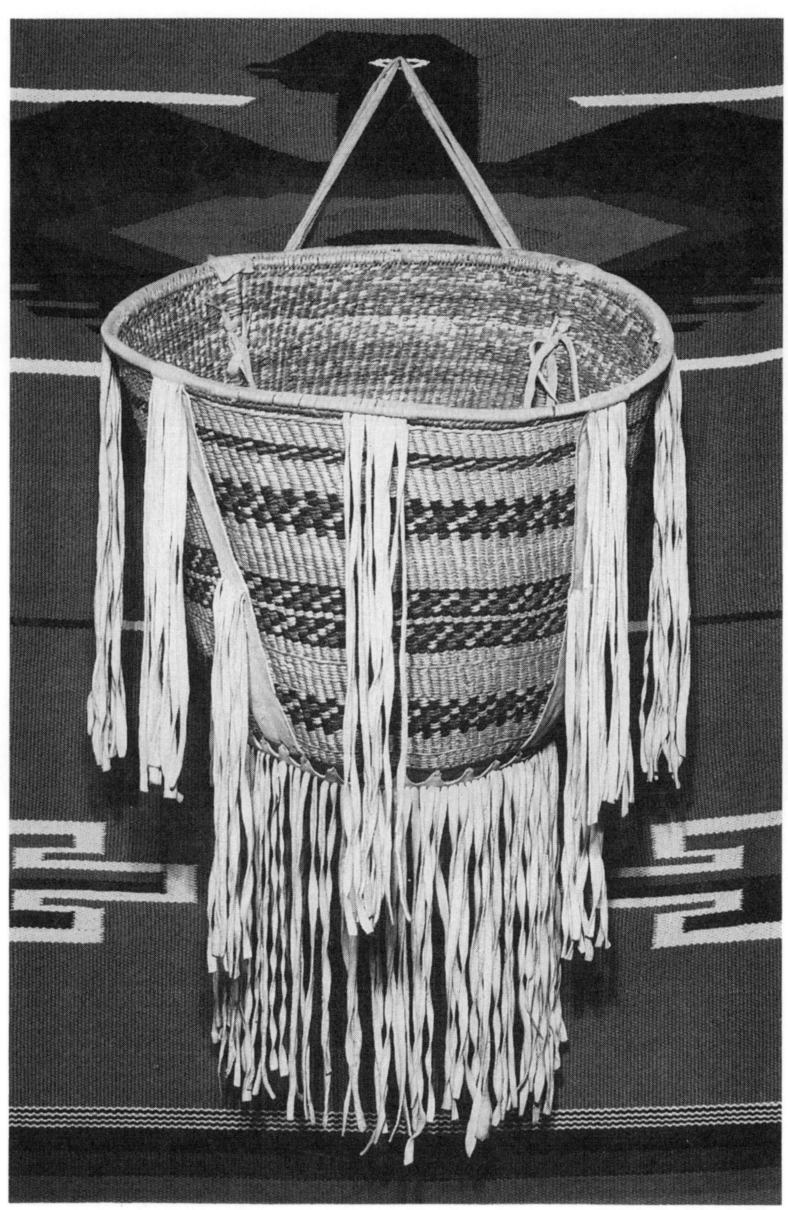

*Burden basket of wild mulberry wood from Fort Apache. The same weaving technique is used in all burden baskets*

PLATE XL

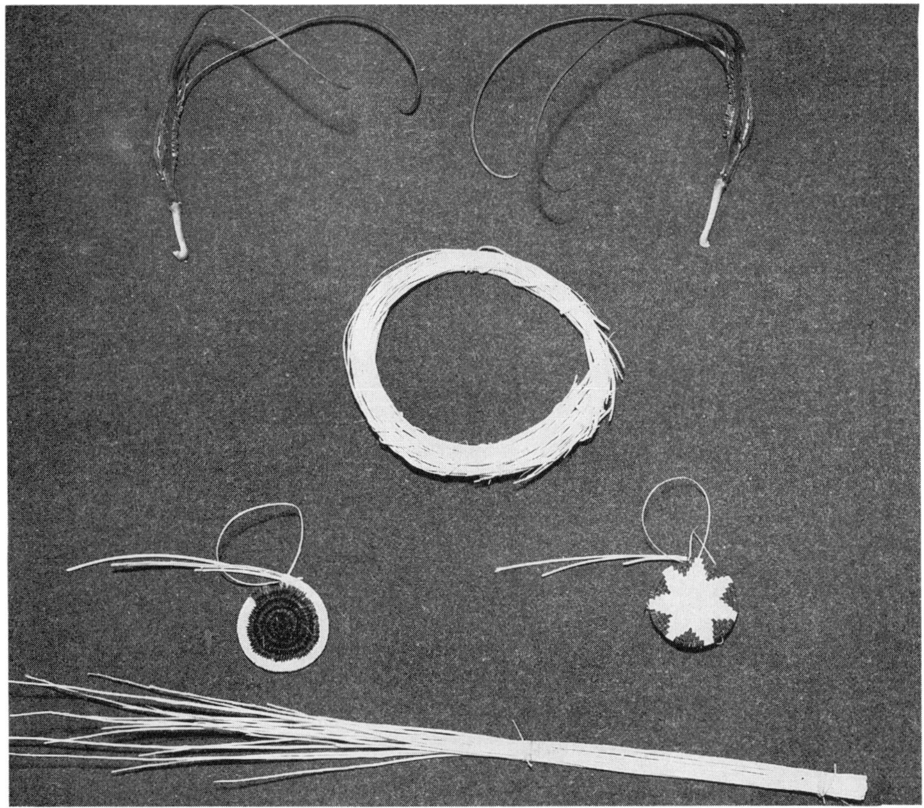

*Shown here are materials used in coiled baskets. At the top are Martynia (devil's claw); in the center is a coil of split cottonwood twigs; at the bottom of the picture is a bundle of whole willow twigs for the warp; just above these are (left) starting of an Apache basket and (right) starting of a Yavapai basket* *PLATE XLI*

larger twig in front of the two smaller twigs the curving of the wall is outward. The twigs are always of uneven length in the bundle and as one is covered by the coiling a new twig is inserted, thus no joints or weak spots occur.

There is much speculation regarding the decorative designs in Apache baskets. It has been mentioned that possibly much of the craft is borrowed from other tribes. This undoubtedly is true of the decorative design. Among Pima and Papago weavers each design is known and recognized by some name. When enlargements of photographs of the baskets shown here were taken to the weavers on the San Carlos Reservation no one could identify them. When the weavers were asked what these designs meant their answer invariably was, "They are to make the basket look nice." When asked why trees, cows, fish, or some other objects were not used, their only reply was, "Because we have always used these designs." No doubt, years ago there was some significance to each figure or symbol but this has been lost to the present generation of weavers. It might be added here that the craft itself has almost been lost, for it is nearer extinction than any of our other basket crafts in Arizona. No Apache baskets are to be found in the trading posts on the reservation, because since tribal cattle sales have recently reached a sizeable amount each year, the laborious task of weaving baskets is no longer required of the Apache women.

When interviewed, Laura Kozi said that her people did not know about these baskets until after the Yavapais came to live with the Apaches.[1] She learned from them to make bowls and dishes which she used about her home. Laura died in 1953, at eighty-two years of age. Miniola Buck said that her family learned to make coiled baskets from the Yavapai women when they lived at San Carlos. Lizette Phillips, Galusha Nasby, and others have said that the Apaches "always made these baskets," so it is difficult to determine how much of the craft is borrowed. This much is true—the materials, the technique, and many of the decorative designs are common to both the Yavapai and the Apache weavers.

The same photographs that appear here were shown to the Yavapai weavers and many of the designs were recognized as Yavapai designs, and could be identified as having some definite meaning. In another chapter of this book are shown photographs of baskets made by Yavapai weavers, a comparison of which with photographs of Apache baskets shown here will reveal the striking similarity between the two. Yet, in spite of the many likenesses existing between them, there also are differences which identify their tribal origin.

The olla shown in Plate XLII was made by a weaver named Boni, living at San Carlos in about 1903 or 1904, according to Miniola Buck. Miniola said that, when the basket reached the height where Boni could not sit comfortably to work on it, she placed it at the rear end of her wagon, sitting in the wagon while she worked. It took two years for her to weave this basket, which is fifty-one inches high and reputed to be the largest known specimen of Apache weaving. It is now in a private collection in Globe, Arizona. The design evidently is an old

1. The Yavapais lived at San Carlos from 1875 to 1900.

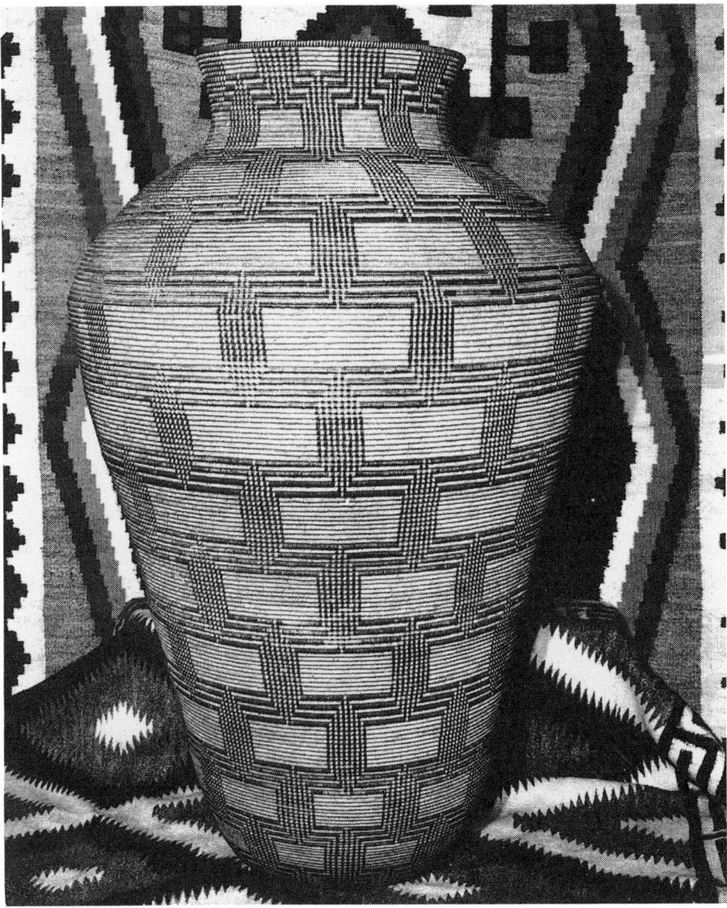

*It took the old weaver two years to make this large olla, which is fifty-one inches high and is the largest known specimen of Apache weaving* *PLATE XLII*

one but none of the weavers at San Carlos could interpret its meaning. Nellie Quail, a Yavapai weaver at Fort McDowell, said the design was very much like the Yavapai turtle back, with possibly some addition made by the Apache weaver.

Both Yavapai and Apache weavers were of the opinion that the arrangement of the designs in Plate XLIII is Apache. The crosses and symbols in the center basket were not used by the Yavapais. All are very fine specimens and typically shaped Apache ollas.

The diamond designs in the largest basket in Plate XLIV are claimed by the Yavapai weavers as originating with their tribe. However, the various interpretations given by weavers of both tribes would make it practically impossible to determine their origin. The designs are interpreted by the Apaches as rays of the sun, hanging clouds, and mountains, and by the Yavapais as representing quartz crystals, which were carried as good luck charms.

The two shallow bowls in Plate XLV are old Apache designs and are excellent specimens of their craft. These bowls are about two feet in diameter. It will be noted that the basket to the left in this picture has a design very similar to that of the olla in Plate XLII. The weaver of this basket is not known.

The star design is very common in Yavapai baskets. It is a sacred symbol with them but has been borrowed in at least one instance by an Apache weaver.

The large shallow bowl shown in Plate XLVI is thirty-two inches in diameter. Such a basket could have no utility value to the Indians.

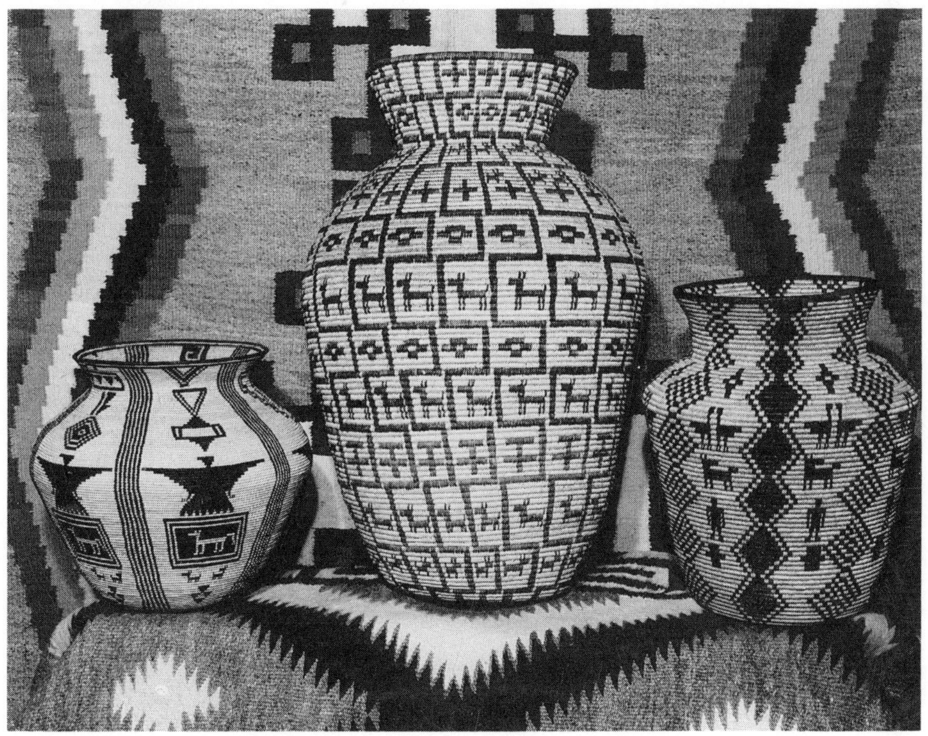

*Three fine specimens of Apache coil-weave ollas. These ollas are identified as Apache by the arrangement of the symbols, particularly in the center basket*

*PLATE XLIII*

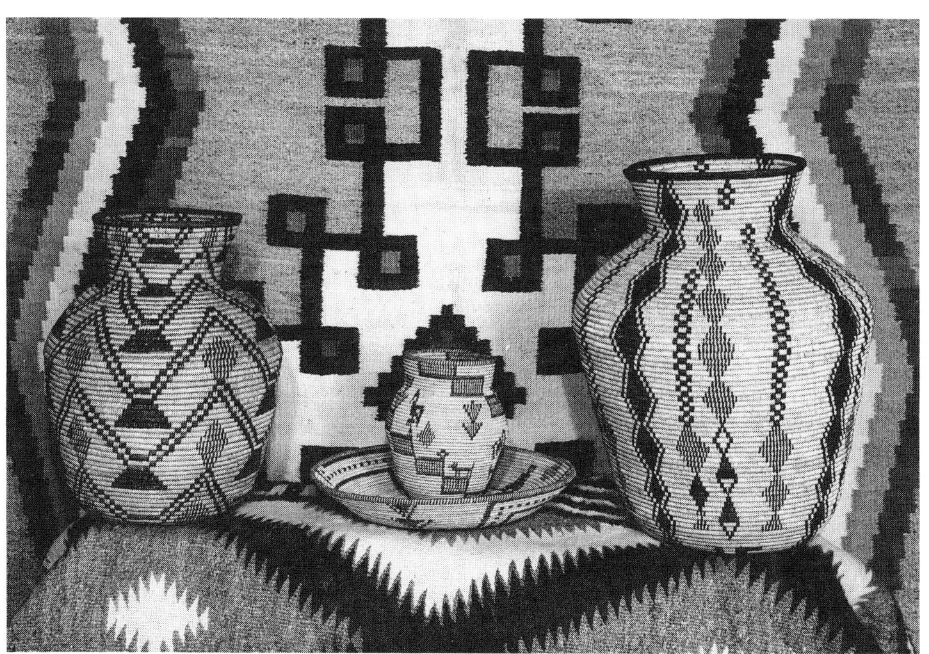

*The small olla and bowl in which it stands are woven together. The Yavapais claim that the diamond designs in the largest basket originated with their tribe*

*PLATE XLIV*

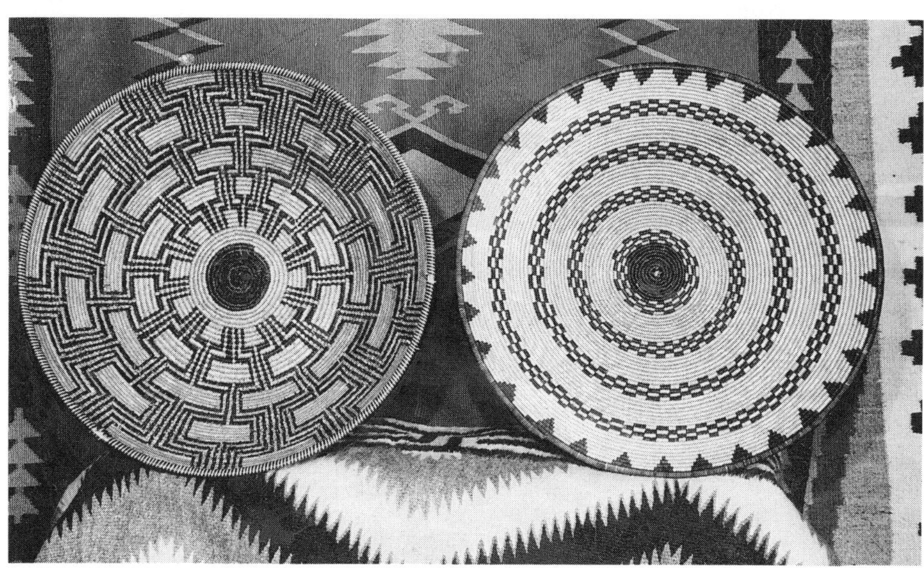

*Two large bowls of Apache design are about two feet in diameter and of excellent craftsmanship. The design in the basket to the left is similar to that of the olla in Plate XLII*

*PLATE XLV*

Like most other Apache coiled baskets shown here, it was made to sell and its large size probably was to fill the order of a purchaser. Both the Apache and Yavapai weavers say that, basically, the design is Apache but the Yavapais point out that a different arrangement of the symbols might place it within the pattern of Yavapai designs. It may be noted that figures of men, dogs, deer, and other animals frequently appear in the decoration of Apache coiled baskets. These same figures appear with the same frequency in Yavapai baskets and are used merely as decorations in both. Neither tribe attaches any significance to these conventional figures, nor do they know anything about their origin. They are used in the same manner in the decorative scheme of the baskets of both tribes: to maintain balance, fill in space, and enhance the beauty of the basic or over-all decorative design. The opinion of most of the weavers is that these character symbols are of a much more recent origin than are the geometric patterns.

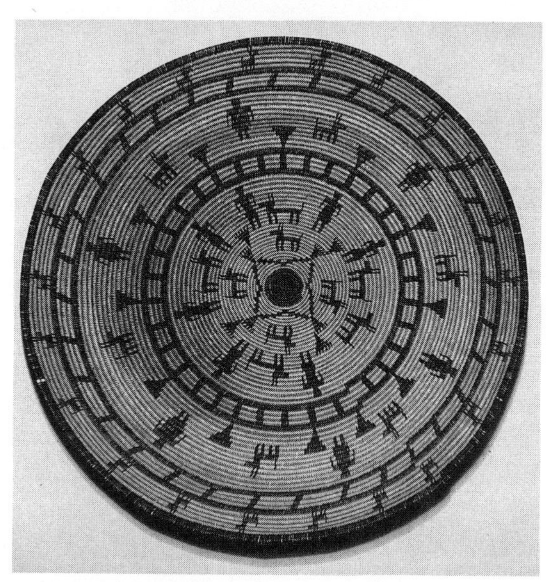

*A large shallow bowl thirty-two inches in diameter. This coiled basket was made to sell, as it is too large to have a utility value to the Indians*

*PLATE XLVI*

In summing up the numerous interviews I have had with Apache weavers, the most outstanding fact established is the complete lack of legend or background which they are able to attach to their craft. Their close association with the Yavapais, even before the latter were taken to San Carlos, indicates that the craft in both tribes was developed simultaneously. As to what the Apache contributed to its development, it is difficult to say.

Susie Dickens, a Yavapai woman at Fort McDowell, who is one hundred and four years old, says that she was weaving baskets when she lived in the Superstition Mountains, long before she and her people were taken to San Carlos, in 1875. Her people used baskets to cook in, and such usage would require a very fine, close weave to make them watertight. It would seem quite probable that the Yavapais contributed to the fine craftsmanship of the baskets, but who developed the decorative designs can be anyone's guess.

# *The Sun People—The Yavapai*

MORE PAGES of history and colorful fiction have been written about the Apache Indians of Arizona than about any other tribe in the Southwest. Yet their nearest neighbors on the west, the Yavapais, have passed almost without notice. The Yavapais always have been closely associated with the Apaches and often have been confused with them; however, no family relationship exists between the two tribes. The Apaches are of Athabascan stock and the Yavapais are a branch of the Yuman family. Sometimes the Western Yavapais were called Yuma-Apaches. Today the remnants of the tribe are located on the small Fort McDowell Reservation, in southern Arizona, and are called Mojave-Apaches. To the average person, they are Apaches and their identity is in danger of becoming lost in the confusion of their names.

The Yavapais (Sun People) were never a strong tribe numerically, their number not exceeding 1,500, but they occupied a rather extensive territory. They ranged as far south as the Superstition Mountains, reaching nearly to the Gila River. Their eastern boundary was the west slope of the Pinal and Mazatzal mountain ranges, with their territory extending north to the east fork of the Bill Williams River and over to the Bill Williams Mountains. On the west, their area bordered that of other tribes along the Colorado River. In all, they ranged over twenty thousand square miles or about thirteen square miles for each member of the tribe.

According to their creation myths, the Yavapais came from under the ground. They crawled to the earth's surface through a great hole in which grew a dogtail pine tree that was covered with grapevines. These were used in making the ascent.

When Hanyiko, the leader of the first people, died he was cremated on a funeral pyre and from his ashes grew a plant which bore many ears of corn; some were eaten and some were saved to plant. This is the Yavapai version of the origin of corn. Their story of the creation has four cycles. The first world was destroyed in a great flood, the second from unknown causes, the third by fire, and the fourth is the one in which we are now living. Other of their myths are similar to those of the Apaches and also neighboring tribes on the west, and almost identical with those of the Hualapai on the north. In fact, the Yavapais say that at one time the two tribes were united but a war brought about a division between them. According to their legend, some children got into a fight and it spread until the older people joined in. As a result, a war occurred and the Yavapais drew away as a separate tribe.

The Yavapais consisted of several bands but there were no distinct tribal divisions such as were found among the Apaches. There were three geographic divisions, namely, Western Yavapais, Northeastern Yavapais, and Southeastern Yavapais, which intermingled and intermarried freely.

In war they fought together as a united people. Runners were dispatched to the various sections, warriors were gathered together, a big dance was held, and the expedition would be under the leadership of one chief. Like the Apaches, there was no closely knit organization of the tribe, each band or group operating independently of any other, except in war. There was no great chief over the whole tribe nor was there a governing council. Leadership was achieved through personal merit based on wisdom, personality, and ability as a warrior. No member of the tribe could become a chief before he had killed at least two enemies in hand to hand combat with club or ax. Shooting them with bow and arrow did not count.

The bow and arrow and club were the common implements of war and, since they were not good horsemen, horses did not play an important role with the Yavapais as they did with the Pimas and Apaches. They used a longer bow than the Pimas, and the average length of the arrow was the distance from the shoulder to the tip of the middle finger. The arrows were made of cane, with a hardwood foreshaft, and the stone point was securely fastened with sinew. The point of the arrow was poisoned with a concoction of rattlesnake venom, spiders, centipedes, abdominal parts of the long-winged bee, and walnut leaves. A wound inflicted by an arrow which had been treated with this mixture was said to cause death within twenty-four hours.

When a chief became old he might no longer lead warriors on the warpath but he retained a place of respect and honor among the members of the band. He might remain at home to direct the defense of the camp in case of attack, while a younger chief assumed command of the raiding party. The Western Yavapais took the scalps of chiefs or important enemies only, who were killed in battle, and upon their return home the scalps were tied to a pole about which the victory dance was staged. They were then discarded.

Among the Eastern Yavapais, scalping was more prevalent and the scalps were dried and kept as trophies in a house some distance from the camp because of superstitions regarding them. The scalp differed from that taken by most tribes, since it consisted of the covering of the entire top of the skull. A line was drawn above the eyes, extending back above the ears and around the back of the head, and the whole scalp removed intact. Prisoners were seldom taken and usually were killed after or during the victory dance.

In a great battle with the Hualapai, their chief, Wachumorma, was killed and his wife was taken captive. After the victory dance she was taken to another village and killed, and her body cooked and eaten by the people. There is also another account of a Maricopa woman and her daughter being taken captive. They were forced to dance all day, then in the evening a log fire was built in a shallow pit and when the coals had burned down the little girl was thrown in alive and her flesh later eaten. The mother escaped. Cannibalism was not practiced because of any taste the Yavapais had for human flesh but more to express hatred and vindictiveness against their enemy. Possibly it incited terror, since the prospect of being cooked alive would cause an enemy to flee when danger of being captured was imminent.

When a war party returned from a raid, any warrior who had killed an enemy in battle had to go into seclusion for four days, during which time he must bathe and refrain from eating meat or salt. He could not scratch his head or body with his hands, for it was believed to do so would cause his hair to fall out. He must use a scratching stick. This taboo was the most common of any among the Yavapais and was applied to both sexes on various occasions. It would seem to indicate that the possibility of becoming bald was an ever-present fear. If a warrior was killed in battle his widow might accompany the next war party on a raid against the enemy in hopes that she might have an opportunity to avenge his death.

The Yavapais were not an agricultural people, depending almost entirely on hunting and the gathering of wild foods for their subsistence. Occasionally they planted some corn along the edge of a stream or in a low place where seepage might give sufficient moisture to produce a crop. No cultivation or care was given after the corn was planted, and they did not practice irrigation. The northern bands planted their corn in the spring, migrating southward in the summer to gather desert foods, and returning in the fall to harvest the corn and gather acorns. The variety of foods was greater than that of most tribes, probably because climatic and other conditions varied so greatly over their vast domain. There was a variation in elevation from five hundred feet in the southern and western part of their area to seven thousand feet in the high mountain areas in the north. Under these circumstances the Yavapais naturally developed nomadic habits, gathering fruit from the saguaro, barrel cactus, and prickly pear on the desert in the summer months, and acorns, walnuts, and piñons in the high forests in the fall.

Mescal was the main staple food and could be gathered at all times of the year. On mescal expeditions the men dug the pits and prepared them for cooking. Such pits were about six feet long, three feet deep, and three to four feet wide. A fire was built and the stones heated in the pit until very hot. The cabbage-like mescal heads were placed on the stones and covered with earth and grass. In this sealed oven the roasting process proceeded for two nights and one day. When the pit was opened each woman claimed her own mescal, having marked all she had gathered in some distinctive manner, as with the outer leaves cut straight across, diagonally, V-shaped, etc., in much the same way a stockman earmarks calves on the range. While the mescal was roasting the women would not scratch with their fingers but used a scratching stick, to prevent bad luck in the cooking. After cooking, the mescal was beaten on a flat rock to break down the fiber and then spread out on trays to dry. The dried food thus prepared was stored in earthenware ollas, where it could be kept indefinitely. Cut into slabs, the mescal was carried by warriors on the warpath.

Saguaro fruits were dried and pressed into cakes and stored in much the same manner as the mescal. The saguaro seeds were parched and ground, and often were carried for food by the warriors. Prickly pears and fruit of the barrel cactus usually were eaten fresh. Sweet acorns were a delicacy when ground into a meal and cooked with meat, preferably venison. Bitter acorns were not used, because the Yavapais had not learned that the bitterness could be leached out.

For meat, they hunted deer, rabbits, woodrats, mountain sheep, and such carnivorous animals as mountain lions, wildcats, foxes, and coyotes. The favorite bird was the quail, although doves, whitewing doves, and smaller birds also were eaten. Two birds not eaten were the hummingbird and the eagle, the first because of its small size and the latter because it was looked upon as sacred. Fish and waterfowl were taboo.

The boys and girls played together without much supervision until puberty. Then the boys were trained in hunting and warfare by their father or paternal grandfather. They played with bows made of willow and arrows without points. Later they learned to make bows of mulberry wood with bowstrings of sinew from the back of a deer.

On hunting parties the man who killed a deer was apportioned one quarter of the meat, the liver, the brains, and the hide. The liver and the brains were used in tanning the hide. The men not only tanned the hides but also sewed all the clothing, which was made entirely of buckskin. The women wore dresses made of two pieces of buckskin sewed together on the sides. The front extended above the bust and was held by a loop around the neck; the back reached only to the waist and was held in place by a belt. In winter, the dress was supplemented with a short tunic with sleeves. The women's moccasins seldom reached above the knees. The men wore buckskin shirts, breechcloth, and moccasins which were longer than the women's, reaching to the hip, where they were fastened to the belt.

Buckskin was an important article, both in domestic use and trade. A man presented it to the parents of his bride-to-be. Usually he gave them two buckskins, but if the bride was especially attractive she might be worth three hides. He also traded buckskins to the Navajos for blankets. The Yavapais did little weaving except baskets and sleeping mats made of willow bark, which were not as warm as the woolen blankets of the Navajos.

There were no family names. The name of a dead person was never given to another, nor was it ever spoken again.

According to a mandatory tribal custom, a child's ears were pierced soon after birth. Yavapai children did not receive the care given to Pima and Hopi children, and occasionally an unwanted child was allowed to die of exposure. Twins were not common, but in the rare cases where they occurred in opposite sex the girl baby sometimes was buried alive.

A woman had little or no voice in the affairs of the community but in the family life she and her relatives occupied a more important position than the relatives of the man. A groom could not converse with his mother-in-law and if she saw him approaching she covered her face, believing if she gazed upon him steadily she would become blind. Neither could the bride speak to her father-in-law.

If the bride died before children were born the husband had a right to marry her younger sister without any gifts being presented to her relatives. Marriages were not arranged by the parents but sometimes the matter might be discussed by the relatives. Marriage at fourteen years was not uncommon for the girls, although they might wait until they were twenty or older. Young girls were taught by their mother or maternal grandmothers to do the many arduous duties which were assigned the women of the camp. They carried wood and water, went on food-gathering expeditions, and prepared and cooked the food in camp.

The Yavapai house was a flimsy structure, somewhat resembling an Apache house. The framework was of poles set in the ground in a circle and lashed together, forming a dome-shaped top, which was covered with brush, and the entire structure thatched with bear grass. An opening left for a door usually was covered with a blanket. There were no furnishings.

On the march, only baskets were carried and all cooking was done in these, except in the lower elevations, when the barrel cactus might be used. This was done by cutting away the top of the cactus, then slashing the pithy part of the stump left standing and bruising it with a stone to extract the water. When the pith was removed it left a hollowed out space partially filled with water, into which the food was placed, then hot stones were dropped in, the same as when cooking in baskets.

In winter, the Yavapais left their flimsy houses to move into caves, several of which are in the Mazatzal Mountains. During the summer and fall months, food would be cached away in these caves, ready for winter occupancy. Neither the caves nor any land was owned privately, all assets of the tribe being shared on an equal basis by its members, with only one exception—an eagle's nest was claimed by the person discovering it.

Eagle feathers were highly prized by the Yavapais. Eaglets were captured when young, and grown to maturity, then their feathers were plucked. They were kept in cages on the ground, and fed on rabbits, woodrats, and bits of meat. The feathers were used more as an insigne of office than as a decoration for the hair, as was the custom of some other tribes. The warriors did not wear feathers, but the chiefs wore three, which signified their rank. A courier might wear a bandolier of feathers over one shoulder and down under the opposite arm. Also, in various ceremonials, eagle feathers had a prominent place.

The dead were burned, together with their personal belongings and the house in which they lived. Sometimes the house was pulled down upon the corpse, then all were burned together, the family moving to a new camp site. The hair was worn long by both the men and the women; and, as a token of mourning, a woman's hair would be cut short and a man's hair cut off above the shoulders. In either case, the hair was burned.

A custom mentioned in the folklore of the Yavapais and which still is in use by some members of the tribe is the sweathouse. This is a low, dome-shaped structure about four feet in height and sufficiently large to accommodate three or four men sitting in a crouched position. It is made of thickly matted brush, and in olden times buckskin or a blanket was thrown over the top. Now canvas is substituted for this outer covering. The sweathouse was used exclusively by the men in a purification ceremony and for treating the sick. Heated stones were placed in the house and sprinkled with water from a stream nearby, to the accompaniment of a chant or song. When the chant was completed the men left the sweathouse and plunged into the stream. This was repeated four times, as there were four songs connected with this ceremony. An old Yavapai told me that members of the younger generation do not know these old songs and that they go into the sweathouse only once or twice, instead of the four times that were required in the old ceremony. These sweathouses can be seen along the Verde River on the Fort McDowell Reservation and are used somewhat as we use a Turkish bath.

## *Yavapai History*

DUE TO THE absence of a prolonged period of Spanish influence the history of the Yavapais does not extend back as far as that of the other tribes. Aside from widely separated visits of missionaries, this tribe had little contact with the Spaniards. This probably was due to the rough country that separated the Yavapai area from the route traveled by the Spaniards in their journeys to and from the Pueblo villages to the northwest. Also, Kino and his followers did not extend their operations beyond the Pima villages, so it was not until the white immigrants arrived from eastern states that the Yavapais figured to any extent in the history of Arizona. Even then their history was so confused with that of the adjoining Apache band that it is difficult to make a definite separation of the two tribes. In appearance, habits, and in economic and social customs, as well as a hostile attitude toward most of their neighbors, the Yavapais resembled the Apaches much more than they did any of their own family group. There is no question about their being warlike and hostile, and they were grouped along with Apache tribes in the records of Indian depredations in this part of Arizona.

They conducted raids against neighboring tribes to both the north and the south but remained friendly at all times with the Apaches along their eastern boundary, even to the extent of combining forces with them in their resistance against the white immigration.

The territory of the Yavapais was so extensive that even defensive warfare brought them into conflict with many early settlements. The towns of Wickenburg, Prescott, Jerome, and Clarkdale, and famous mines such as the Vulture, all were within Yavapai country. General Crook's campaign, in the fall of 1872, was, to a great extent, in Yavapai territory. While it is recorded as an Apache campaign, many of the engagements involved the Yavapais. The Wickenburg massacre was actually committed by the Yavapais, and in the famous battle of Skull Cave, north of the Salt River, Yavapais and some Tonto Apaches were involved. After this campaign the resistance of both tribes was broken and the Yavapais were brought into Camp Verde and placed under the protection and control of the American Army. The word protection here is used advisedly, for at about this period in the history of Arizona, white renegades and outlaws were a menace to both Indians and whites; especially were they guilty of many unjust and brutal attacks on the Indians, regardless of whether they were hostile or friendly.

The original plan for the Yavapai tribe was that they would be held at Camp Verde and taught the white man's way of subsisting themselves through their own efforts. During the period of their training the government would provide food, clothing, livestock, and implements. However, this plan was abandoned in the interest of economy and the Yavapais, along with several bands of Apaches, were located on the San Carlos Reservation.

Sam Etchesaw was one of the Yavapai warriors taken to San Carlos, and, upon arriving there, joined the Indian scouts. He is now the only living Yavapai scout. He has told me of serving in four campaigns against Geronimo and his band and eventually of seeing them brought over the border for the last time. He now claims to be one hundred and six years old, yet he is alert and active and still remembers clearly events of eighty years ago.

Two other members of the tribe, who have told me much about those days at San Carlos, are Charlie Dickens, age ninety-three, and his mother, Susie, who died in 1950 at the age of one hundred and eight. Susie was one of the most interesting old ladies I have ever met. Her vision had been gone for many years but her memory was surprisingly keen. Through her son, who speaks English well, she told about the night raids by the Pimas, in which her relative who later was known as Dr. Carlos Montezuma was captured.[1]

### *Fort McDowell*

In 1875, more than one thousand Yavapais were sent to San Carlos. When they were released twenty-five years later, only two hundred members of the tribe remained, aside from a small, undetermined number that had straggled back to the Verde Valley at an earlier date. The white man's diseases had almost destroyed the tribe. Those who survived were an unhappy broken people without a home. While they were away the white settlers had appropriated most of the vast territory at one time claimed by the tribe, so most of the Yavapais returned to old Fort McDowell. Asked why they came to Fort McDowell, some of the old people reply that when sent away they were promised the old army reserve when it was no longer needed for military purposes. No doubt that was true.

Fort McDowell was an army post established in 1865 by five companies of California Volunteers. It figured prominently in Crook's campaign and that of General Alexander and others in bringing hostile Indians in this area under control. It was abandoned by the army in 1890 and, a year later, was turned over to the Department of the In-

1. See Oren Arnold's *Savage Son,* University of New Mexico Press, Albuquerque, 1951, for the complete story of Carlos Montezuma. Mr. Arnold calls Montezuma an Apache, but, as a matter of fact, he was a Yavapai.

terior. White settlers took up most of the best farm land along the river above the fort. When the Indians returned, in 1900, and it was decided to set aside the old army reserve for their reservation, these claims, along with the irrigation canals and other improvements, had to be purchased from the white owners. This finally was consummated and, in 1903, the area, comprising 24,680 acres, was set aside for the use of the Mojave-Apache Indians. This evidently was an error, for all three divisions of the Yavapai tribe were thrown together on the reservation and undoubtedly it should have been called the Fort McDowell Yavapai Reservation.

About two thousand acres of the reservation are irrigable, and in the adjudication of water rights on the Verde River the reservation was allotted 390 miners inches, continuous flow, of water to irrigate this area, although only 250 acres are under cultivation. These Indians are more interested in stock raising and have some good Hereford cattle. Their main source of income is through labor on construction jobs, in mines, and on ranches in the territory they once occupied. There are no mineral or timber resources on their reservation.

On the whole, the tribe is more primitive and recalcitrant than other Indian groups in southern Arizona. This is due, in a large measure, to the feeling of injustice done them, and when we consider that their number has dwindled from 1,500 to 200 and their territory has shrunk from 12,000,000 acres to 24,000, we realize the foundation for such feelings.

The Fort McDowell Reservation is under the jurisdiction of the Pima agency at Sacaton, from which the affairs of the reservation are administered. The tribe is organized, and is governed by a tribal council consisting of five members elected to serve terms of two years. Elections are held and balloting is conducted in much the same manner as might be followed in any other community in our country.

All the buildings of the old fort have been replaced by a stockman's cottage, a one-room school, teacher's cottage, and a community building. The stockman assists and advises the Indians in their agriculture and cattle raising, while in the one-room school building the teacher gives about thirty little Yavapais their foundation in the three R's. When the children advance beyond the fourth grade they are sent to the Indian boarding school in Phoenix to complete their education.

The teacher and stockman, together with an Indian policeman, who maintains law and order, which generally is not a difficult problem, are the only government personnel on the reservation. A public health nurse makes periodic visits to check on the health of the little community and any serious cases are given free hospitalization at the Indian Service hospital at Sacaton. The women of the community are organized into a women's club, under the direction of a government home demonstration agent; they contribute materially to the welfare and improvement of this Indian group. The decline in population, that has wrought such havoc in the tribe, has been stopped and the Yavapais slowly are approaching the normal increase that is prevalent in the surrounding communities.

## *Yavapai Baskets*

THE ONLY ART WORK now being done by the Yavapais is the weaving of baskets, and this is on a very limited scale. The beautiful work done with white buckskin, that the old people tell us about, is completely lost to the present generation. The indications are that it is only a matter of time until the Yavapais will join the long list of other tribes whose native arts have been lost to posterity. Yavapai baskets no longer are used for cooking as they were in olden times, having been replaced by modern utensils. Baskets are now woven exclusively for sale to the white trade and find a ready market.

Yavapai coil baskets are constructed of cottonwood, devil's claw, and willow all of which are gathered, prepared, and stored in much the same manner as by Pimas and Apaches. The willow twigs are not split but are used whole in the warp of the basket, around which the devil's claw and cottonwood materials are coiled. They vary in size according to the size of the basket or the fineness of the weave. In an olla such as Mable Osife weaves, some of these twigs were as large as a lead pencil, but in the finer baskets woven by Minnie Stacey, some of the twigs were no larger than a darning needle.

Like the Apaches, a peculiarity of the Yavapai weaving is the bundle of warp around which the coiling material is bound. This bundle always contains three willow twigs, two of which are small and one larger, through which arrangement the variation in the contour of the baskets is controlled. For instance, in a shallow bowl when the center or bottom of the basket is completed, the curving upward of the bowl is accomplished by placing the larger twig on the back of the

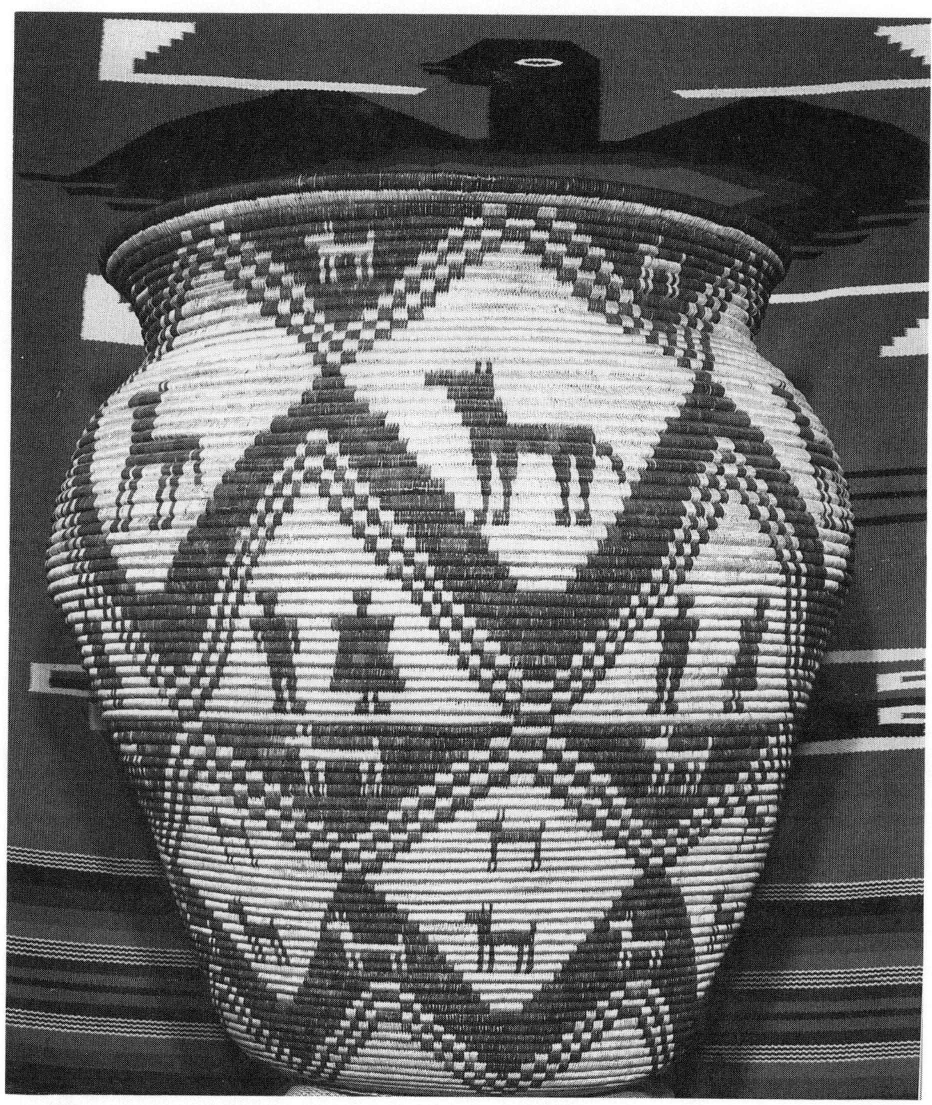

*This Yavapai olla, woven thirty years ago, still is in excellent condition. The figure designs are used merely as decorations and have no other significance*

PLATE XLVII

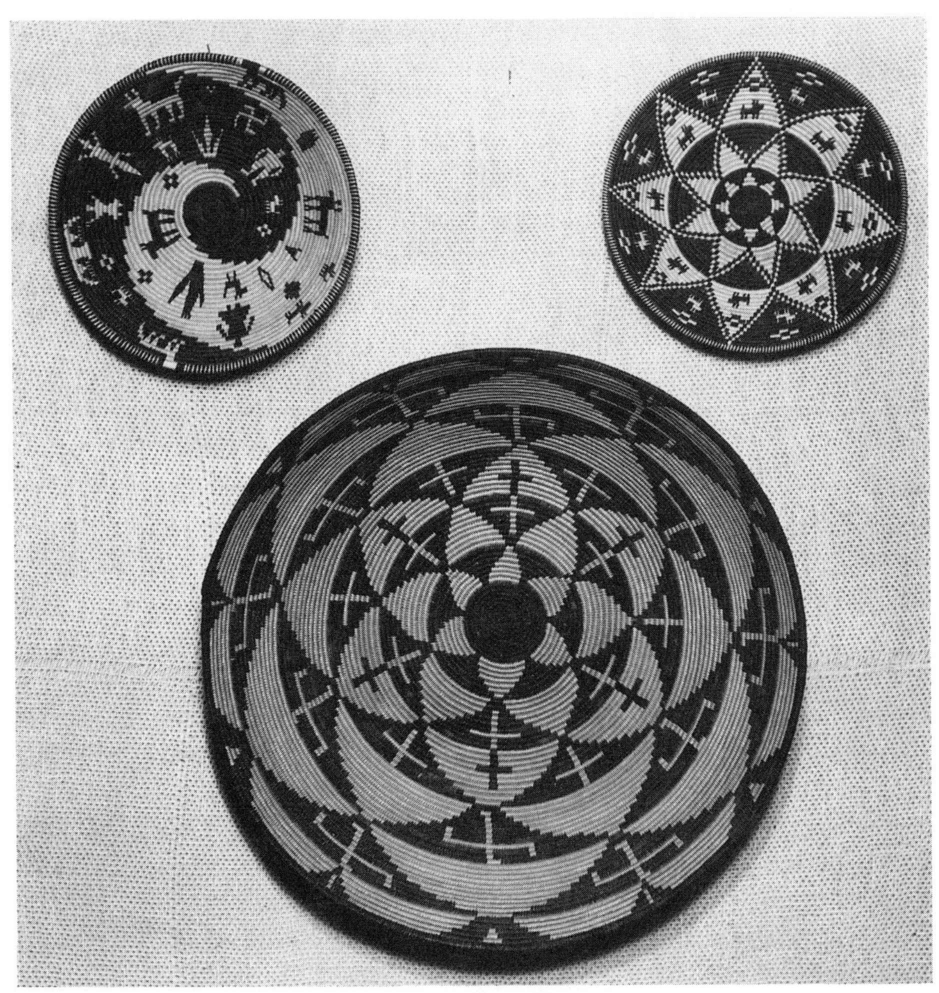

*Yavapai basket designs—Upper left, whirlwind; right, seven-point star; lower, thundercloud. Geometric designs are not common with the Yavapais, and the thundercloud shown here is a fine example of the exception*

PLATE XLVIII

bundle and threading the coiling material between the larger twig and the top twig. When the coiling material is drawn tight, the desired curvature is accomplished. In like manner, in an olla where the contour of the basket would curve upward toward the neck, the placement of these willow twigs would be reversed, with the large twig on the front of the two smaller ones. Although the twigs in the finished coil are hidden, the weaver knows how to insert the thread of her weaving material so that it passes between the twigs in the manner she desires.

Because of their resemblance to each other, baskets of both Yavapai and San Carlos Apache tribes are thrown together in the curio stores and classed as Apache baskets. On the other hand, the work of the Pima and Papago weavers is distinguished easily, even though the shape or type of basket may be very similar. The principal difference in the baskets of the desert weavers and those of the mountain country is that, among the Pimas and Papagos, we find classic designs that probably are centuries old and constitute the full decorative pattern of the basket. With the Yavapais the decorations are mainly character and symbolized designs, and the placement or number and kind of designs used are entirely optional with the weaver. In other words, geometric designs, which are common with the Pimas, are the exception with the Yavapais. A very fine example of this exception, however, can be noted in the lower basket of Plate XLVIII. This is the thundercloud design, and anyone who has seen the white thunderheads billowing up behind the Mazatzal Mountains on a summer afternoon may recognize the inspiration that created this design.

The symbolized design might be classed in two categories, as Minnie Stacey has explained it. There are designs that date back to the legends and folklore of the Yavapai people, and are held sacred by them as signs of good omen. The most widely used design in this class is the star design, which appears in the center or bottom of most Yavapai baskets (Plate XLIX). The swastika also is a sacred symbol sometimes used. Another symbol that is held sacred is the diamond or triangle that frequently points inward around the border of the basket. This design originated from the quartz crystals which were sought for in the mountains and were carried by the Indians as good luck pieces. This design is used also by the Apaches (see p. 81). Another symbol that is very sacred, and not so frequently used, is the eagle. This bird plays a prominent part in the old myths of the Yavapais, and, because of superstitions, some of the weavers will not use this design. Other figures such

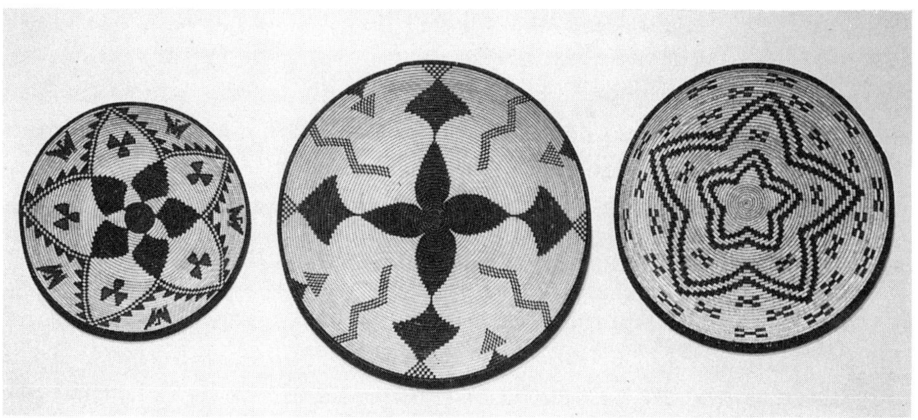

*The eagle and the star symbols are considered sacred by the Yavapai weavers. They are widely used because, presumably, they bring good luck* PLATE XLIX

as deer, men, dogs, gila monsters, buzzards, cacti, arrowheads, etc., while being tribal in character, are not considered sacred by the weavers (Plate L) .

Since each weaver creates her own over-all pattern by placing or arranging the different symbols to suit her own artistic taste (Plate LI) , she, in a way, develops her own personal pattern. We found this occurred frequently with Papago weavers and that, through their code

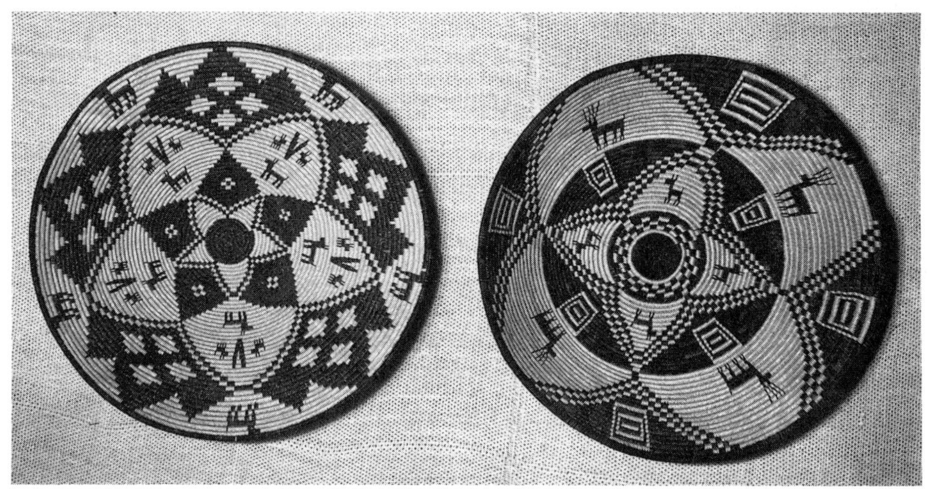

*Character designs, such as dogs, deer, and cacti, are extensively used for decorative purposes in Yavapai baskets. They are not considered sacred* PLATE L

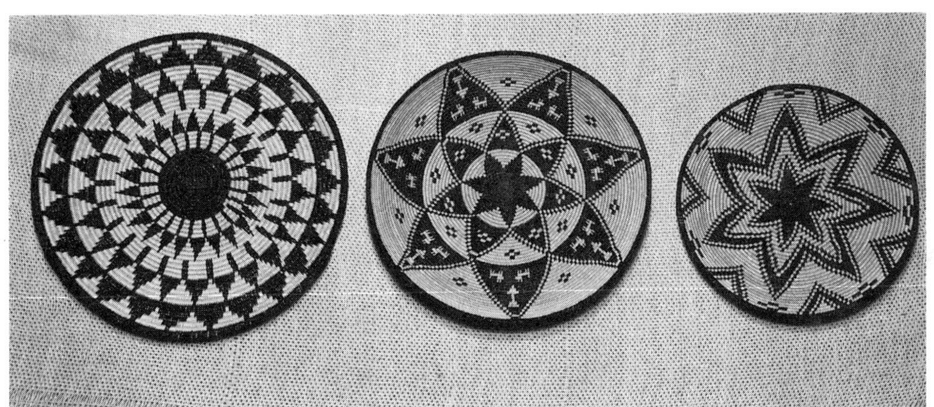

*The arrangement of the decorative designs in a Yavapai basket is always original with the weaver. Any weaver is free to use the arrangement, however* PLATE LI

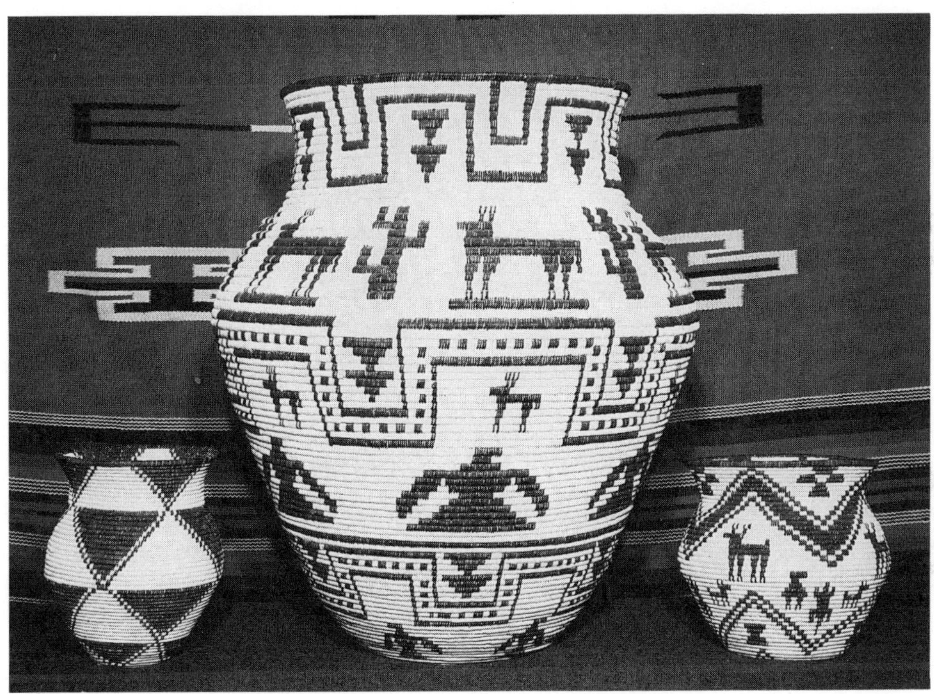

*The large olla shown here is more than three feet high. Smaller ollas of fine workmanship are more popular with the white trade* PLATE LII

of understanding, one weaver would not copy a pattern used by another weaver. I have asked Yavapai weavers if that same code existed among them and they say it does not. Any weaver is free to use any design or arrangement of design without fear of criticism from anyone.

Yavapai baskets are not made in a large variety of shapes but shallow bowls, flat plaques, and ollas are quite common. Most of their deep baskets are of the olla shape and some of them are three feet or more in height (Plate LII). Such a basket will require several months to make

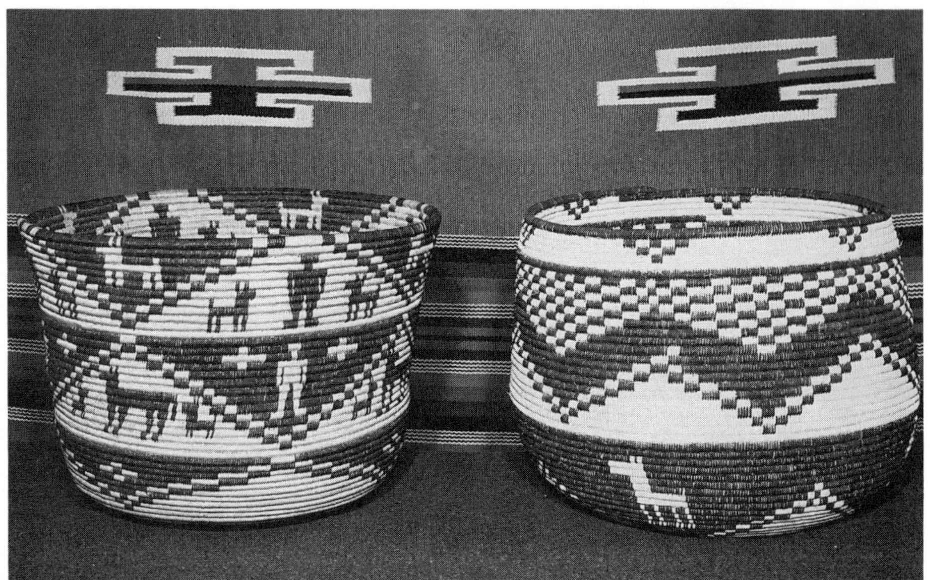

*Two deep baskets of distinctive Yavapai shape and design. The same symbols and designs are used in all types of Yavapai baskets* *PLATE LIII*

and when finished will sell for more than $100. Not all deep baskets are of this shape, however (See Plate LIII). The same designs and symbols are used in the decoration of all types of Yavapai baskets, with adjustments being made in the size of the decorations in relationship to the size of the basket. The Yavapais do not make any miniature or covered baskets.

In many ways the art of the Yavapai basket weavers remains untamed by the influence of the white man. The profusion of characters and symbols leaves many an unanswered question in our minds about the weavers and the wild mountain country from whence they came.

Aside from a few acres of tilled land along the Verde River at the site of old Fort McDowell, time has brought little change to this section of the old Yavapai territory. The lowlands are still dotted with giant cactus centuries old, and in the foothills of the Mazatzals are thick growths of manzanita and scrub oak, with juniper and some piñon on the higher elevation. To the east, Four Peaks Mountain marks the location of the great Roosevelt Dam, which impounds irrigation water that has created a rich inland empire in the valley below. But to the north, the Yavapai country is still the hinterland it has always been. It is off the beaten trail as it was in the time of Coronado and of Fr. Kino and the civilization that followed.

Among the people themselves there are some changes, possibly not as many as in many neighboring tribes, where isolation, lack of natural resources, and a deep feeling of injury have not been retarding factors. In these changes many of the traditions, customs, and crafts of the old Yavapai culture are being lost. The changes are occurring among the young people who have gone away to school and have learned many things from the white man but have learned little or nothing about the tanning of buckskins or the weaving of baskets.

# *Weavers of The Agricultural Country*

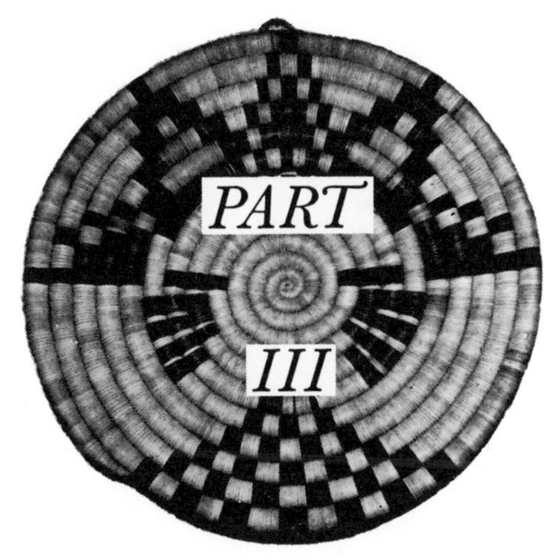

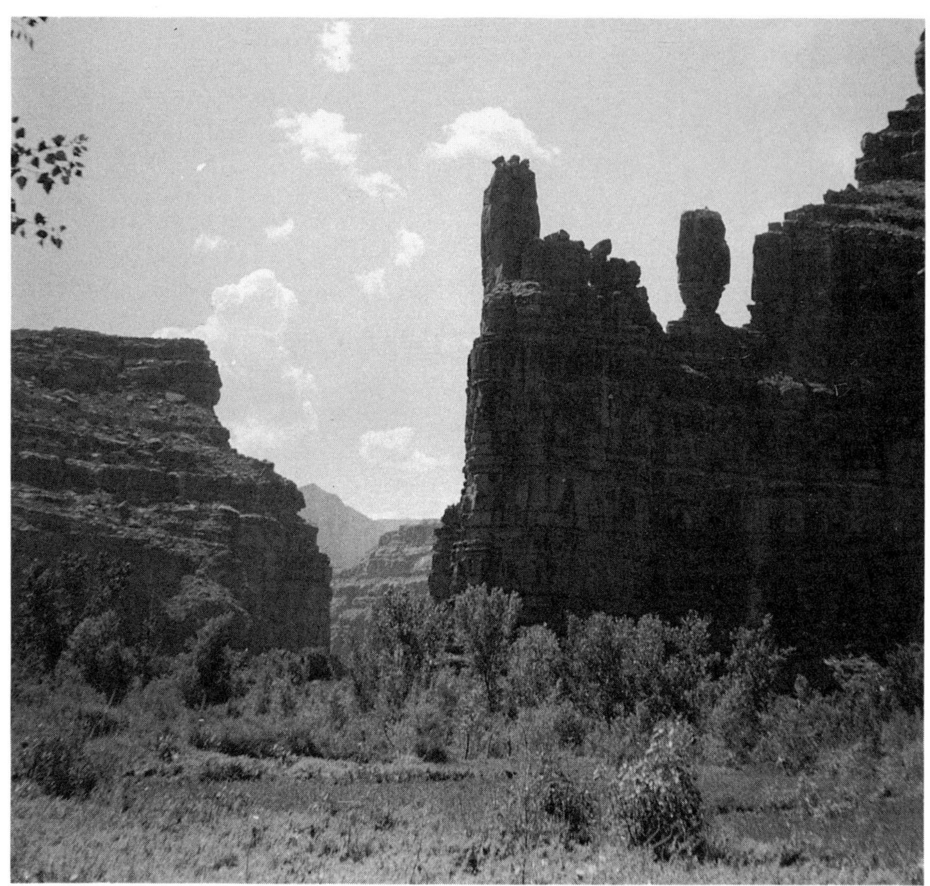

*Wiggl-ee and Wiggl-i stand, overlooking the Havasupais' valley, as a lesson to members of the tribe who might be tempted to disobey the gods*

PLATE LIV

# *Tedjupa and His People*

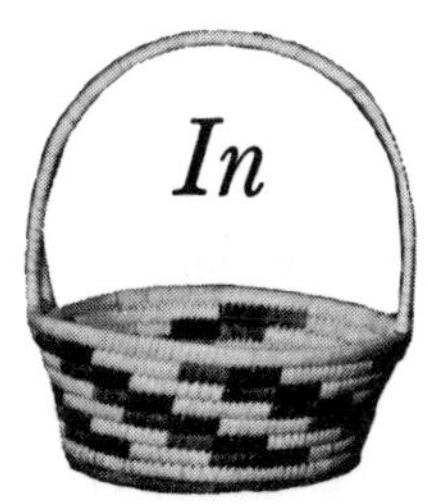


In THE NORTHWEST corner of Arizona, the Colorado River, after rushing past the towering walls of the Grand Canyon, makes a sharp bend to the south and then flows more leisurely down through its vast agricultural empire to the sea. In no other place on this continent do we find a greater variety of products grown than in the semi-tropical valleys along the Colorado. Here, we find great fields of cotton, cereal grains, flax, grain sorghums, alfalfa, citrus fruits, dates, nuts, melons, and all kinds of winter vegetables, and we might continue on down the long list of foods which make up the greatest menu of any living animal, that of man himself.

Back to the north, as if caught in the bend of the river, there lies an arid plateau crossed by short mountain ranges and steep valleys from which the short seasonal rains disappear with amazing rapidity. This plateau is the native habitat of the Walapai Indians. Anthropologists tell us that the Walapais are relatively new in this district, that they are a branch of the Yuman family, and were preceded here by a prehistoric people, whose ruins of villages and abandoned turquoise mines are found over this part of Arizona.

The old legends of the Indians relate a different story. They say that after the great water that covered the earth had disappeared through a hole in the ground, two gods came up through the mud at the base of Wikame Mountain. They climbed to the top of the peak and there it was agreed that Hamatavila, who was an old man, should allow Tedjupa, who was young and strong, to rule the world. But there were no people, so Tedjupa went down to the river and brought back a cane stalk which grew near the water's edge and he broke this cane stalk into six pieces. He named these Mojave, Havasupai, Piute, Hopi, Walapai, and Yavapai. He took this bundle of pieces of cane to the east and laid them down on the ground and they became alive and turned into people, and they all lived together around the base of the Walapai Mountain.

One day old Hamatavila accidentally stepped on a frog and crushed it with his foot. This made him sick at his stomach and he died, and the people placed his body on a funeral pyre and burned it for four days, after which he was supposed to come to life again; but when he did not, they buried his body in the ground. Four days later they found beans, squash, melons, and corn growing on his grave and all the people gathered these foods and feasted. From what was left they took seeds for planting, and they continued to grow these crops for many years. Finally they began to quarrel among themselves, so Tedjupa thought it was time to separate them. He gave each group some seeds to plant and then he sent the Mojaves to the south and told them to live along the Colorado River; he sent the Piutes across the river to the north, in what is now Utah; the Havasupais went down in Cataract Canyon, to live along the Havasu River, from which they got their name. The Hopis went to the east, where they now live on the Hopi mesas. This left only the Walapais and the Yavapais living at the foot of the mountain. One day some children began throwing mud at each other, and when one of them was hurt he picked up a rock and threw it; then all the children began throwing rocks; then two of the men joined in the fight and when one of them was killed the fight became general. In the end, the Yavapais drew away and went down to live where the cities of Clarkdale and Prescott now stand and along the Verde Valley. Thereafter, the Yavapais were bitter enemies of the Walapais and frequently made war upon them. However correct this old legend may be, anthropologists have found that the Yavapais and Walapais are a closely related people of the same linguistic stock, and undoubtedly at some time in the past there was a separation that brought about these two distinct tribes.

The old Walapais lived almost exclusively on wild foods. The rainfall was insufficient to produce crops, and the absence of any flowing streams made irrigation on a large scale impossible. Among most primitive people the distribution of food is the controlling factor in the concentration of population, but on this plateau the available water supply was the controlling factor. There were numerous springs at the foot of the mountain ranges, and at the headwaters of certain creeks the water flowed for a distance and then sank into a bed of sand farther down the stream. Wherever water was available, the Walapais dug small irrigation ditches with shovels made from the horns of mountain sheep, and irrigated small plots of ground. Usually, most of the crop was consumed at a feast which the owner gave to his friends and relatives at harvest time. What was left over, if any, was put into a bag made of mountain sheep skin and hung under a ledge or in some cave for winter use.

The people built their houses near to their farming plots and thus small villages sprang up wherever there was a spring or other source of water. These villages were limited in size by the amount of water available, averaging about twenty-five persons to a village. Each family built two houses. One was a summer house made of brush and the other a more permanent structure in which the family lived in winter. The summer house was very flimsy, sometimes consisting merely of brush leaning against the lower branches of trees to give some shade from the summer sun.

Other shades were made somewhat similar to the *ramada* used by the Papagos and Pimas. This was made by setting four posts about ten to fourteen feet apart in the form of a square, each post having a fork at the top. These posts were obtained by building a fire at the base of a juniper tree and burning it off. Poles would be laid in the forks of the posts, making a framework, with other poles laid crosswise and brush thrown over, which formed a structure with a roof, all sides being open. The winter house was more substantial. It was made by taking four tall juniper poles of four to six inches in diameter and setting them in a rectangle or square about ten to fourteen feet apart. The tops were bent over and lashed together with yucca fiber. Smaller poles were then set to make the framework of the wall. The tops of these were lashed to the center, making either a round or oval frame, with a door in one side facing the east. The framework was thatched with arrowweed or small branches, or covered with strips of juniper bark. Whatever the thatching material might be, it was tied down and held in place with light ropes made of yucca fiber. When the house was completed, it was a fairly efficient shelter. The Walapais were so much attached to their homes that the older people were reluctant to go on a long journey for fear they might die away from home. A homesite or a plot of ground might remain in the possession of a family for several generations.

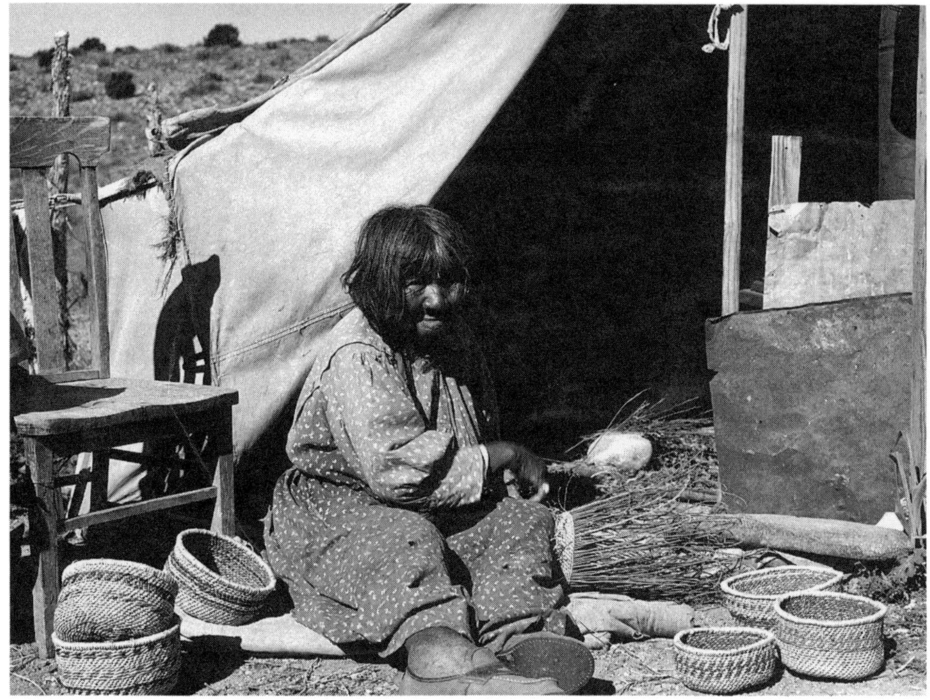

*Sometimes a tent serves as summer quarters for the Walapais on the range. Most modern Walapai baskets are small and bowl shaped as shown. When well made they are very strong* *PLATE LV*

The native foods which made up the diet of the Walapais covered a wider range than those used by other tribes of the area. The plant foods embraced the various kinds of cactus fruit, seeds of desert plants, beans from the mesquite, palo verde, catclaw, and screw bean trees, the Spanish dagger and mescal, acorns, berries, and nuts.

For the most part, the plant foods were gathered by the women and girls, with the exception of mescal, which usually was gathered by whole families or groups of families and prepared in much the same manner as the Yavapais and the Apaches gathered and prepared this food. The gathering of piñon nuts was carried on by groups or parties which went into the mountains for this purpose. The cones were picked with a long stick having a hook on one end, and then roasted over a fire; later the nuts were threshed from the cones by beating them with a stick. The cones were picked in the morning before the piñon gum had become soft from the heat of the sun, for this resin gum is very sticky as it oozes from the trunk and branches of the tree.

Seeds and berries were harvested with the aid of a seed beater, which was an instrument shaped somewhat like a long spoon but woven of basket material, with the outer end cupped to direct the seeds or berries into the basket that was held under the bushes. The warp of the seed beater was bound together to make a handle like the handle of an old-fashioned carpet beater. Cactus fruits, such as saguaro and prickly pear, were dried, also yucca fruit. With few exceptions, the plant fruits that were stored for winter were ground into a coarse meal and stored away in bags made of buckskin or mountain sheep skin. When used, these foods were mixed with water and drunk as a gruel, either with or without cooking.

The animal foods covered even a greater scope, for these Indians ate almost all forms of flesh. There were few exceptions, such as fish and frogs, that Tedjupa had told the people long ago they should not eat; also snakes and small lizards, unless they were near starvation. However, the chuckwalla was eaten. This is a large, bright-colored lizard, sometimes a foot in length, found among the rocks in the lower mountain areas all over Arizona. Of the animals commonly found in this country, the skunk was the only one these Indians eliminated from their menu. Among the birds, the eagle and the hummingbird were the only ones that escaped. Like the Yavapais, the Walapais considered hummingbirds too small and the eagles were sacred.

The larger game, such as deer, antelope, and mountain sheep (elk and bear were not used because they were difficult to kill), usually was hunted by a number of men, working together, with those who were the best marksmen being located in positions where they might get a shot at the game while other members of the party drove the animals to them. The hunter killing the animal was given the hide and the brain and spinal cord to tan the skin, also the sinew along the backbone, which was used for a bowstring, and perhaps a hindquarter, but the meat always was divided among all members of the party. In fact, all food was shared throughout the group.

When an animal was killed, it was skinned immediately and the intestines removed if the kill was made at some distance from camp, but nothing was discarded. The Walapais used all parts of the animal. Hides were tanned and made into clothing and moccasins, and all other parts were used as food, the intestines being given to the old people. The main meat supply was provided by rodents, such as rabbits, rats, mice, gophers, and other small animals falling in this class. Carnivorous animals that were common to the region, such as mountain lions, coyotes, foxes, bobcats, and badgers, also were eaten. Rabbit skins were cut into strips and woven into sleeping blankets. The skins of other small animals also might be pieced together and made into blankets. With the exception of the larger ones, most of the animals mentioned were cooked whole, with only the skin removed. All other parts were eaten, the viscera and internal organs being given to the old people. Many of the smaller animals were trapped with stone deadfalls. Rabbits sometimes were driven into nets made of fiber of the Spanish bayonet, and wild pigeons were caught in snares made of yucca fiber. Birds used for food were plucked immediately when killed and the heads fastened to the yucca-fiber belt of the hunter and brought into camp ready to be cooked. They were cooked whole and the carcass distributed in the same manner as the animal, the old people always coming in for the intestines of any animal foods. The men prepared the meat and the women did the cooking. Notwithstanding the great variety of foods which the Walapai used, the primary occupation of the whole family was gathering foods for the family subsistence.

The position of the woman in the Walapai home was comparable to that of the Pima and Papago women and much more favorable than either the Yavapai or the Apache women. She associated more freely with the members of the family and visitors who might come in. After she prepared the meal, she sat down with the family and ate with them. There were no mother-in-law taboos. She was responsible for the training of the girls and the care of all the children until the boys were old enough to go with their father on hunting trips. She taught her daughters to be strong and industrious and to maintain good behavior.

When the girl reached the age of fourteen to fifteen years she was eligible for marriage, and this usually was entered into by agreement between the young people concerned. When a young man became interested in a girl he killed a deer and took it to her father's house. Later, he might give her father a buckskin or some food, and if the girl did not respond, the father might speak to her. Even though she had some other choice, the girl would marry the man her father requested her to take and then later might run away with the man of her choice. Marriage consisted simply of cohabitation. There was no ceremony, and usually the young couple lived in the home of the girl's parents. This might continue for some time or until the first child was born, then they would live with the boy's parents. If neither parent needed their help or support, the young people would establish a home of their own.

The boys were taught by their fathers to be good hunters, and the virtues that were most prized in a young man were his thriftiness, ability as a hunter, and his abstinence from gambling, which was the chief vice of the Walapais and remains so even today.

The Walapais practiced polygamy, but as a usual thing it did not extend to more than two wives. In such cases, both wives lived in the same house with the husband.

Divorce proceedings were no more difficult or involved than was the marriage ceremony. When a couple separated, a division of personal property was made, the wife taking her baskets and pots and the man taking his own personal effects. If there were children, they too were divided equally, the oldest going with the father, for in their old age each parent would need the help and support of the children. There were practically no bachelors or spinsters among the Walapais, and one of the primary responsibilities of all persons was the care of their parents when they became old. Children were given a name when they were about six months old, but later, when twelve to fifteen years of age, they might change that name to suit their own fancy. This practice, which prevails in many Indian tribes, often presents a difficult problem in maintaining statistical records. The names selected for children usually were patterned after some unusual thing or happening, but an effort was made to select a name that had been given to no one else. After death, the name of a deceased person was never mentioned, and to do so in the presence of relatives of the deceased constituted an insult to them. When a person died, the body and all personal belongings were burned on a funeral pyre of dry juniper wood, and the house which had been occupied by the deceased also was burned. If the deceased had been a man, his horse was killed but not cremated. Friends always prepared the dead for cremation, after which they washed their hair and bathed with yucca root soap and burned their clothing.

The Walapais did not have a tribal chief, and there were no subtribes or large geographical divisions as among the Yavapais. Even in warfare, they were not bound together in a co-ordinated group, but, rather, in a collection of small groups. Each village had its headman or chief and this position was hereditary and passed to the oldest son. If there was no son to assume leadership, then the father's brother might take over or, in some cases, an influential chief in a neighboring village.

As in our own political life, leadership was attained through aggressiveness and ability to talk. The powers of the chief were more advisory than dictatorial. He gained his position and reputation through haranguing the people along the lines of proper conduct and industry, but the power of suppressing evil and wickedness rested entirely with the people themselves.

A thief might not be punished, but the person losing the property would, in turn, try to steal it back. If a wife were unfaithful, the first offense might pass without any action being taken. If the offense were repeated, a small bit of scalp from the back of her head might be cut off by the irate husband but he could not kill her. He could burn the house of her "boy friend" or kill his horses, but seldom did he kill the man himself. In case of murder, the relatives of the murderer would be asked by the community for permission to kill him. Such permission always was granted and a relative of the murderer's victim would carry out the execution.

After death, the spirits of the good people went to Tedjupa, who lived in the west, where the sun set, and there they lived in plenty. The insane and wicked people, such as murderers and other vicious characters, went down to Matial, where they lived as people here on earth. There was no fire and brimstone in the underworld but they believed that their people must work and strive for a living in a manner similar to that which they had endured in life. Anthropologists, as well as the Indians themselves, question the amount of influence white contacts may have had regarding the version of these beliefs which the modern Walapais give us.

Walapai religion seemed to have centered mostly in their belief in the spirits who were supposed to work through the medium of a medicine man. These spirits were thought to inhabit the mountains in the Walapai country, and the spirit of Wikame was considered the strongest and most important of all. The position of the medicine man, if not inherited, was obtained by an individual through pilgrimage to the mountains to commune with the spirits and be vested with their power. Equipment of a medicine man was a gourd rattle, a number of songs and incantations, and a considerable amount of hocus pocus. When called to aid a sick person, he would sing to the patient to the accompaniment of his gourd rattle, or he might apply his lips to the part of the body giving pain and then exhibit a small stone which he had drawn into his mouth. He would promptly swallow the stone, and the theory was that the bad spirit that had caused the sickness would in this way be carried away by the medicine man. Sickness was supposed to be the result of the spirit of some deceased relative coming back and entering the body of the patient. The medicine man was paid for his services in buckskin and was regarded with about as much fear as respect, for the people believed that he could not only cure but could induce sickness and disease. If he failed to cure his patient, another medicine man could be called in or, if the patient died, the relatives of the deceased might kill the medicine man. Apparently, this provision kept the ranks of the medicine men relatively small. But, even so, they held a rather important place in the community group, so important that they sometimes accompanied the warriors into battle in order that they might treat those who were wounded.

The Walapais were not a warlike people and most of their warfare was defensive rather than aggressive. They maintained friendly relations with the Mojaves, to the west, with whom they traded buckskin for corn, beans, and other farm products, and with the Hopis, to the east, with whom they traded for blankets, some of which had been obtained from the Navajos. The Piutes, in the north, were not friendly and occasionally caused some trouble. The traditional enemies of the Walapais were the Yavapais, who lived to the south. The weapons used by the Walapais were the bow and arrow, and a war club made of hardwood studded with quartz crystals found in the mountains. The warriors who fought with the war club were called the "brave men" and they advanced against the enemy to engage in hand-to-hand combat. They used a shield in the form of a curtain, rather than the round shield of bull hide carried by the Pimas. This buckskin curtain was held in front of the advancing warrior and used primarily to deflect arrows aimed at him. Arrows were poisoned with a sticky, paint-like substance made by boiling scorpions and a poisonous plant in deer blood. The arrow had three feathers in the top instead of the usual two, and the shaft was either cane or arrowweed. If the shaft was made of cane, the stone arrowhead was set in a short foreshaft made of hardwood and set into the cane. Stones with straight, smooth grooves were used to straighten arrows by drawing them back and forth through the grooves. Such stones were supposed to be found where a rainbow touched the earth.

## *The White Man in the Walapai Country*

THE WALAPAIS, like many other Indian tribes of Arizona, received their first introduction to the white man through a visit from one of the early Spanish missionaries. He was Fr. Francisco Garcés, who visited many of the tribes living in the Colorado River valley during the latter half of the eighteenth century. In 1775-76, Fr. Garcés made a trip from the Mojaves, on the Colorado, to the Hopi villages to the east and, en route, passed through the Walapai country. He described them as inferior to the Mojaves, but peaceful people, who received him with all friendliness. He did not attempt to establish missions among them and, apparently, his contact was merely by way of passing through their territory.

Nearly a century passed before white immigration penetrated to any extent into this remote section of Arizona. Early army records show that in 1852 Captain Sitgraves passed through the Walapai territory on a march from the Zuñi villages to the Colorado, but, like Garcés, his contact with the people was limited to merely passing through. Several years later, Lieutenant Joseph C. Ives made a more detailed survey and report on the Walapai country and its people. He found them to be poor and miserably clad, mostly in skins, and living upon wild foods and game, both of which were scarce. The Indians offered no objections to the survey and, according to Lieutenant Ives, seemed to be more occupied with the problem of obtaining a living than anything else.

There were no hostilities on the part of the Indians until 1866, when their chief, Wauba Yuma, was killed by a white man. It was claimed that some of the old chief's warriors had killed a white man, but the accusation later was found to be questionable. In going back over the history of Indian tribes, it is interesting to note how frequently the peaceful relations existing between the two races were broken by such an incident as mentioned here. Almost invariably the white man was the aggressor in the beginning and, according to Indian code, the relatives of the slain warrior would be obligated to avenge his death. Our principles of law were entirely foreign to them. Their law was an "eye for an eye and a tooth for a tooth," and invariably this brought on retaliation that, in the end, precipitated a long and desperate struggle. From the time old Wauba was killed, the Walapais went on the warpath and in the following years many depredations against miners and white settlements were credited to them.

In 1866, our government granted the Atlantic and Pacific railroad all odd numbered sections of land in this vast territory. This railroad later became the Santa Fe, and, until 1942, this land grant was a bone of contention between the railroad company and the Indians or the government in their behalf. In that year the grant was set aside and the lands became part of the Walapai Reservation.

The policy of the government in the early seventies, in condensing Indian population on selected reservations, caused the Walapais to be moved onto the Mojave Reservation early in 1874. This can only be credited as another error in the management of our Indian people, for the Walapais were a mountain people who were accustomed to the higher elevations, and the burning heat of the Colorado River desert brought untold hardships and disease upon them.

Their stay on the Colorado River, however, was of short duration, for in less than two years they moved, in a body, back to the area formerly occupied by them. Because of dissension between the Indian Service and the army, they were not followed, nor was any attempt made to have them returned.

By now, another problem had arisen. Many mines had sprung up in their territory, and the best grazing lands were covered with thousands of cattle belonging to white cattlemen. This further reduced the native food supply, which had become critically scarce. The Walapais sought employment in the mines and from the white ranchers and tried to subsist themselves, but their condition became so desperate that rationing again became necessary. These rations were issued at Hackberry, and flour from the Hayden mill on the Salt River, together with beef, corn, and tobacco was given them. This flour was ground from wheat which Mr. Hayden purchased from the Pima Indians, on the Gila River.

During all this time, efforts were being made to find a definite location that could be assigned to these Indians. Finally, in 1883, a much reduced area, compared to their former holdings, was set aside for them. It contained approximately 800,000 acres of their early holdings. The Indians claimed that all of the best land was excluded from the reservation, and, for anyone knowing the territory in question, this statement is very difficult to deny. The eastern part of the reservation is high, reaching an elevation of six thousand feet, and covered with a growth of inferior quality pine on the higher elevations. The western part slopes to the Colorado River, and here desert conditions are encountered. About one-third of the reservation consists of brakes into the Colorado and this broken eroded area is of little value. There is practically no agricultural land on the reservation.

The Walapais relied almost entirely on labor on the railroad, in the mines, and on ranches for their subsistence, and, by 1900, had adjusted themselves to the extent that they were earning seventy-five per cent of their maintenance; the other twenty-five per cent consisted of flour rations issued by the government. Outside labor still furnishes the larger part of their income.

About the only industry that is possible on their reservation is stock raising and this is now being promoted through government assistance and supervision. In 1916, fifteen families were made allotments of ten cows each, for which they were to pay within a period of five years. From this small beginning, the cattle industry on the reservation has been developed until in 1953 the Walapai sold $1,182,000 worth of beef cattle and their carry-over on the ranges numbered approximately 3,300 head. The reservation has been increased until it now extends over approximately one million acres and has a carrying capacity of about seven thousand head of beef cattle, but development of additional water reservoirs is necessary before any appreciable increase in the present herds can be made.

The Walapai tribe is thought never to have exceeded one thousand members, and in the years immediately following occupation of their country by the whites this number was greatly reduced. In fact, their number declined until about fifteen years ago, when education and medical service offered by the government checked their high rate of mortality. They now are slowly approaching a normal increase. There are about five hundred Walapais, and the 3,300 head of cattle mentioned are fairly well distributed through this group. The bulk of holdings of individuals range from twenty to seventy-five head for each cattle owner. A herd of 1,200 head belongs to the tribe and is operated under direction of the tribal council. Other cattle herds on the reservation are operated through cattlemen associations, and these Indians are generally credited with being good cowboys. Providing water for livestock sometimes involves the hauling of water in barrels for many miles during extreme drought periods.

It is estimated that there are 100,000,000 board feet of ponderosa pine on the reservation, most of which is ripe and ready for cutting, but at present no commercial sawing is being done.

Walapai children attend school on the reservation through the grades and then are sent, for their high school work, to Indian boarding schools at Phoenix, Riverside, and Santa Fe.

A tribal council similar to that mentioned as the governing body of other Arizona tribes has taken the place of the talking chief of olden times, but the exercise of its control over the people is not rigidly enforced.

## *Walapai Arts*

THE PRIMITIVE STATE of the people extended even to their arts and crafts. There are no beautiful designs or highly developed craftsmanship as are common with so many of Arizona's aboriginal groups. They made both pottery and baskets for utility purposes only. Their pottery consisted mainly of cooking utensils, serving dishes for food, and spoons without handles. Also, water jars were made, and possibly the most unusual item was the pottery pipe in which they smoked their native tobacco. These pipes were straight and ranged from three to six inches in length, the mouthpiece tapering from the bottom of the bowl to a size small enough to be taken into the mouth. There was no reed or cane stem, but while the clay was soft a hole was made from the bottom of the bowl down through the mouthpiece. The pipe had to be tilted upward when in use. Tobacco grew wild in the Walapai country, but was not cultivated. To prepare for smoking, the leaves were dried and rubbed between the hands until fine and the contents of the intestines of a young rabbit were dried and ground fine and mixed with the tobacco when it was put into the pipe. A boy was not allowed to smoke until he had killed his first coyote. If he did not observe this rule, he would remain lazy throughout his life. Other safeguards to the Walapai youth in this old custom are obvious, because the boy should attain some degree of maturity before indulging in the use of such a tobacco mixture.

The basketry of the tribe has undergone an extensive alteration, both as to type of basket woven and materials used. In olden times, the women made conical burden baskets of willow or squawberry bush (Plate LVI). They also made a coil weave basket of mulberry wood, which usually was in the shape of a shallow bowl. These were tightly woven and sometimes were smeared with mush to make them even more water tight. Water jugs, similar to the *tus* of the Apaches, also were made of basket material and smeared inside and out with the gum from the plentiful piñon tree.

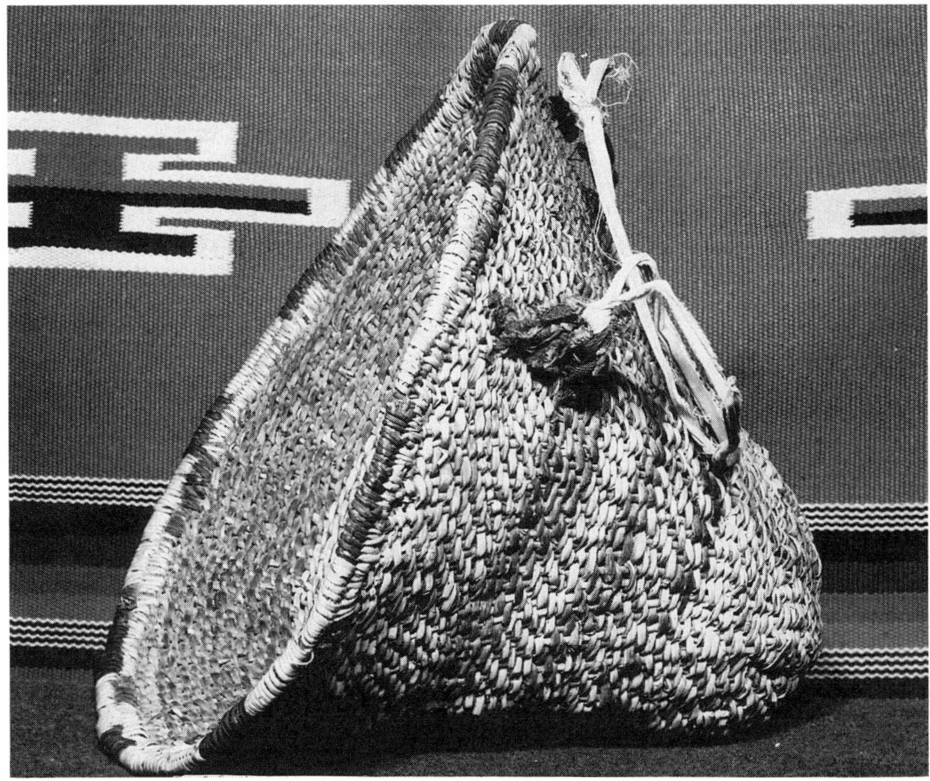

*Walapai burden baskets are almost extinct. This type was made in olden times from willow or squawberry bush* *PLATE LVI*

Another implement made of basket material was the seed beater. This was shaped somewhat like the elongated bowl of a spoon. The ribs or warp of the beater consisted of twenty or more rods extending the full length of the beater, which was twelve to eighteen inches. These rods were bound together with a wicker weave and when the beater, which was three to six inches in width, with a bowl three to four inches deep, was finished the rods of warp were bound together at the lower end, making a handle. The outer end of the bowl was cupped inward so that in beating seed or berries from bushes, they would be directed into the burden basket held under the bushes.

All of these baskets now have been discarded, along with the pottery used in the old Walapai camps. Today, baskets are made entirely of sumac twigs. They are very strong and durable but exhibit, probably, the least native art of any of our Arizona baskets, yet they are by no means unattractive. The dyes used in the decorative band are aniline dyes purchased at the traders and lack the soft shades reproduced in the decorative designs of the Hopi baskets. Both the warp and the woof are of the same material, which grows abundantly on the Walapai Reservation. Many Walapai weavers are fortunate in having to go only a hundred yards or so, to the top of ridges near their homes, to gather material for their baskets. The best period for gathering this material is in September when the twigs which came out from buds in the spring have fully matured.

The Walapai women probably give less time to the preparation of their basket material than other Arizona weavers. I have seen them gather twigs from the sumac bushes and immediately start weaving them into baskets, with an occasional leaf still clinging to the twig.

In starting a basket, the weaver takes a bundle of three rods or twigs and crosses them, with the ends extending like the spokes of a wheel. At the point where they cross, or the hub, they are bound firmly together, and then a loop of the weft is placed around one rod and the two ends are then twined over and under the rods where they extend from the hub. The warp or ribs are immediately worked into the starting of the basket. These ribs are twigs twelve inches or more in length and measure about one-eighth of an inch in diameter at the base. The weaver splits and chews this piece for about one inch and bends the split portion like the fingers of a half-closed hand. The upper end of the split section is placed in position and firmly bound by the twining of the weft, and as this continues around the center of the basket, other ribs are inserted until the framework is firmly bound together with the ribs radiating from the center. The split twigs which stand up in the inside of the basket are trimmed away when it is completed (Plate LVII). The weaving continues with the framework remaining flat until the bottom of the basket is woven, then the ribs are turned upward and the weaving on the sidewall begins. When the wall is completed, the basket is finished by placing a twig in hoop-like fashion on both inside and outside of the upper edge of the basket. This is bound

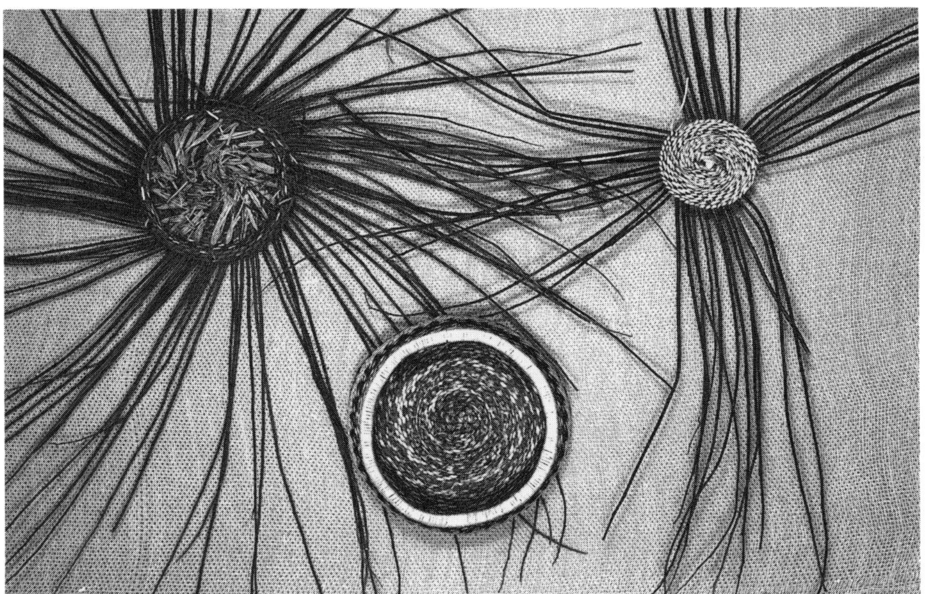

*The starting of a Walapai basket. Top left, inside view —note the protruding ends of the ribs or warp; top right, outside view of bottom of basket; bottom, finished basket*

*PLATE LVII*

firmly in place with the weaving material in a coiling stitch passing through the basket and over the two rods, binding all firmly together and giving a smooth, broadened rim to the top of the basket.

With rare exceptions, the modern Walapai baskets are bowl shaped. Since the weft is merely split sections of the round twigs which are not carefully sized, the Walapai basket lacks the smooth even finish of the other Indian baskets of Arizona. Likewise, the warp is not sized and, therefore, there are variations in it as well, so it is probable that the art and craftsmanship of the modern Walapai baskets do not equal that of baskets made in olden times. They do, however, possess strength to a greater degree than other baskets. I have seen a Walapai bowl six inches in diameter placed upside down and a man stand on it without any injury to the basket. This is due to the strong ribs all radiating from the center of the bottom of the basket to the outer rim, hence the man's weight was distributed over several score of these ribs.

I have a group of Walapai baskets which I have collected over a period of thirty years. The largest basket of the group was obtained from the weaver in 1926, but it is difficult to distinguish any difference between this basket and others of the group, several of which were brought from the reservation in 1946. Two of these baskets are vase shaped and are not true to type, but are efforts of a Walapai weaver to please her public. With a glass or tin insert, these baskets make beautiful flower vases.

The Walapais, like the Papago weavers, have gone further in their efforts to meet the demands of the white trade than most other Arizona basket weavers. They have changed material, craftsmanship, decorative designs, and type in order to create a basket that can be easily and quickly made and, therefore, sold at a lower price. Most of the tourists who come into the Indian country are not students of Indian art, and a basket that can be made in a day and for which the weaver asks only two or three dollars is oftentimes more attractive to them than a masterpiece that required several weeks to weave and is priced at several times as much. The Indian weavers are only following the competitive trend of the civilization of which they are a part. In the final analysis, the changes they have made in their craft are merely the adjustments necessary to their participation in the white man's way of living, and upon this participation rests the destiny of the Indian people.

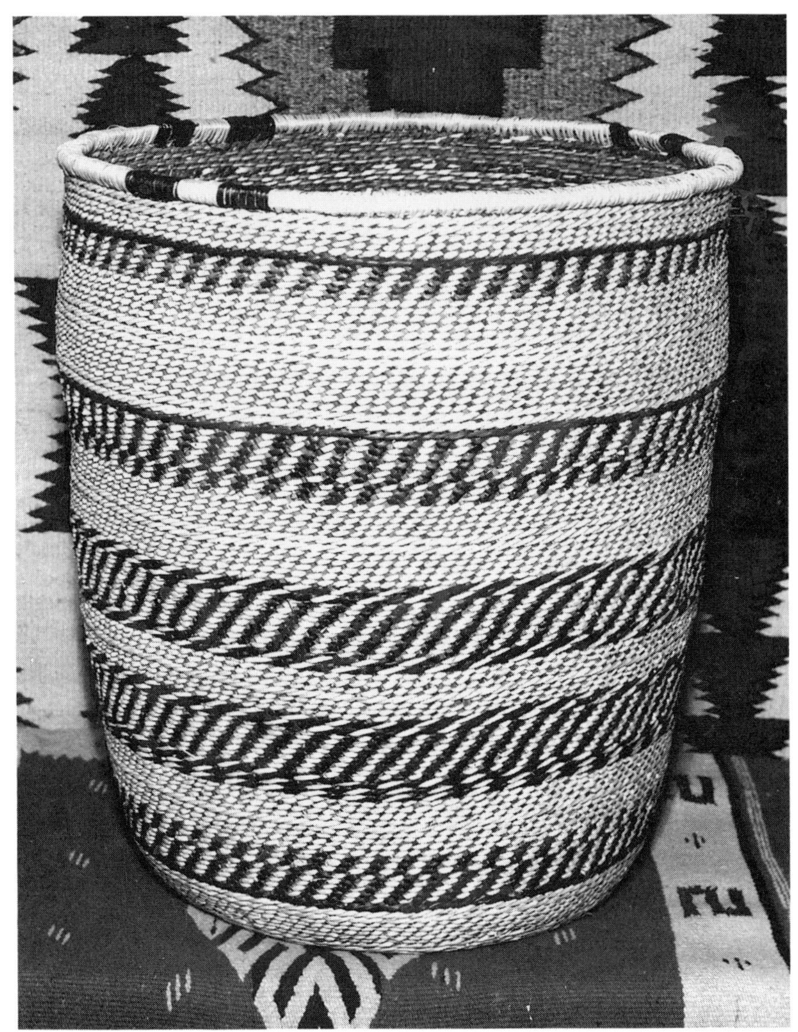

*An unusually large Walapai basket—Baskets of this shape and size seldom are made by the present-day Walapais*

PLATE LVIII

# *The Land of the Willows*

THE HAVASUPAIS are of Yuman stock, closely related to their nearby neighbors, the Walapais, and are considered an offshoot from that tribe. The Walapai creation myth credits their hero, Tedjupa, with giving the Havasupais corn, beans, and squash seed and telling them to go down into the canyon and plant their fields along the river of the blue-green water. No other reference to the separation of the tribe is found in Walapai folklore, but if and when the separation came it evidently was not attended by hostilities, for the two tribes have remained friendly with each other to the extent of frequent intermarriages between them.

The language and culture of the two tribes are almost identical, but their economy is quite different. The Walapais depended on wild foods almost exclusively, while the Havasupais were an agricultural people and used wild foods only to supplement those grown on their small plots of land in the canyon. Environment, no doubt, played a large part in the adoption of the economy which each followed, for the arid conditions prevailing in the Walapai country made farming impossible and, likewise, wild foods were difficult for the Havasupais to obtain from their isolated canyon.

The first white man to visit these people was Fr. Garcés, who came into the canyon in 1776, and nearly another century passed before Captain Ives made a survey and report of this isolated canyon and its people. Even today, the Havasupai village probably has fewer visitors than any other spot in the Indian country, for it still is inaccessible except for two narrow trails, the Topacobia and the Walapai. Only the hardier visitors will brave the long walk or horseback ride down these trails that follow along the narrow ledges of the canyon wall. However, the grandeur and scenic beauty of this canyon will repay the traveler for the soreness he may experience for several days after his trip to Havasupai.

The Havasupai Indians, according to ethnological studies, never greatly exceeded 250 in number, which is about the present census of the tribe. They have, at times, dropped below this number, but improved facilities have brought about their recovery and an approach to the normal increase of most other tribes. Their lands form a narrow strip along each side of Cataract Creek, which runs through their narrow valley and then plunges over a succession of falls into the Colorado River, 1,500 feet below.

The Havasupais irrigate their lands with water from the stream, and there always is an abundant supply for their needs. In ancient times, their crops were confined to corn, beans, and squash, but they secured peach trees and other fruits from the Hopis, with whom they carried on trade. In fact, they had livestock and fruit trees, which had been brought to the Hopis by the Spaniards, long before any member of the white race had reached the Havasupai country. Figs and other fruits have been added since. Their corn was of several varieties and colors—black, blue, red, white, and mixed—and while they might plant all different colors in a field, each would have its own separate plot. The whole family assisted in planting the fields and cultivating the crops. Irrigating was done by the men, with the women doing the greater part of the harvesting. When the crops were gathered, in the fall, they were stored in stone granaries located along the base of the canyon wall but well above any danger of floods from the stream below. These granaries were natural recesses in the rock, in front of which stone walls were built, and the interior sealed with a plaster made of bat guano to protect the food stores from rodents.

In the olden times, after the harvest was finished and the food stored away, the Havasupais ascended to the plateau—taking with them small buckskin bags of corn and other food—where they constructed winter homes in the thick cedar brakes and piñon trees that covered the area. There they spent the winter hunting and gathering nuts and wild seeds, occasionally making a trip back to their granaries for additional supplies. In the early spring they returned to the canyon, and April found them preparing their fields for the spring planting. There are only about five hundred acres in the canyon, of which less than one hundred acres are in cultivation.

Inheritance follows in the male line only, a man's son inheriting his land or, if he has no sons, his brother or his nephew may be the heir. The widow or an unmarried daughter may share in the crop but the ownership of the land is vested in some male member of the family. One rather peculiar custom involves the ownership of fruit trees. A person planting a tree on land owned by someone else retains ownership of the tree with, possibly, the landowner sharing to some extent in the crop.

Upon the death of any member of the household, the home was burned. If the deceased were a man and had a growing crop, one-half of the crop would be cut down and as soon as it was dry it would be burned. If he owned livestock, two or three of the horses would be killed and the rest of the stock driven away. His saddle might be burned or left on one of the horses that had been killed, but his bow and arrows, war club, and other personal belongings would be buried with him. His fields would be allowed to lie idle for a year or two, and his wife could not remarry for an equal period of time without bringing criticism upon herself from the family and the community as a whole. The custom of never mentioning the name of a deceased person was not rigidly observed by the Havasupais but names of deceased persons were never mentioned in the presence of their relatives.

The Havasupai family was a closely knit unit, independent of any other group, and it was about the only associated group in the community. Unlike the Hopis and the Navajos, there were no clans; and no bands or tribes, as were common among most Western Apache tribes. The whole community associated freely together and their continual visiting, which they carried on throughout the small tribe, possibly accounts for the absence of any separate groups within the tribe. The man was recognized as head of the family, with the wife sharing greater privileges and prerogatives than the women of most Arizona Indian tribes.

The care of the children was shared by both parents but was sporadic and incidental, lacking a set plan. Children were treated with affection and were said to be generally easy to manage. Punishment was administered often and usually a slap or a lick with a switch was sufficient. In stubborn or difficult cases, the child was sometimes held by the heels face down in a smudge of burning manure until almost suffocated, which seems a rather drastic treatment. At birth, the baby was placed on a cradleboard and was kept there until nearly old enough to walk.

The mother and grandmother taught the girls to be industrious and to bring wood and water for the camp, grind corn, cook, and do other household duties. When a girl reached the age of seven or eight years, she was taught to make baskets. This was a domestic art that provided a great number of household articles and it formed an important function of the female members of the household. When a girl reached adolescence, she was watched carefully and cared for by her mother until marriage, which occurred during the teen age. These marriages were not arranged by the parents and while they might express their attitude toward a marriage, the final decision rested with the young people concerned. There were no marriage laws; the man simply took up habitation in the girl's home and they were accepted as belonging to each other. The girl might elope with a young man and later the couple would receive the parental blessing very much as we handle such cases in our own society. The newly married couple lived with the girl's parents for a year or two or until one or two children were born. During this time the boy worked in his father-in-law's fields and shared in the foods produced. However, neither he nor his wife shared in any land holdings. At the end of his stay in his father-in-law's house, he went to his own parents and built his home near them, for eventually his inheritance in land would be in his father's holdings. There were no divorce laws, and a man might drive a woman away from his home or she might go with another man without serious consequences, but such occurrences were the exception rather than the rule. The Havasupais rarely were polygamous but, if so, the entire family lived in one house. There were no restrictions or taboos with respect to mothers-in-law or any other member of the family, but all associated freely together.

The boy's training was taken care of by his father, grandfather, and, to some extent, by his father's brother. He was taught to hunt, to work in the fields, and to make clothing and moccasins for himself and other members of the family. The clothing was made of buckskin, and was quite similar to that worn by the Yavapais and the Walapais. His first hunting was for rabbits but, as he became older and more skilled, he hunted deer. The Havasupais relied more on skill than on prayers and amulets for success in their hunting.

The property rights of the Havasupai family were quite unevenly divided. The women owned the baskets, pottery, and personal effects, but had no share in the land, house, and other property.

Two types of structures were in common use. One was a circular or dome-shaped structure made by constructing a framework of poles and thatching the sides and roof with bundles of willow branches, held in place by small flexible poles lashed through the thatching to the framework underneath. Willows grew abundantly along Cataract Creek. The roof of the structure was covered with earth, which usually washed off during a heavy rain. The other structure was a rectangular house made by setting four posts in the ground with forks at the top in which poles were laid lengthwise and other poles crosswise, with brush on top similar to the Papago and Pima houses. The roof was covered with earth and the sides thatched with reeds or willow. No provision was made for the smoke to escape, and, except during the rainy weather, all cooking was done outside.

As with most tribes, cooking pots were in general use but the Havasupais also used baskets in cooking certain gruels and mush. They, like the Yavapais, also used the barrel cactus for boiling meat. Antelope, mountain sheep, and deer were the principal animals eaten, but, when game was scarce, mountain lions, raccoons, and foxes might be utilized. Most of these animals were taken when the tribe was in winter quarters on the plateau. Other game, such as rabbits, quail, and doves, usually were found in the canyon near their farms.

The sweathouse, similar to those used by the Yavapais, was another institution that had an important place in the everyday life of the men. The sweathouse might be somewhat removed from the creek, for the Havasupais did not always plunge into the stream after leaving the sweathouse, which was the Yavapai custom. These small structures were about six feet in diameter and four feet in height, with the floor scooped out to a depth of six to eight inches. The framework was made by setting twenty-five to thirty small poles in the sand about eight inches apart, forming a circle, with the upper ends bent inward and lashed together to make the dome-shaped top. Two hoop-like bands of poles were tied to the outside, one near the ground and one about three feet above, as a brace to the frame, making it strong and rigid. Blankets were thrown over the framework to make a thick covering, almost airtight. The floor was covered with green twigs, except for a small space at the left side of the narrow door which admitted the bathers. Each house would accommodate four men sitting with legs crossed, but a lesser number could use the house if they desired. When the men were seated on the floor, stones were heated in a nearby fire and placed on the left side of the door. The stones were then sprinkled with water and the opening sealed with a blanket. The men remained in the sweathouse for about ten minutes and then emerged and went bathing in the stream or laid around on the sand awaiting their turn to re-enter, which they might do four times during an afternoon.

The entire family worked in the fields throughout the morning, and during the long summer afternoon the men went to the sweathouse or laid around on the sand and visited. The women and the younger men went to the shade of the cottonwoods along the stream and gambled or visited, and, in general, the tribe led a rather carefree existence. There seemed to have been no serious attempt at cultural improvement but, rather, an attitude of allowing each day to take care of itself. The lack of organization extended to the point that no control was exercised by any group or individual.

The governing head, if he might be called such, was called "Chief," and in the community there could be several such individuals, some called "Big Chief" and some "Little Chief." The Big Chief earned his distinction through some deed of daring or because of superior wisdom and influence over the people. The position of chief was hereditary only if the person inheriting the chieftainship was considered worthy of the position. The chief's control over his people originated through his own dignity, industry, and ability. There were no great war chiefs, most of the wars being defensive, since numerical strength never was sufficient to wage aggressive warfare against the more powerful tribes of that region. They were an agricultural people, living in permanent homes, and almost invariably we find tribes having an agricultural economy were less inclined toward warfare than roving or nomadic tribes that depended upon wild foods for a living. The incentive to engage in warfare was lacking, for food was the objective of most tribal wars and the food supply of the Havasupais was more nearly adequate than that of most of their neighbors. They sometimes joined with a neighbor against a common enemy but, for the most part, remained peaceful in the seclusion of their isolated canyon.

Weapons were the bow and arrow and the war club. The war club was made of hardwood with rounded head and a short handle for use in close, hand-to-hand combat. Their armor consisted of buckskin worn in front and back. Sometimes they held a curtain-like shield of the same material in front when advancing upon an enemy. They ground up red ants, scorpions, and poisonous bugs with which they poisoned their arrows; and their bow was somewhat different from the bow of other tribes we have mentioned. It was called the "sinew back" bow and was made of seasoned oak or other hardwood, with sinew from the deer being glued on in thin layers on the back of the bow. They also used another bow made from a young ash tree of one to two inches in diameter. They did not use a lance, nor was a sling considered an effective weapon.

In scalping an enemy, they followed the pattern set by their kinsmen, the Walapais—that is, they took practically the entire covering of the head. When a scalp was brought into camp, an old woman washed the hair with soapweed and then tied it to a pole set in the center of a dancing arena. The whole community, dressed in their best apparel, made a circle about the pole and yelled, tapping their mouths with their hands, as they danced. The dancers held their bodies in an erect position and the dance step was merely a shuffling sidestep, instead of the feverish gyrations of the warriors in most dances of this sort.

Aside from the occasional victory dance, little in the way of rituals or ceremonial dances was practiced by these people. There was a dance at harvest time, late in August or September, to which the Walapais, Hopis, and sometimes the Navajos were invited, but this was more in the form of a social function than a ceremonial. This dance is said to have lasted for a period of four days, and sometimes visitors from a distance remained even longer to share in the bountiful food supply produced by the Havasupai farms. Some of the older people say prayers for rain, and good harvests were offered during this dance, but the extent of religious implications in the affair seems to be quite vague. The same might be said of their religious beliefs as a whole, for little thought was given to religion. They were not inclined to believe in the supernatural and they had no important deities or much idea of what occurred to the soul after death. They did believe that a man's soul rested in his heart and that after death the spirit went to the north, but they offered no explanation of the separation of the good from the evil spirits if, indeed, they had such belief.

## *The Medicine Man*

WHILE THE HAVASUPAIS seem to have been lacking in a religious creed, they had implicit faith in their medicine men. This is the only tribe known that had medicine men who specialized in certain activities. They had medicine men to produce rain and to cure the sick, and others who specialized in injuries, broken bones, snake bites, etc. They used the gourd rattle and songs, much the same as Walapai medicine men, in the treatment of their patients, but often they requested the relatives of a sick person to stand by all during a night's sing, and occasionally they were called upon to shout, tapping their mouths with their hands, all of which was supposed to assist in driving away the evil spirit. They believed sickness often was caused by the spirit of a dead relative entering the body of an individual. Sometimes more than one medicine man would treat a patient, and there was, apparently, no professional jealousy among them. If a medicine man had a long list of failures to his credit, he might be driven away or even killed by the community. A medicine man could inherit his powers from his father or a relative, or he might acquire them through dreams. In the case of inheritance, the novice must chant correctly the songs of the person from whom he had inherited his powers. It is interesting to note the relentlessness with which the Indians have clung to their old customs and traditions. The medicine man probably has been more universally held in the confidence of the older people than any other institution. Even today patients are coming into the modern hospitals on the reservation with burns on their bodies that have been inflicted by the medicine man in an effort to drive out the pain. This is understandable, for we, too, have our home remedies. It is doubtful if many of our older people have escaped the mustard plaster, sulphur and molasses, or sassafras tea prescribed by our grandmothers. The medicine man still may have a place of limited importance among the Havasupai people but many of the old traditions and customs are gone, for the white man's civilization, bringing better medical care, has penetrated even into the depths of this remote little canyon.

## *The Havasupai Indian Reservation*

IN 1882, CATARACT CANYON was set aside as the Havasupai Reservation. When the survey was made, the old chief insisted that his people should not claim any of the surrounding plateau but only the floor of the canyon on which their homes and their little plots of farm land stood.

He argued that larger holdings would invite trouble; some other tribe—maybe the white people—would come and want to divide their land and take some away, but if they claimed only the small area of the canyon, no one would molest them and they could live in peace. Hence, the Congressional Act of March 31, 1882, set aside only 519 acres of land as the Havasupai Reservation, but subsequent acts have added about 34,000 acres of grazing land on the plateau above.

The Havasupais still irrigate their fields by means of brush-and-rock dams placed across Cataract Creek, but they have many modern improvements, even a small tractor. The one thing that has not changed is their transportation lines, and the narrow trails winding along the canyon walls present a difficult problem. All supplies must be packed down one of two trails, and heavy materials and machinery must be completely disassembled and separate parts packed in on horses and again reassembled at the bottom of the canyon. Lumber is delivered in eight-foot lengths at the rim of the canyon and packed in. There are stoves, mechanical refrigerators, and many other articles of modern civilization in the canyon, and even a piano at the school, which recalls an interesting story.

A few years ago, a firm in Phoenix advertised a sale of pianos, which they agreed to deliver anywhere in the state. The official in charge at Havasupai purchased a piano and when asked where he wished to have it delivered, he replied, "Havasupai." The firm made good on its agreement, and the piano was hauled to the rim of the canyon at the Topacobia Trail. This is the longer of the two trails, being about fifteen miles in length, but was easier to negotiate with such a load. Crews of men were organized to carry the piano down into the canyon. One crew carried the piano until they were tired and then was relieved by another crew. In this manner, the instrument finally was delivered.

The elevation is 3,200 feet at the school and 6,500 feet on the plateau above. During the summer and early fall there are frequent rains, sometimes of cloudburst proportions. Floods often damage the fields and sometimes the homes. In the Supai village, the yearly rainfall varies greatly, ranging from five to fifteen inches. The summers are semitropical, temperatures sometimes reaching above 100°, but when the days begin to shorten, the shadows from the canyon walls permit only short periods of sunshine on the canyon floor below. The days are short and the chill and dampness rising from the stream make the winters in the canyon rather uncomfortable. The migration from the canyon floor to the upper plateau, that formerly occurred in October, is no longer a routine occurrence. Like other Indian tribes, the Havasupais have adopted a single place of abode throughout the year.

A few cattle graze on their range land on the plateau above the canyon. The little herd, numbering about 150 head, supplements the products of their small farms with meat deprived them by the passing of the antelope and mountain sheep.

This little group of Indians probably is one of the lowest income groups in our nation. Their income is estimated at about $130 per year per family. In spite of this, there is less real want than one finds existing in our large cities. Their needs are quite simple and their appetites have not been attuned to a great variety of foods. Corn, beans, dried fruits, and a little meat provide them with their simple requirements, and, apparently, they are happy. Cushing, Spier, and other writers who have visited the Havasupais have mentioned their almost continuous eating habits. On entering a house, a visitor was fed and if he continued on through the village the procedure was repeated at each successive home visited; yet the Havasupais are of a slender, sinewy physique.

## *Havasupai Craft*

THE HAVASUPAI WOMEN rank high among the weavers of fine baskets in Arizona. There is some similarity in their weaving to that of the Yavapais but it is entirely different from the work of the Walapais. The ancient Havasupais used baskets for every purpose for which they were used by other tribes, with some uses individual to the Havasupais alone. They made burden baskets, food bowls or trays, parching trays, cooking baskets, water jugs, and a small watertight bowl used for drinking. Water jugs, burden baskets, and parching trays were made of a twine weave; and bowls, food trays, and cooking baskets were made of the coil stitch, similar to that used in modern Havasupai baskets. The burden basket was conical in shape and made of acacia twigs, with an occasional combination of willow and cottonwood (Plate LIX) . They were about two feet in diameter at the top, with a loop of buckskin inserted about six inches from the upper rim of the basket on either side, to which was fastened a headband of the same material. This band passed over the forehead of the carrier, and the basket was somewhat flattened where it rested against the back of the woman carrying it. The bottom of the basket was protected by a covering of buckskin.

The Havasupais made water jugs of different shapes. Some were large with flat bottoms, like the *tus* of the Apache. A smaller water bottle for use on the trail was of an hourglass shape, being pointed at both ends; the upper end or opening was fitted with a corncob for a stopper and the lower end covered with buckskin. These water jars were car-

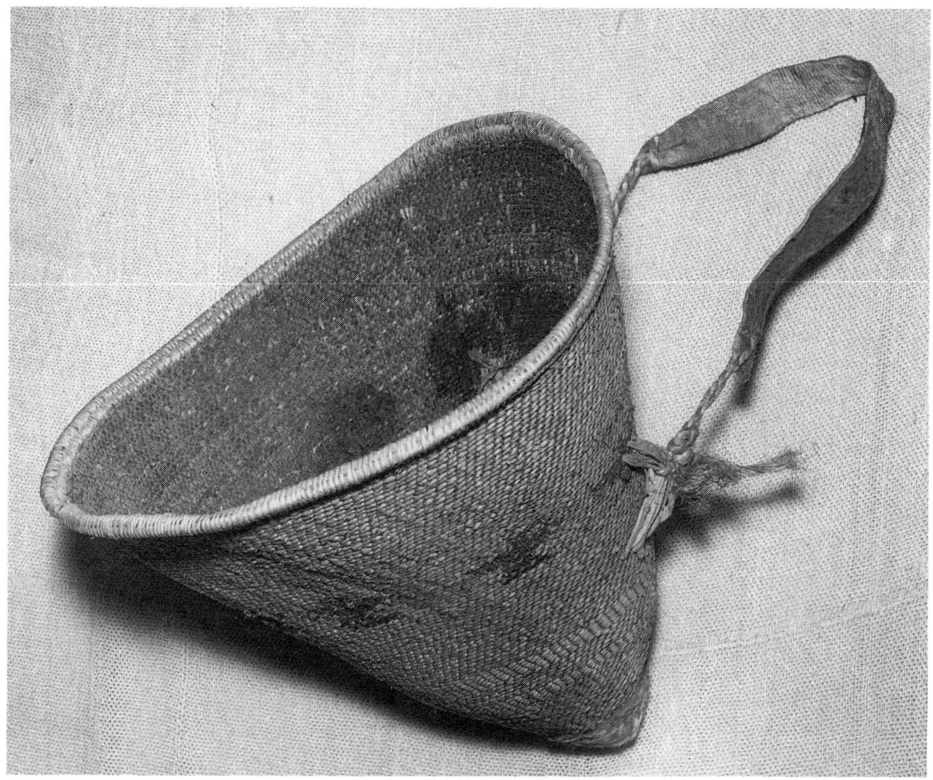

*Havasupai burden basket, showing attachment of head-band. This basket, about two feet wide at the top, also shows the bottom protective covering of buckskin* *PLATE LIX*

ried under a yucca-fiber belt, which was a common part of the Havasupai dress. Soapweed was worked into a paste and rubbed over the water jugs before a coating of piñon pitch was applied.

The parching trays sometimes were coated on the inside with soapweed, or even clay, to protect them from the live coals.

The baskets mentioned here, formerly a part of the equipment of every household, are now extremely scarce. A dozen or more such baskets were kept for use about the home and in the fields, but now dishes and pans and other containers that are common in our homes also have found their way down to the Havasupais.

The present type of basket is made primarily for sale to the white trade. This is a coil type basket, the weft of which is coiled over a three-rod foundation or warp, and both weaving material and foundation are carefully worked to a uniform size. In starting a basket, one end of the rods of the warp are softened in water, mashed or chewed, and tied into a knot. The rods are then bent around this knot and sewed to it, with the coiling proceeding from right to left, which is common in most coil baskets (Plate LXI) . The weft is made of willow twigs that are split and scraped to proper size, and the decorative designs are worked in with the black devil's claw. Two species of this plant grow in the canyon, with the variety bearing white seeds and having the longer tentacle being the most popular with the weavers.

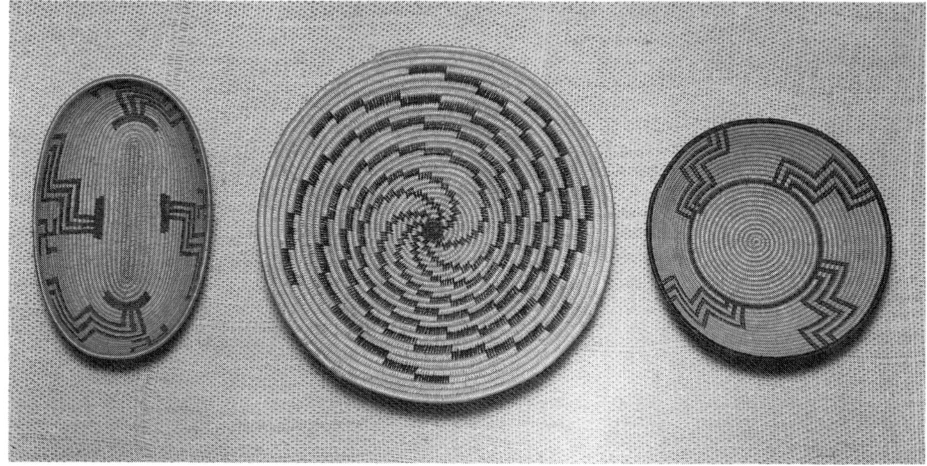

*Oval trays are quite common among Havasupai baskets. The type of basket shown here is made primarily for the commercial trade. They often are shipped by mail* PLATE LX

Some of the popular decorations used by the Havasupai women are simple geometric figures, with the arrangement or combination of such figures determined by the weaver. In construction, Havasupai baskets are almost identical with those made by their kinsmen, the Yavapais. Some of the figures, such as triangles, stars, etc. (Plate LXII) , are very similar to designs used by the Yavapais, but the profusion of symbol and character designs so common in Yavapai baskets are lacking in the Havasupai craft. The outstanding characteristics of these baskets are the beauty of design and smoothness and evenness of contour, all of which is the result of careful preparation of weaving material, as well as of craftsmanship.

The Havasupai weaver no longer has to carry her baskets over the steep trail to the canyon's rim and then another long trek of twenty miles to the nearest market, for Uncle Sam maintains a post office at Supai, and several of the baskets illustrated here came by way of the postman. Thus, the most inaccessible village in all the Indian country has become just another station on one of the nation's rural routes.

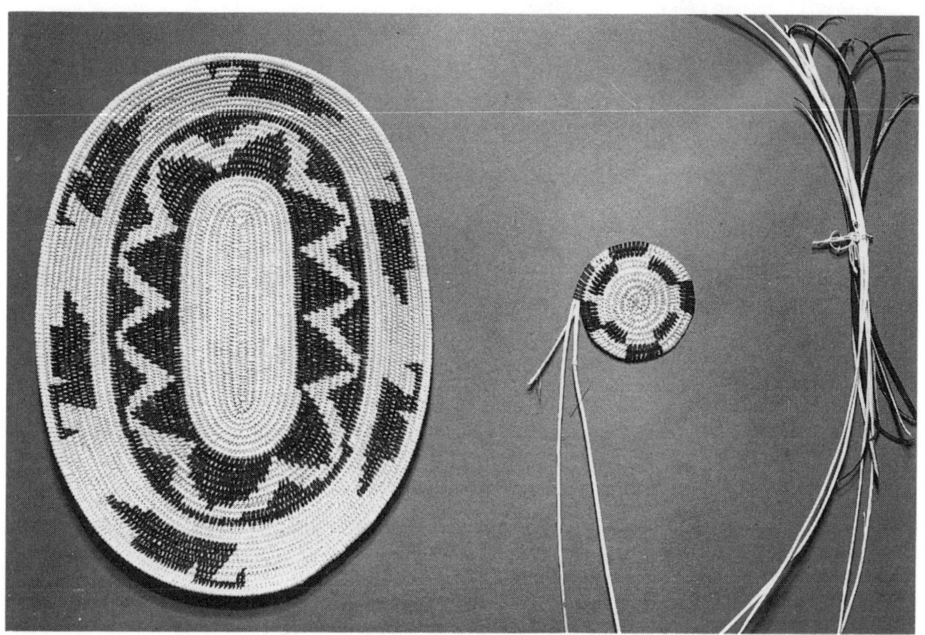

*Present-day type of Havasupai basket—Shown here are (left) finished tray; (center) starting of basket, showing three-rod foundation or warp; (right) willow and devil's claw weaving material*

*PLATE LXI*

## *The Wig-li-wa*

NO DOUBT WIGGL-EE and Wiggl-i (Plate LIV) look down upon all this in bewilderment. Geologists will tell you that these two are only monoliths or pinnacles of stone that erosion of countless ages have left standing at the head of the canyon, but the legend of the people tells a different story.

When the world was new, the earth was covered with water except for one mountain peak in the north, which rose above the surface of the water. Deep within this mountain were four great caverns, in which all the people of the earth lived until a great chief led them up through the different levels of the caverns and through a hole in the

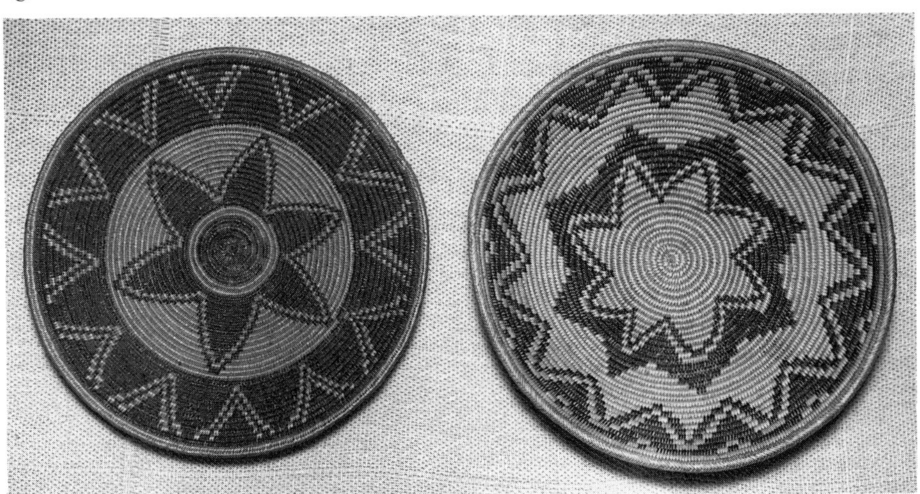

*The star in the center of the Havasupai shallow bowl often has six or eight points, as shown here. Some of the Havasupai designs are very similar to designs used by the Yavapais*

PLATE LXII

mountain out into the sunlight. But the chief was overcome with the sunlight and died. Coyote was there and told the people that if they would burn the body of the chief and scatter the ashes on the water it would dry up and disappear. The people said they had no fire, so Coyote told them he would go and search for some. After he had gone, Blue Bottlefly, who was resting on a twig, told the people he could make fire for them. He rubbed his wings together until the sparks flew and ignited the twig on which he sat. The people then made a pyre of dry wood, placed the chief's body on it and set fire to it. Coyote was a long way off when he saw the smoke, and hurried back, but all except the heart had burned when he arrived. This angered him and he dashed into the fire and grabbed the heart and ran away with it. The fire was still very hot and Coyote's face and forepaws were burned, and that is why the face and forepaws of the coyote are black to this day.

Coyote ate only part of the heart and buried the rest, and where it was buried a stalk of corn grew, bearing six ears of corn. The corn was of different colors—black, blue, red, yellow, white, and mixed. As the people came out of the mountain, the gods distributed this corn among them, giving some black corn to the Apaches, blue to the Hopis, mixed colors to the northern tribe, etc. When the Havasupais came along, only one small red ear was left. As this was insufficient for the needs of all the people, Coyote told them that they would have to hunt for food part of the time, like he did.

After the water had disappeared, the earth became very dry and great cracks opened up on its surface. Water was then very scarce and all of the people went out searching for it. Finally, the Havasupais came to a canyon through which the river of the blue-green water flowed. Here they planted their fields and built their homes. It seems that they were then forbidden to leave the seclusion of their little canyon, but the wife of one of the chiefs grew bored with the isolation of the place and longed to see what was going on in the outside world. She persuaded her husband to go away with her. As they climbed along the ledges toward the rim of the plateau, they were discovered by the Havasupai

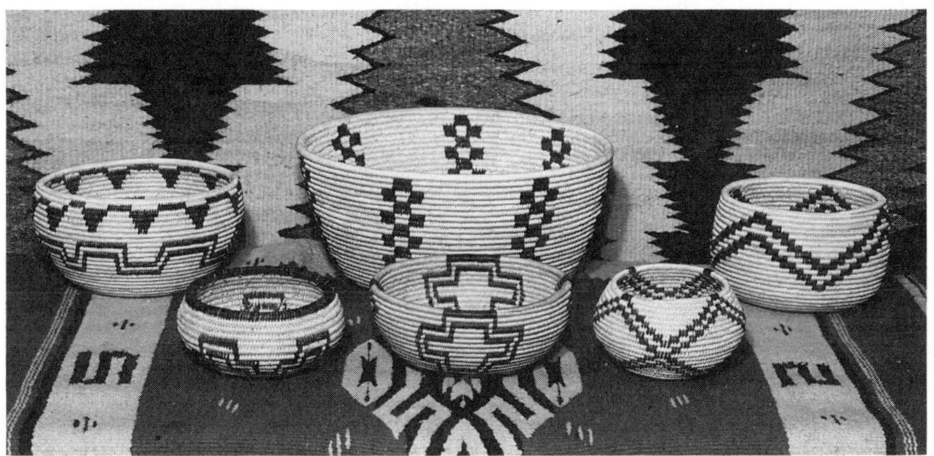

*Havasupai bowl-shaped baskets usually are small, but are outstanding in smoothness and evenness of contour, due to careful preparation of material and excellent craftsmanship* *PLATE LXIII*

gods. Angered at the disobedience of the chief and his wife, the gods turned them into two pillars of red sandstone. And today, Wiggl-ee and Wiggl-i, which are the ancient names given to them, still stand on a rocky promontory overlooking the valley below. They are in full view of the village, where they are pointed to as a lesson for those who would disobey. The people believe that they have stood there since the beginning of the Havasupai tribe and will stand until the end. For if one or both of the Wig-li-wa should fall, then that will be the end of the Havasupais.

# *Chemehuevis on the Colorado*

WHEN THE WHITE man came into the Southwest, the area which is now western Arizona was occupied by the Yuman tribes. South of the Hualapai country, the Mojave territory extended along the Colorado River down to the Yuma holdings. There were other small tribes or bands and, with one exception, they have been absorbed into the tribes above mentioned. This exception is the Chemehuevi tribe, which is a small Shoshonian band, whose territory lies on the California side of the Colorado River and who had formed a close alliance with the Mojaves. How or when this alliance came about is not known. It has been recognized by the Mojaves to the extent that the Chemehuevis share in the land holdings of the Colorado River Reservation. In the early times the Shoshonian group occupied large areas in California, Nevada, and Utah, about one-third of California originally being occupied by these tribes.

Some of the first accounts of contacts between the Chemehuevis and Americans are contained in the reports of Lieutenant A. W. Whipple,[1] who passed through their country in 1853-54, while making a preliminary survey for the Atlantic and Pacific railroad. Whipple estimated their number at 1,500, which seems rather large for the small area of the Chemehuevi Valley and is much larger than any subsequent figure given. He describes them as an agricultural people and mentions that their hunting was carried on more for pleasure and pastime than for their subsistence. However, this does not wholly conform to other reports and to the general practice of most Indians in the area. He found that wheat was being grown, along with their native corn, beans, melons, and squash.

A later report, made in 1858 by Lieutenant J. C. Ives, gives a further account of the Chemehuevis' agricultural pursuits. In his expedition up the Colorado River, he stopped in their valley and traded beads and calico for corn and beans, when his provisions ran low.

Both Ives and Whipple described these people as inferior in many respects to the Mojaves and other tribes of the area. They lacked the stature of the Mojaves, the fierceness and cunning of the Apaches, and

1. A. W. Whipple and others, *Report Upon Indian Tribes,* Senate Exec. Doc. 78, 32nd Cong. 2d Sess. Govt. Printing Office, Washington, 1856.

the honesty and dependability of the Pimas and Papagos. They were referred to as "knaves," but, like the Walapais, the extreme difficulties under which so many of their people existed might have accounted for this trait. Only that portion of the tribe living along the Colorado River had any reliable source of food supply, for the western section of their land holdings was all desert.

## *The Explorer*

IT MIGHT BE interesting here to mention the manner in which Ives explored the Colorado River, since he commanded a steamboat, "The Explorer," probably one of the few military craft ever to navigate this river. It was a flat-bottom, stern-wheel river boat, more than fifty feet long, with a four-inch howitzer mounted in the bow. Those who are familiar with the shallow, sandy channel of the Colorado can hardly visualize a steamboat, with a three-ton boiler and heavy iron plating on the hull, finding sufficient draft to navigate this stream. The Explorer was built in Philadelphia, dismantled, shipped around South America, up the Gulf of California and reassembled for the Ives expedition.

No doubt this old wood burner, with its flashing paddle wheel, was an object of great curiosity to the Indians as she plowed her way up stream, pulling in to the shore at night to make camp and replenish her fuel supply. At such times, Indians in large numbers would appear, and it was on these occasions that trade with them was carried on.

The Chemehuevi tribe occupied the lands lying at the head of the Colorado River valley. The many ways in which they differed from the other tribes encountered was expressed by Ives in the following manner: "They are altogether different in appearance and character from the other Colorado Indians. They have small figures, and some of them have delicate, nicely cut features, with little of the Indian physiognomy. Unlike their neighbors, who, though warlike, are domestic and seldom leave their own valleys, the Chemehuevis are a wandering race, and travel great distances on hunting and predatory excursions. They wear sandals and hunting shirts of buckskin and carry tastefully made quivers of the same material."

The Explorer encountered considerable difficulty in the shoals adjacent to the Chemehuevi Valley, for here the river was broken by numerous islands, and the intervening channels were not of sufficient depth to navigate. The Chemehuevis, however, experienced no such difficulty, since they used rafts constructed of bundles of reeds tied together and propelled by a pole. Like all other tribes along the Colorado, they did not have canoes.

The Chemehuevis are the only California tribe that migrated across the river before the coming of the white man and at a time when the territorial holdings of each tribe rather definitely fixed their location, excluding immigration from other tribes. Even the old legends of the tribe tell nothing about the coming of the Chemehuevis to the Mojave territory. In fact, less is known of the Chemehuevis than of any other of the tribes of Arizona. The Chemehuevi Valley extended about five miles along the river, and was the only agricultural land belonging to the tribe. The far greater part of their territory extended to the west, taking in the eastern half of the Mojave Desert. This represented the largest area in California occupied by a single tribe in primitive times. It was also the most thinly populated area, and the most worthless.

There is nothing known of the primitive political, social, or family organizations of the Chemehuevis. They evidently were ruled by a chief. How he acquired his position or what power or authority he held is not a matter of record. Their houses were crude structures, little more than shelters from the desert sun. Whipple mentioned their clothing as consisting of a bark petticoat worn by the women and a breechcloth worn by the men. Ives says they wore buckskin hunting shirts, and moccasins of the same material, and feather caps. The difference in the apparel as described by the two men can be explained by the fact that Whipple visited their country during the summer months, while Ives' trip up the Colorado was during January and February. Babies were bound to a cradleboard but the material or manner of construction of the cradle is not given.

Their food was similar to that of the Walapais and other tribes living in arid regions. Lizards, with the exception of the chuckwalla, used by the Walapais, generally were taboo. Their diet consisted of seeds of desert plants, mescal, and such game animals as deer, antelope, and mountain sheep, together with rabbits, desert rats, and other small desert animals. In olden times, each Chemehuevi carried a crooked stick, something like a shepherd's crook, with which they dug out rodents from their burrows wherever they found them.

Their main weapon was the bow and arrow. Their bow was especially well made, with recurved ends, painted, and sometimes decorated on one end with the skin and rattles of a snake. Their arrows were fitted with a foreshaft in which was set a flint point, evidently similar to the arrows of the Yavapais. They also made a stone knife shaped somewhat like a large arrowhead, having a short handle fitted to the head and bound with sinew.

The medicine men acquired power through dreams, and were called upon to treat the sick. There seems to be no record of religious ceremonies or rituals as distinctly belonging to the Chemehuevis. Culturally, they leaned more toward tribes of California and the great basin, but associated more with the Mojaves, Yavapais, and other Yuman tribes than with their kinsmen, the Paiutes. They buried their dead but burned all possessions of the deceased. The men and women wore their hair short-cropped in front, bound together at the nape of the neck, and hanging down their backs. They were not a warlike people and the only conflict mentioned in what meager history we have of them was a war with the Mojaves in 1867. They were greatly outnumbered but put up a good fight and, although they were driven out of the Chemehuevi Valley, they later returned and have lived peacefully with the Mojaves since. There are no records of any serious conflict with the white settlers who came into the Colorado River valley.

In 1853, Whipple placed the population of the tribe at 1,500. A little more than a decade later, Thomas gives an estimate of only half that number. In 1903, Hodges gives their number as 300. The census of the Colorado River Reservation, in 1944, places the number of Chemehuevis at 371. About 100 of these are living off the reservation in Needles, Banning, Barstow, and other California cities, where they are employed.

## *Chemehuevi Reservation*

THE CHEMEHUEVI Reservation was established in 1907, giving the tribe about 32,000 acres of land in eastern San Bernardino County, California. About 3,000 acres of the Chemehuevi Reservation along the river were irrigable. With the completion of the Parker Dam, all of this land was under about forty feet of water. In 1940, the Metropolitan Water District of Southern California purchased the land from the tribe for $108,000. Through their old affiliation with the Mojaves, the

Chemehuevis are permitted to acquire land in the vast irrigable area on the Colorado River Reservation. Many of them have been allotted lands in this area and have prosperous little farms. Others who wish to do so may receive assignments of land from the Colorado River Tribal Council.

Title to land allotments on an Indian reservation is held in trust by the government. The Indian has full control and unrestricted use of his land with the exception of change of title by sale or otherwise. This means that when he dies, his allotment is divided among his heirs. After two or three generations this results in an allotment being divided into many small fractional holdings. Since the Indian Reorganization Act of 1934, no allotments have been made. Instead, assignments are made by the tribal council, which administers the land holdings of the tribe. Any landless Indian may acquire land by applying to the tribal council for an assignment. Such assignments provide that, prior to the death of the assignee, he will bequeath his land to one heir. This procedure prevents the fractional heirship tangle so common among Indian tribes.

The Chemehuevi is, possibly, the only tribe whose reservation lies in one state and the people live in another, and on another reservation. The Chemehuevi Reservation is in the eastern edge of the great Mojave Desert, where the rainfall is sufficient in only one out of ten years to produce a sparse forage crop of desert feed; for this reason the reservation has been abandoned. On the Colorado River Reservation, the Chemehuevis have been allotted land in areas with the Mojaves. These lands are fertile and there is an abundant supply of irrigation water. With this combination, both tribes are prospering. Through intermarriage and free association with each other, it is difficult for the casual observer to distinguish one from the other.

## *Chemehuevi Baskets*

THE CHEMEHUEVIS have adopted cultural habits of both the Mojave tribe and the white people who have come into the valley. True to Indian tradition, they have clung to certain features of their own culture. This is especially true of their arts and crafts. The Mojaves do beautiful beadwork, in which the Chemehuevis do not participate. On the other hand, the Chemehuevi women always have

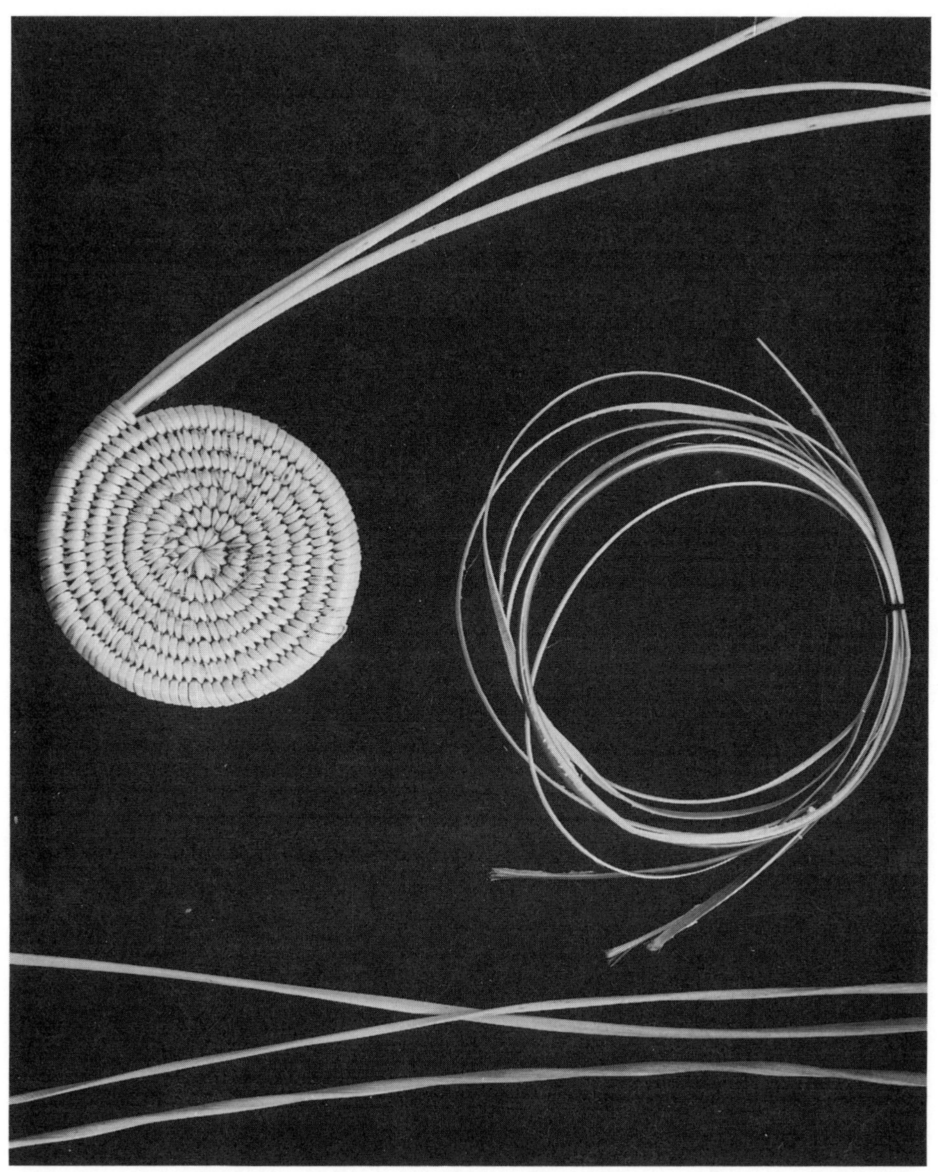

*Junkus weaving material and starter of Chemehuevi basket. Note that the coiling proceeds to the right, a technique used only by the Chemehuevis*

PLATE LXIV

been noted for their beautiful baskets. These baskets are of coil type weave and the technique used is similar to that employed by the Yavapais and Havasupais. The same three-rod warp or foundation of willow twigs is used. Over this warp, split willow, or sometimes the juncus, is coiled for the background of the basket, with the design being made of devil's claw. The juncus is a rush that grows in marshy land in the mountains near Banning, California, and is imported by the Chemehuevi weavers. The juncus twigs are green when gathered but when dried they take on a variegated brown color. Thin sections of the outside of the twigs are used in weaving. This combines well with the black *Martynia* and produces a very attractive basket. One characteristic peculiar to the Chemehuevi craft is that the coiling pro-

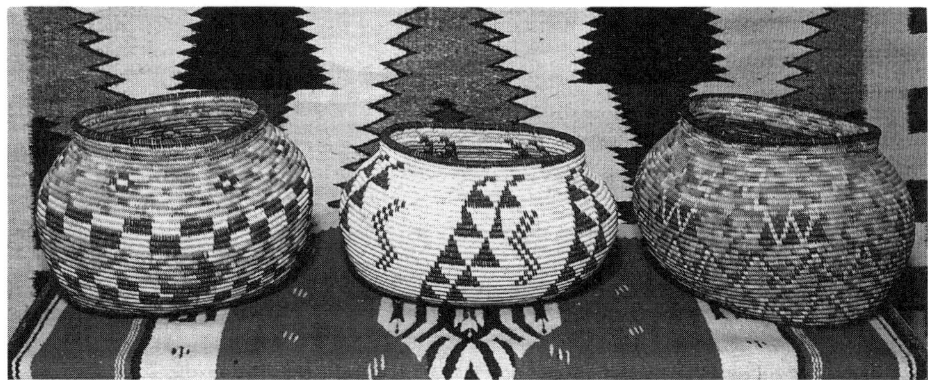

*Oval ollas are more common among the Chemehuevi baskets than those of other Arizona tribes. Decorative designs in Chemehuevi baskets cover a wide range and are original with the weaver* — *PLATE LXV*

ceeds to the right (Plate LXIV). They are the only Arizona weavers who use this technique.

The decorative designs in the Chemehuevi baskets cover a wide range, including geometric figures such as diamonds, blocks, and heavy zig-zag lines representing lightning (Plate LXV). The combination or arrangement of these figures originates with the weaver. There are no distinctive tribal designs such as are found in the geometric patterns of the Pimas. Instead, a design belongs to the weaver who originated it and cannot be used by other weavers. Besides geometric designs, they use bugs, snakes, butterflies, stars, and ocotillo, which is a familiar desert plant. Most of their work is exceedingly smooth.

Their craft is highly commercialized, and in trying to meet the demands of the public they have made about all the shapes and styles found in Indian baskets. However, these usually are of a size that might find some utility purpose in the purchaser's home, and shallow bowls, ollas, and the plate shapes are common. Large scrap baskets or waste-paper baskets seldom are seen. A type of basket that rarely is found among other Arizona tribes is the oval olla, shown in Plate LXV.

On a visit to the Colorado River Reservation, the writer met many of the Chemehuevi weavers. Probably the most interesting, as well as the most famous, was Mary Snyder, who, records show, died in 1951. In Plate LXVI, she is shown at her home with her weaving material and a basket she has just completed. The most famous of her creations

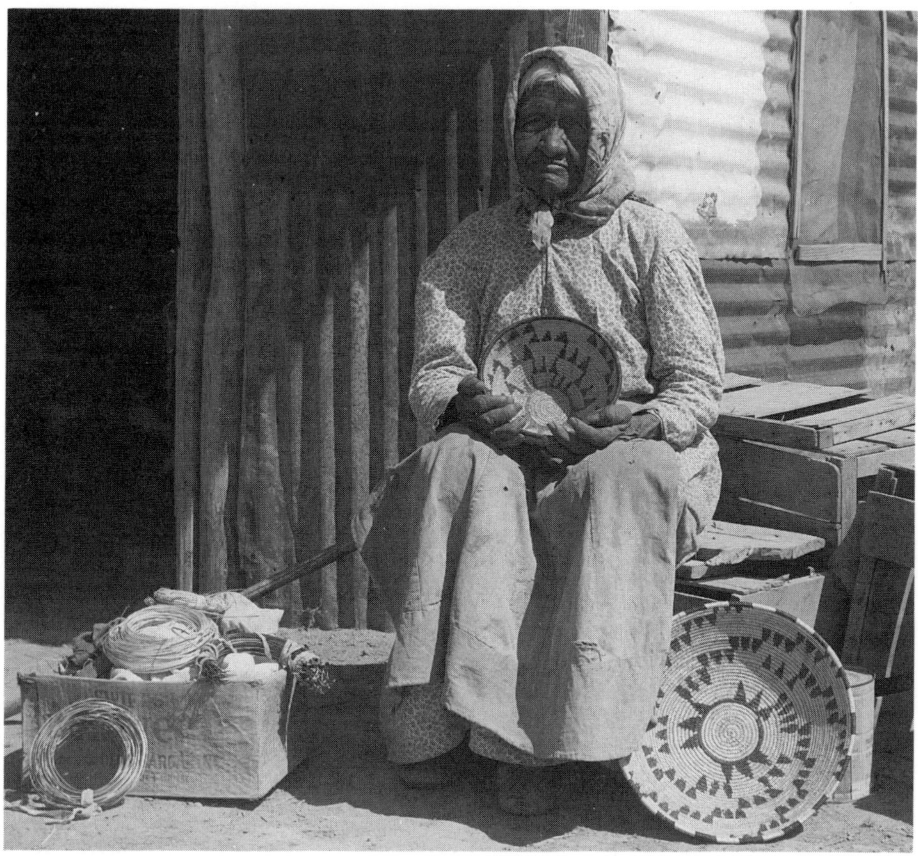

*Mary Snyder, the most famous Chemehuevi weaver, was born in 1852, according to tribal records. She is shown here at her home with her weaving materials and a basket which she has just completed*

*PLATE LXVI*

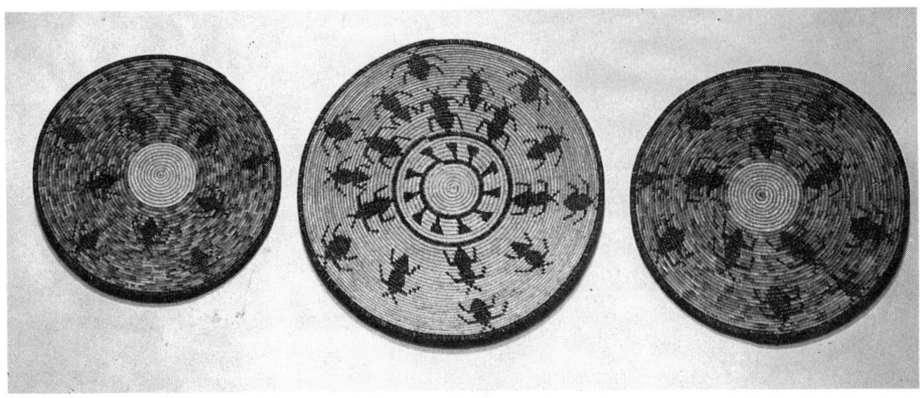

*Shown here are fine examples of Mary Snyder's bug designs. These and Mary's snake designs, shown in Plate LXVIII, are her most famous creations* PLATE LXVII

are her snake and bug designs (Plates LXVII, LXVIII) . When talking to the other weavers it was found that, regardless of the popularity of these designs, no one but Mary could use them. Although the baskets shown here were collected over a period of fifteen years, they were all credited to Mary Snyder, for these are her designs.

In discussing with the weavers the designs shown here, it was revealed that, with few exceptions, no significance was attached to them.

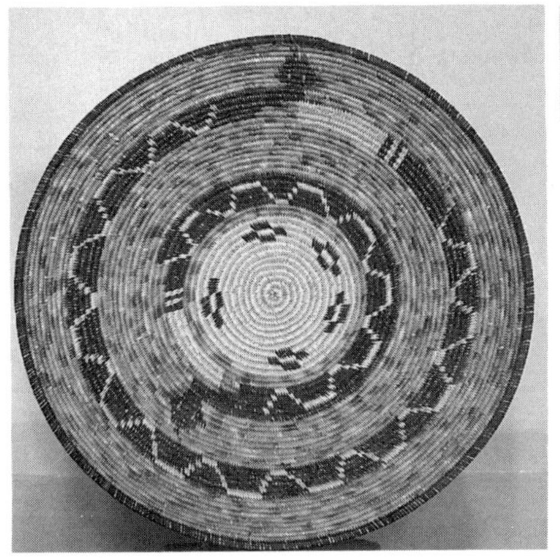

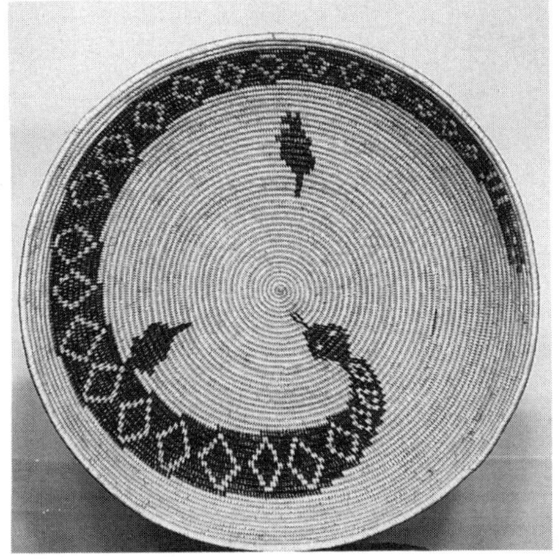

*Coyote tracks and mice have been added to the snake design in these baskets made by Mary Snyder. Her popular snake and bug designs are hers alone, and may not be used by any other weaver* PLATE LXVIII

All said the designs were only to make the baskets look nice. Mary Snyder's bug design is said to have some connection with an old legend but the interpretation given was very confused and difficult to understand. Mary does not speak English. In Plate LXIX, the butterfly design is said to mean spring, and this design would be made at that time of the year. When showing the weavers the different basket designs, it was remarkable how quickly they recognized the weaver of any particular basket. This would indicate that a strong code of ethics exists, which forbids the use of another weaver's design.

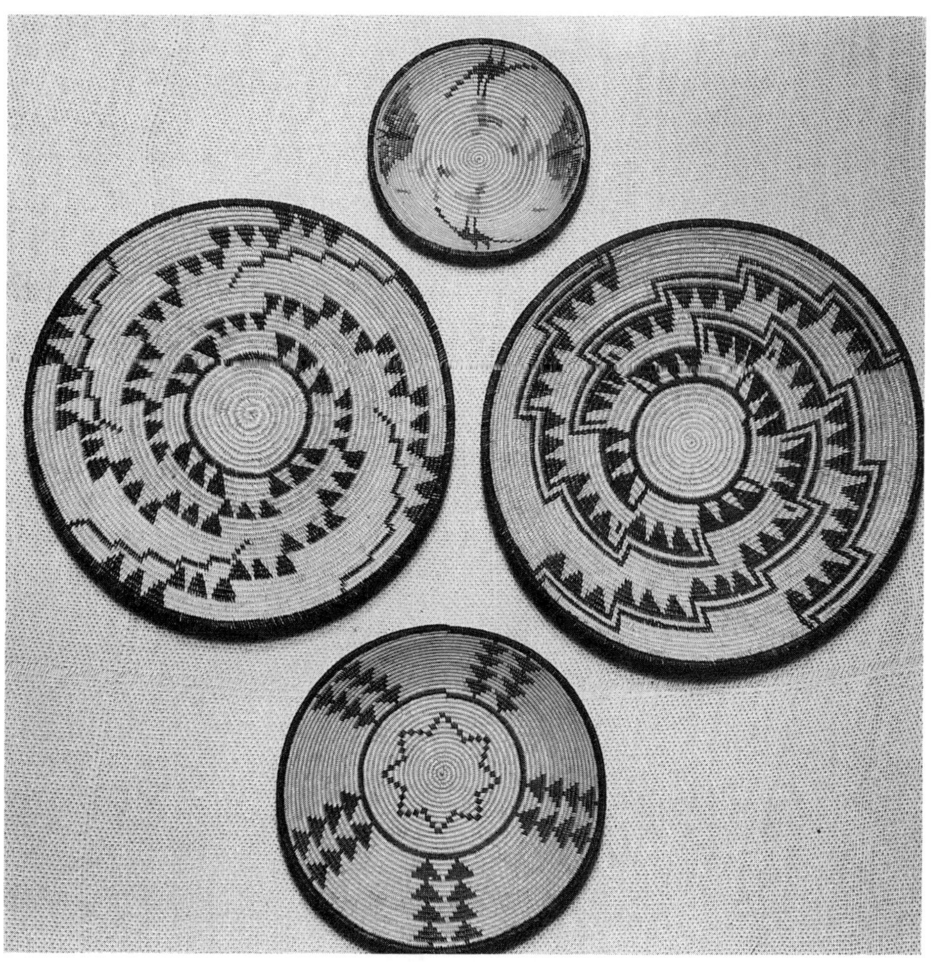

*The butterfly design in the basket at the top denotes spring, and is made only at that time of year. Most Chemehuevi designs have no significance beyond identification of the weaver*

*PLATE LXIX*

# *The People of the Mesas*

ABOUT 170 MILES north and west of the rugged Apache country lie the Hopi mesas. There probably is no spot in all the Southwest more steeped in the legend and romance of the past than these rocky wind-swept plateaus. They extend like three great fingers from Black Mesa, to the north, down onto the desert floor, from which they seem to rise abruptly, and with their teeming villages on the top they stand like monuments to the vigor and strength of the Hopi people.

These three peninsula-like formations of rock and sand are called First Mesa, Second Mesa, and Third Mesa, and on them are located nine villages. On First Mesa are the villages of Hano, Sichomovi, and Walpi; on Second Mesa are located Shipaulovi, Mishongnovi, and Shongopovi; and on Third Mesa the villages of Old Oraibi, Hotevilla, and Bacabi. At the foot of First Mesa is found Polacca; New Oraibi is located at the foot of Third Mesa. To the casual observer, the boundaries of these villages would seem very indefinite, but they are, in reality, separate and distinct communities, even to the extent of having some language differences. In ancient times each village had its own chief and warriors.

There was a time when the Hopis numbered probably 20,000, but drought, pestilence, and the raiding of their more aggressive and warlike neighbors reduced their number to about 2,000 by 1904. In the forty years that followed they doubled that population, and a steady normal increase still continues.

The village of Old Oraibi is the oldest in the group; it has also the distinction of being the oldest town in the United States that has been continuously occupied. Archaeologists say the Hopis have lived there since about A. D. 1150, or perhaps earlier, and beneath the village lie the remains of two other cultures that preceded that of the Hopi. During its long existence, immigrants from Old Oraibi have founded five other Hopi villages. The earliest of these villages were upper and lower Moencopi, which were founded by old Chief Tuba and his followers, about 1870. The next villages to originate through migration from Old Oraibi were Hotevilla and Bacabi. This migration was made necessary because of a feud that developed in the old village. When the two factions became so divided that no reconciliation was possible, it was decided that one or the other must leave. Instead of resorting to bloodshed, the Hopis decided to settle the matter by a tug of war. A line was cut in the stone surface of the mesa, and, on September 8, 1906, the opposing factions faced each other across this line. The faction led by Chief Tewaquaptewa was victorious and his opponent, Yokioma, took his band and moved over and founded Hotevilla, with one group of his party moving on and settling in what is now Bacabi.

The last village to originate with settlers from Old Oraibi is Kyakotsmovi (New Oraibi), which is located at the foot of the mesa. It has grown up partly because Chief Tewaquaptewa decreed that Christian converts should not live in Old Oraibi, but possibly its main source of development has come through its younger people, who have become Americanized and built their homes at the foot of the mesa rather than climb the long winding trails to the top. Nearly a half century has passed since the tug of war occurred between the two chiefs but the line cut in the stone surface of the mesa is still very plain and above it are inscribed these words:

> Well it have to be this way now that when you pass
> me over this line it will be DONE.—September 8, 1906.

Not far away old Tewaquaptewa has a little shop where he makes kachina dolls and gourd rattles. He will even demonstrate his wares for you if you will buy, giving a few shuffling steps of some old dance as he chants a song to the rhythmic beat of a gourd rattle. His old opponent, Yokioma, died several years ago, but Tewaquaptewa, despite his age, is still a virile, dominant factor in every phase of village life.

After the Indian Reorganization Act was passed, in 1934, the Hopis, like many other Indian tribes, organized a tribal council composed of representatives of each community. An attempt was made to form an over-all government for all the villages. Due to the differences existing between the communities, this was not successful. They now have reverted to their old form of government. A kik-mon-wi, or spiritual leader, directs the religious or ceremonial activities of a community, and most normal government functions are left to Indian Service officials.

Due mainly to the pressure from their neighbors, the Navajos, whose land completely surrounds them, the land holdings of the Hopis are much reduced from what they formerly were. The Hopis are in no way related to the Navajos or the Apaches, but belong to the Pueblos, and are the only members of this group in Arizona.

The Hopis are primarily farmers. Water is extremely scarce, and sheep, their principal domestic animal, can range only on limited areas where water is obtainable. Water is supplied, principally, by springs, and since the villages are located near those springs, serious overgrazing has occurred in their vicinity. The Hopi men are the shepherds of the tribe. Some range cattle are grazed, but this does not have the important place in their economy that sheep raising has. The sheep provide not only meat but wool for the weaving of blankets. While these blankets are not as colorful or as famous as those woven by the Navajos, they are, nevertheless, worthy of mention. Unlike the Navajos, the men are the blanket weavers of the tribe.

The Hopis are truly expert farmers. When we consider that the Hopi country has an elevation of about 6,000 feet, with a mean temperature of 52° to 55° and an average rainfall of from 9.5 to 12:5 inches per year, some of the obstacles to farming become apparent. Corn, beans, squash, melons, garden vegetables, and fruit are the principal crops grown.

On the toe of the mesa, below the village of Hotevilla, are found extensive terraced gardens which are irrigated from a nearby spring. All of the soil has been carried in and poured on the rocky slope to provide the seedbed for these gardens; and this process has gone on for centuries until now a considerable area is being cultivated. Rock walls hold this terraced soil in place, and we found only women working in these plots (Plate LXX).

Corn and beans are grown in small fields which usually lie adjacent to the washes. Hopi corn is native to the Hopi country. The long slender ears of blue, red, white, and variegated colors, which are stored away in the Hopi's home are indeed his treasure. He always keeps a supply on hand sufficient for a year or more, in case a drought may come and the crops fail. The kernels on the Hopi corn are not like the corn of the Middle West, but are rounded and more of the shape of a drop of water, with the sharp pointed end attached to the cob. While corn makes up more than 70 per cent of the Hopi farm crops, the average yield is but five bushels to the acre. The farmer's tools are a planting stick and a hoe. In April or May he takes seeds selected with great care by his mother or grandmother and, making a hole in the sand to the depth of ten or twelve inches, he drops in from ten to twenty grains of corn. The seeds are covered by only two or three inches of sand and as the plants grow, the hole is gradually filled in. Of course, cutworms, wind, and rodents will destroy the larger portion of the young plants, but the farmer anticipated this when he placed the ten to twenty kernels in the hill. Instead of the rows being three feet apart like they are in the corn belt, these rows are from two to five yards apart and the plants in the row are separated by a like distance. This widely spaced

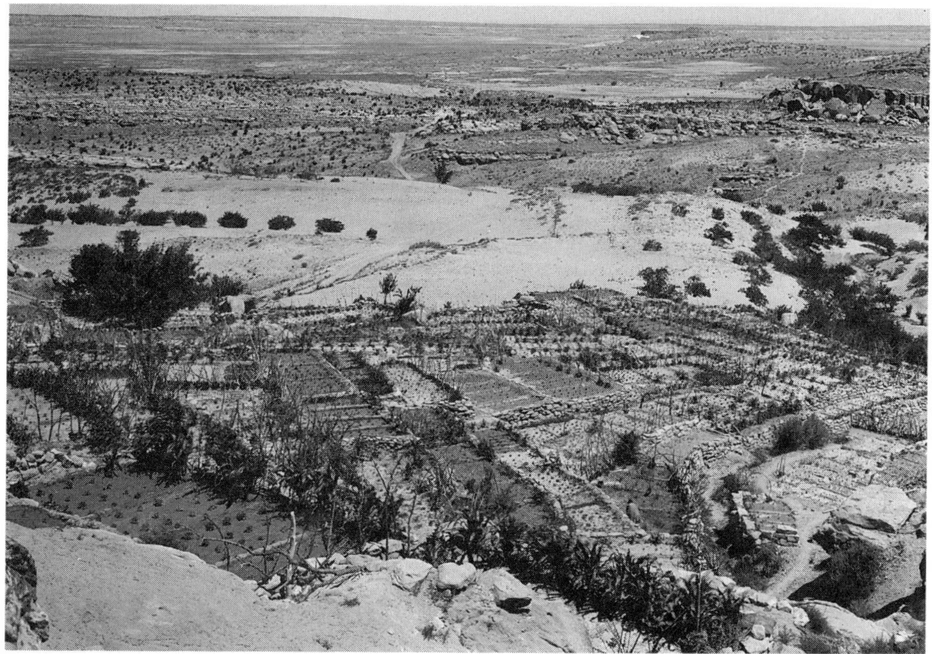

*Hotevilla gardens–Picture taken from the rim of the Mesa. The soil for these gardens has all been carried in and spread on the rocky slope* *PLATE LXX*

planting is necessary for the corn plant to have sufficient moisture, and the Hopi farmer will tell you that the roots of the corn plants in his field cover the entire space. The ears form close to the surface of the ground, and the whole plant does not average more than three to five feet in height.

Beans are next in importance among the Hopi farm crops. They, too, are native varieties which the Hopis have grown for hundreds of years. The young, tender plants are protected by placing flat rocks upright by each hill as a windbreak and are spaced about the same distance apart as the corn. This again illustrates the tremendous effort the farmer must put forth to produce a crop. The yield is about the same as corn.

The fruits grown in the Hopi country are peaches, apricots, pears, plums, apples, cherries, and grapes. Peach trees were sent as a special gift to the Hopis by Queen Isabella of Spain and the Hopis call them "*supaula.*" These same peaches are still grown today and make up the greater portion of the peach crop. For hundreds of years the Hopis have preserved peaches by drying them on the flat rocks of the mesas, and have used this dried fruit, not only as a food for themselves, but as a medium of barter and exchange with other tribes.

The first contact the Hopis had with the white man was in 1640. Coronado, in his search for the Seven Cities of Cíbola, had arrived in Zuñi. There he heard about the Hopi villages and sent Pedro de Tovar with a few men to investigate. They arrived in July, and the records of the expedition recount how the Spaniards feasted on green corn, melons, and fowl. The fowl undoubtedly was native turkey, since no other domestic fowl now used for food had been introduced into America. These early Spanish explorers are credited with introducing horses, sheep, cattle, and, possibly, swine into the Hopi villages. The padres received these animals to distribute among the people, for here, as elsewhere, the Spaniards laid claim to the land in the name of Spain and the church. Evidently the Hopis accepted the livestock with much more enthusiasm than they did the white man's religion.

Many books have been written about the struggle the Hopis made to retain their old rituals and customs. Their whole culture has always centered about their religious ceremonies, which control every phase of their home and community life.

## *Hopi Arts and Crafts*

THE ARTS AND CRAFTS of the Hopis were given special mention by the Spaniards. Beautiful shawls made of native Hopi cotton and dyed with their own vegetable dyes, as well as pottery and baskets, were among the gifts which were presented to the white visitors. The weaving of cotton cloth no longer is practiced, since these materials are easily obtained at the village trading posts. Now the weaving is done with woolen yarn from their own sheep. They make blankets, shawls, and dresses for the women, and sashes and belts for the men.

The Hopi women are noted for their baskets and the pottery which they make from the white clay found in the canyons. These two crafts are peculiar to the three mesas. The women of First Mesa make decorated pottery; those of Second Mesa weave baskets of yucca and galleta grass, and the women of Third Mesa weave highly colored baskets of wild currant and rabbit brush.

In the decorative design of Second Mesa baskets, only four colors are used together with the white background. They are pale yellow, green, black, and red. The first two are natural colors and the latter two are dyed. The background is the natural white of the inside leaves of the yucca plant, the green is the outside leaves, and the yellow is the white leaves dried in the sun. The black dye is obtained by boiling sunflower seeds with piñon gum and native ochre. The prepared yucca strips are dipped in this solution and smoked over burning black wool. The red dye is not a brilliant red but of a shade frequently called Indian red, and is obtained in the following manner: Either of two native plants which the Hopis call *"si-i-ta"* and *"ho-hoy-si"* is boiled, strained, and the color set with native alum. The fiber then is dipped in this solution and smoked in a closed container over burning white wool.

Second Mesa baskets (Plate LXXI) are of a coil type weave and the yucca thus prepared is bound over a foundation of galleta grass or shredded yucca, and the stitches are not interlocking. The underlying

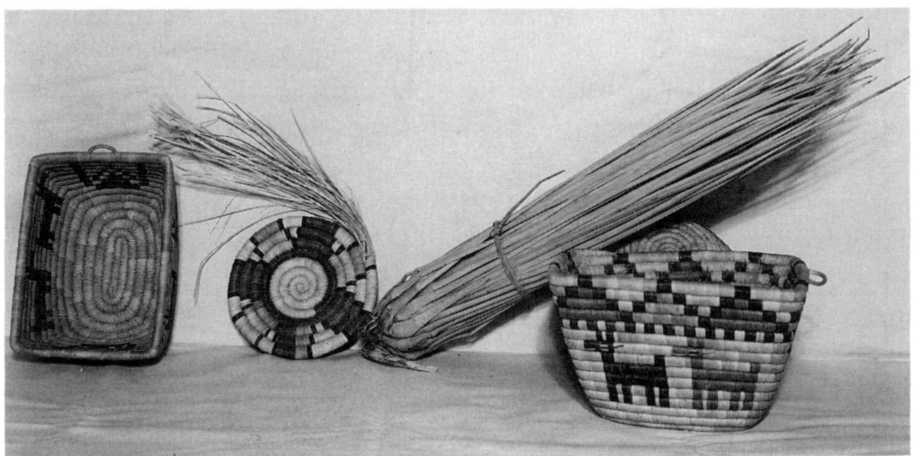

*Hopi Second Mesa baskets with starting of basket and bundle of yucca material. Four colors and white are used in decorative design by Second Mesa weavers* *PLATE LXXI*

coil is pierced by an awl and the stitches are drawn tightly around the grass filler, making a strong, durable basket. The decorative designs are either conventional geometric figures, or the masks or the full figure of some ceremonial character. Sometimes conventional bird designs are used. In the geometric figures, the sections of the design may be single or in pairs or in zones. The mask may be that of one of the characters of the dance or ceremony in which the basket is used. Originally Second Mesa baskets were made in round plaques or shallow ceremonial baskets only and were made specifically for ceremonial or household use. Through the influence of the white traders, deep baskets are now being made on Second Mesa, for commercial purposes.

While Second Mesa lies only ten miles from Third Mesa, there is no similarity in the baskets woven on the two mesas. In the first place, the materials used in Third Mesa baskets are wild currant bush and rabbit brush. The bark is peeled from the round stems or twigs of the rabbit brush and they are dyed and used whole. Another difference is that the baskets are constructed of a wicker weave. The method of dyeing the rabbit brush is the same as is used in Second Mesa baskets but a greater variety of colors is used. In addition to the black and red dyes described in Second Mesa baskets, a yellow dye is obtained from the flowers of the rabbit brush, pink from amaranthus, purple and carmine from the purple maize, greens from indigo and the flowers of the rabbit brush, and purplish blue from sunflower seed. White is simply whitewash made of white clay. Many color tones and shades are obtained by blending these dyes, which accounts for the brilliancy of Third Mesa baskets.

The framework or warp of these baskets is of wild currant bush or, sometimes, a plant or grass, common to the locality, which the Hopi call *si-wi,* and through these are woven the dyed stems of the rabbit brush. The finished product is the most colorful of any of the baskets made by our Arizona weavers, since both the background and design are made of highly colored material. Like the Second Mesa baskets, these too were originally made only in two shapes—the plaque, and shallow ceremonial baskets. Now, deep baskets, as shown in Plate LXXII, also are made by Third Mesa weavers to meet public demand. The edges or rims of Third Mesa baskets are finished with yucca. A noticeable characteristic of these baskets is the hump that appears in the center of the bottom. In starting the framework, two sets of three or more bundles of branches of the wild currant are fashioned together

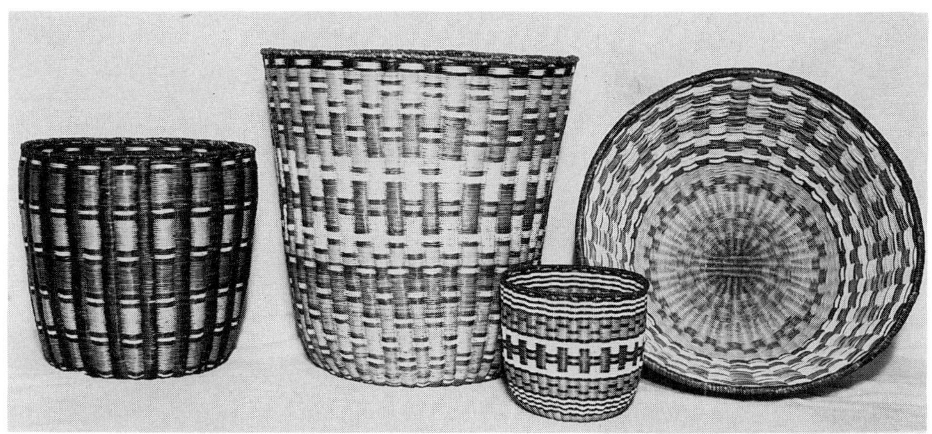

*Hopi Third Mesa weavers originally made only shallow baskets and plaques, but now, to meet public demand, the deep baskets shown here also are made* *PLATE LXXII*

crosswise and produce this hump. As the weaving progresses from the center, other warp is inserted.

The decorative design may be a figure or may be only the mask of a ceremonial figure. Also, conventional bird designs similar to those of Second Mesa are used. Most common among these is the eagle, with wings and tail spread wide. However, geometric designs which are distinctly Hopi in character and individual to Third Mesa probably are most frequently used.

Another type of basket made in all of the Hopi villages is a loosely platted basket of coarse yucca material, which is made for utility purposes. One of the principal uses for this basket is to screen the sand from corn which has been parched in hot sand. These baskets (Plate LXXIII) are bowl shaped and range in size from six to fifteen inches in diameter and three to four inches in depth. Because of their rugged construction they make excellent containers for fruits and vegetables and find some sale among white trade for this purpose.

## *A Hopi Wedding*

OF THE CEREMONIES in which baskets are used today, one of the most colorful and beautiful is the wedding ceremony. When it is evident that two young Hopi people want to get married, the parents get together and pass judgment on the match. The young man is judged

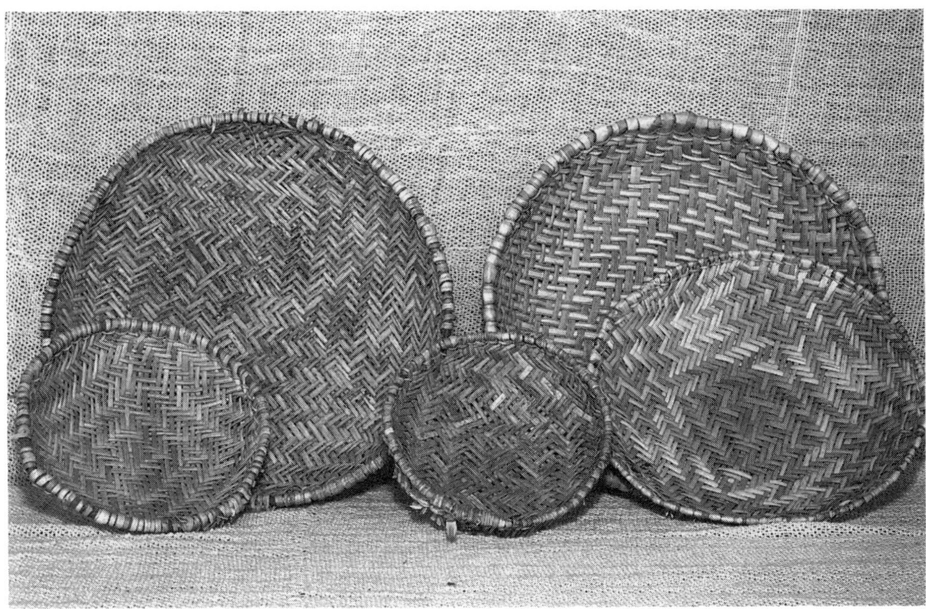

*These screening baskets, made in all the Hopi villages, are used to screen the sand from corn which has been parched in hot sand* *PLATE LXXIII*

by his industry; and the girl by her ability as a cook and homemaker. When approval of the match has been given, the girl goes to the home of the boy's mother,[2] where, for the first four days, she grinds corn on the grinding stone, and does the cooking and other household duties to prove her domestic talents. When her presence in his home is discovered by the boy's aunts, they come with pots of mud, which they throw on the boy's parents, and the girl too if she has not been hidden away before their arrival, which usually is the case. This is done in mock remonstrance against the boy's parents for giving him up, but is only in fun and the whole affair evidently is enjoyed by all.

The bride's wedding garments always are a present from the male members of the groom's family. When the girl comes into the home, the groom's father takes a sack of cotton in the seed and distributes small amounts of it to all the neighbors in the village. They pick the seed from the lint and return both to the boy's father, who takes the lint around to different kivas, where it is corded and spun into thread by the men. Four men then are selected to make the bridal garments, which consist of a pair of moccasins, usually of white buckskin, the

2. Hopi women always own the house.

tops of which reach almost to the knees, two white cotton blankets, and a white sash with a long fringe. The smaller of the two blankets later is fashioned into a dress. The blanket is folded in half lengthwise; where the two upper corners meet they are stitched together for a short distance across the top; then, leaving a space down the side for an armhole, the two ends of the blanket are stitched together. The dress is put on over the head, with the right arm through the opening in the side, and the left shoulder and arm bare. The other blanket is worn as a shawl, and the wide sash is looped around the waist so the fringe hangs down the side.

After the bridal garments are made a feast is prepared, to which all of the men who helped make the garments are invited. When the men have feasted and the women who helped in the preparation of the food are fed, any remaining food is given to the guests to take to their homes.

The marriage rites are performed by the mothers. Early some morning, after the roosters crow, the mother of the girl comes over to the boy's home, where her daughter has been staying, and the two mothers fill a bowl with water, in which suds are made with the root of the yucca plant. The heads of the two young people are then washed together and their hair intwined, indicating they are now joined together. The girl's mother washes the groom's hair and the boy's mother washes the bride's hair and then combs it in the style worn by the Hopi married women. Thereafter, she must always wear her hair in this fashion, which differs from the style of hairdress worn by the unmarried girls.

Dressed in her wedding garments, with the exception of her sash, which she carries wrapped in a grass mat, the bride returns alone to her mother's home. The groom must then go out onto the desert and cut firewood and carry it to his mother-in-law's home. He then takes up his abode there as a member of her household. This cutting of wood and carrying it in is not as simple as it may sound, for the house to which he brings it is perched high on a rocky mesa and he may have to travel out onto the desert to find this wood.

Sometime after the wedding, when the bride and her mother and other relatives have completed a number of wedding baskets, the final act of the marriage takes place. The bride will have ground a large amount of corn, to which will be added ground corn contributed by her girl friends, some of which she will pay back at their wedding ceremonies. The bride, followed by her relatives and all carrying baskets heaped with the ground corn, proceeds to the home of the groom's parents. These laden baskets all are given to the groom's mother, with the exception of the basket carried by the bride. This basket, which is the largest in the group, is given to the groom to be kept until his death and is buried with him.

In August of each year, the brides of the year dress in their bridal costume for the "home dance," after which these costumes are kept for a burial shroud or are buried with them.

As the Hopi people are, for the most part, farmers, and, during the growing season, their time is taken up with the crops, it is only during the winter months that elaborate wedding ceremonies are performed. Even though either party may marry again, the Hopi wedding ceremony occurs only the one time. Bachelors are rare and spinsters are almost nonexistent.

The whole social order of the Hopi people centers about the home, clan, and religion. The Hopi family is more highly organized than in any of the other tribes of Arizona. The family organization takes in the whole relationship and each member has certain prerogatives, responsibilities, and functions in the family group. There are some rather striking differences in this family organization as compared with most family relationships. For instance, the right of succession passes not from father to the oldest son, but from the father to his wife's brother—in fact, the women, and not the men, might be regarded as the head of the home.

Children always are welcomed in the Hopi homes, and, contrary to the preference which many races have toward boy babies, the girl baby is most favored. This preference probably developed in ancient times when the Hopis were being harassed by their warlike neighbors and they saw in each girl baby a potential source of increase in the strength of their tribe and replacement of their warriors lost in battle.

The little girls are carefully reared and taught by their mothers and other members of the family group, including aunts and grandmothers; in fact, the whole family organization has a definite responsibility in the rearing and training of all the children. The child has not only his parents and grandparents but godparents and clanparents as well, and each have certain responsibilities in the care, training, and development of the child. The little girls of the family are well clothed but the little boys may go about entirely nude until they reach the age of three to four years. One Hopi writer tells of having been rolled in the snow while nude, by his uncles. This treatment was considered a toughening process for little boys. He told of playing in the snow with his only garment being a blanket thrown about him.

When the boys reach the age of five to six years they join their fathers in the kiva and go with them to work in the fields and to tend sheep. In the kiva they learn the many things Hopi boys must know to be wise in the traditions of their people.

## *The Kiva*

NO DISCUSSION of the Hopi Indian would be complete without a description of the kiva. It is unique and, in many ways, the most important institution in the community life of these people. It is a subterranean chamber hewn in the floor of the mesa or built along its wall on a projecting ledge, and is reserved for the use of the male members of the tribe, serving as a ceremonial room and men's club. Each clan has its own kiva, and many religious rituals are performed there. It is also the workroom where the weaving of blankets and garments is done. It serves as a place of barter and exchange with the members of other kivas, and is the social meeting place universally used by the men; in fact, most of their leisure hours are spent there.

There seem to be no set dimensions for these underground rooms. They usually are rectangular in shape and are often of a size that will accommodate thirty or more men. One thing which they all have in common is a rectangular opening in the center of the roof. A ladder is placed through this opening to the floor below and is the only means of entering or leaving the kiva. In cold weather a fire is built directly below the opening, which serves as an escape for the smoke.

## *The Hopi Pahos*

A HOPI BELIEVES that life is shared alike by all living things, and this includes animals, birds, and insects, as well as trees and all plant life. While we accept them in the form in which we see them, he believes that in their own world they take on human form. Therefore, he must use them only to satisfy his actual need. For instance, if he is going hunting he must prepare a *pahos* or prayer offering for the particular animal he wishes to kill. A *pahos* is made by tying bird feathers, preferably from an eagle, to a stick which can be stuck into the ground. The evening before the hunt, he places the *pahos* where the animal people will be sure to find it. It will convey to them his great need which causes him to kill one of their people for food, and the animals, knowing this, will willingly give up their earthly lives for him. The spirit of the animal killed will return to the animal kingdom and can never again leave, but its descendants which are left on earth will continue to grow and multiply. If a Hopi wishes to gather some particular plant for his own use he takes with him the proper prayer offering and places it at the first specimen of the plant that he finds. He does not gather from this plant, however, for it will convey to other like plants his great need. He goes on until he finds other plants which he gathers to satisfy his needs.

## *Awatobi*

THE EARLY SPANISH priests built churches in the Hopi country in an effort to Christianize them, and, for a time, the Hopis offered only passive but, nevertheless, effective resistance to this new faith. In 1680, they joined with the other Pueblo people in their revolt and killed all of the priests and destroyed the churches. Today one will find the great carved beams of the church in the village of Old Oraibi lying abandoned on the mesa. They give mute testimony to the wreckage of another conquest of old Spain. Catholic missions were never again established in the Hopi country.

After the revolt, the padres were not permitted to return to any of the villages except Awatobi, which is located at the head of Bluebird Canyon. Here, about 1700, missionary priests returned and again made converts among the people. This so infuriated the villagers in Walpi and Mishongnovi that they attacked Awatobi. The men were all in a kiva at a meeting. According to the old Indian story, the ladder was pulled up through the opening in the kiva roof, leaving the men trapped in the chamber below, then burning pine knots were thrown down through the opening and the men were suffocated. The women and children were taken back to Walpi and Mishongnovi and the entire village of Awatobi was destroyed. It never has been rebuilt, for, among the old Hopis, it still is considered a place of evil.

In many ways, the Hopi is the most colorful and the most advanced member of his race. The complications of his economic, social, and religious organizations are almost beyond our understanding. He has built his culture in the face of hunger, drought, pestilence, and aggression from the warring tribes that surround him. In spite of all these obstacles, he has emerged strong, self-reliant, and self-sufficient. If you visit him today, you will find him friendly and gracious in the hospitality of his simple home. You will be seated in the best chair the home affords. You will be shown every courtesy by all members of his family. One thing you will notice is the large number of happy little youngsters whose respect and politeness toward their visitor is quite remarkable. When you depart, their shrill little cries of "Goo bye" will follow you far down the winding trail toward the desert below. Then as you leave these enchanted mesas and watch them fade into the northern horizon, there is a hope—yes, a prayer in your heart that all this will never change, that this always will be the land of the Hopis.

# CITATION FOR MERITORIOUS SERVICE

## ALAMBERT E. ROBINSON

upon retirement after more than thirty-two years of service in the Department of the Interior.

Mr. Robinson was first employed in the Government by the Bureau of Reclamation in 1916 and served two years on the Salt River Project in Central Arizona. In 1921, he was appointed to the Bureau of Indian Affairs in Sacaton, Arizona, where he remained until he retired on October 15, 1951, from the position of Superintendent of the Pima Indian Agency. In this capacity, Mr. Robinson was responsible for the economic, educational, and social progress which has marked the development of the Fort McDowell, Maricopa, Salt River, and Gila River Indian Reservations, comprising his jurisdiction. Under his able direction, extensive land subjugation and irrigation, administration of a good school system, rendering of excellent medical service, modern and scientific farming operations, and many other benefits have accrued to the Indian people residing on these reservations. Beloved among the Indian families of his agency, Mr. Robinson wisely counselled and guided them in their economic and domestic difficulties. He is also an authority on Indian basket weaving among the Southwestern tribes. His personal collection of baskets is considered to be the best in the world. In recognition of his contributions to the welfare and development of the Indian people under his jurisdiction and to an important phase of Indian arts and crafts, Mr. Robinson is deserving of the Meritorious Service Award of the Department of the Interior.

Signed: OSCAR L. CHAPMAN
*Secretary of the Interior*

# Index